Simon Wooldridge was born in '
for sport began as a young boy atte ..
and Wembley Stadium where he witnessed Evel Knievel
attempt to jump thirteen London buses on a Harley Davidson.
He has lived in England and Australia, and has worked in publishing
and educational filmmaking. This is his first book.

I LIKE TO WATCH

STORIES FROM THE STANDS

SIMON WOOLDRIDGE

SANDHURST

Sandhurst Consulting
PO Box 4062
Bendigo VIC 3550
Australia
Email: iltw1979@gmail.com
Ph: +61 (0) 400 984 814

ISBN: 978-0-6480246-0-6

I LIKE TO
WATCH

STORIES FROM THE STANDS

**For everyone whose company I've enjoyed in the stands
and on the terraces**

Ian Wooldridge, Veronica Wooldridge, Henry Wooldridge,
Louis Wooldridge, Kevin Wooldridge, Max Wooldridge,
Sarah Wooldridge, Gill Wooldridge, Nick Batt, Steve Batt,
Andy Richards, Mark Scarborough, Ken Baiden, Andy Figiela,
Richard Hicks, Owen Francis, Witold Zdybicki, Peter Yale,
Brian Doran, Lee Izzard, Rob Woodcock

Carl Prinzel, John Matthews, Phil Silver, Carla Langley,
Darryn Mawby, Gill Francis, Norman Francis, Valerie Morrow,
Jim Green, Anne Lenehan, Peter Moody, Amanda Moody,
Martin Cross, Clive Richards, Mark Taylor, Dino Antoniades,
Paul Robbins, Richard O'Connor, Bobby Spasevski, Denis Heenan,
Lisa McPherson, Denis Spilar, Jim Kernaghan, John Curtain

Tara Langley, Noel Langley, Jean Langley, Glenn Harvey,
Zack Harvey, Darryl Stevenson, Charlie Wade, Mark Cherrie,
Gary Charalambos, Nick Hellman, Ivan Pryce, Mick Cantillon,
Seamus Kerr, Sebastian Carr, Allan Payton, George Parry, John Will,
Alan Coles, George Cheney, Brendan Conlan, Billy Drinkwater,
Josiane Tabone, Paula Thomas, Donna Clarke, Jimmy Carroll,
Paul Rooke, Peter Walsh, Mark Lavin, Rebecca West, Rene Kunisch,
Paul O'Shea, Louise Harnby, Breffni O'Connor, Guy Simpson,

Nick Ball, Pat Rice, Mark Shearwood, Michael Sherwin,
Mark O'Sullivan, Juliet Matthews, Peter Kay, Tony Molloy,
Chris Ferns, Clive Lawson, Fred Scarborough, Sid Scarborough,
Harry Sheahan, Robert Beat, Duncan Beat, Brian Evans,
Brian Mackie, Tom Corrigan, Joe Keneally, Andrew Abbotts,
Christopher Morgan, Bruce Clark, Adam Porter, Paul Ryan,
Pete Coyle, John Coyle, Sandra Volk, Ross Fodie, Sandy Harman,
Mark Hamilton, Lisa Tancredi, Dave Speedy, Dee Powell,
Gemma Cottle, Dwayne Trusty, Andrew Connelly, Penny Clark,
Evan Clark, Vincent Thompson, Peter Stancliffe, Martin Addison,
Ajay Aggarwal, Christine Henderson, Jo Grech, Gabrielle Harvey,
Adrian Lock, Xavier Lock, Buster Hall, Sarah Pollard, Stuart Grant,
Nick Mawby, James Mawby, Caroline Byrne, John Evans, Stewart
Frost, Stuart Conway, Cameron Hallowell, Tony Prentis, Barb Prentis

And anyone I may have unwittingly omitted.

Contents

Riga   inbox ×   🖨 ⬀

From: Simon Wooldridge   Sent: Wed 14/09/2011 9:38 AM
To: Owen Francis
Cc:

Moose

The Latvian top division is called the Virsliga. Skonto (the only Latvian team I've ever heard of) are at home on the Sunday afternoon we're there, but it'll be too late for our flights and much as I'd like to do it, I don't really fancy staying another 24 hours and paying about £100 more getting back just to get the ground done. It holds about 8500 and is never full – I read something in WSC recently.

Cheers,
Simon

Riga again...   inbox ×   🖨 ⬀

From: Simon Wooldridge   Sent: Wed 14/09/2011 10:23 AM
To: Owen Francis
Cc:

Ok I looked again. There's another division called Liga 1 and on the Saturday we're there, there are 5 games. There's a team called Rigas Futbola Skola who are playing at home. They're third in the division and the ground holds 650 so it could be a bit low key. One of the other clubs is called Ogres / FK 33. Their ground holds 2500 but after 16 games this season they only have 1 point and have a goal difference of -70. There might be some other Riga-based teams out of the 5 teams at home. At least it looks like we have some options...

Introduction

Ealing, West London, Saturday 12 May 1979, about 7 p.m.

I let myself into the house. I was just back from my twenty-seventh Arsenal game that season, the FA Cup Final – the 'Five-minute Final' against Manchester United.

My parents were in the living room, drinks in hand. They had friends over. They were pretty sociable – even in those few months before their marriage ended.

"Great game!" My mother said, enthusiastically.

I beamed. I was at that awkward age. Young mind in an almost adult body. Mature, but immature.

"Tell us about it." My father said.

I didn't. I couldn't say much beyond a muted, low-key "it was amazing".

I moved to leave the living room, go to my room and the sanctuary of my Clash cassettes.

"You don't have much to say," rebuked my father. "You've just been to the greatest Cup Final since Matthews…"

In my room I lay on the bed, my red and white woollen bar scarf still tied tightly around my neck. I knew I'd seen something special. It took a few years of *no trophies* for me to realise just how special that afternoon was.

My love affair with football didn't start that afternoon. It began a few years earlier when my father took my brothers and me to Highbury for the first time. We saw Arsenal beat Stoke City 2-1 – a rare afternoon out, just us boys with our dad.

Between that first Arsenal game and the 1979 FA Cup Final I got to Test matches at Lord's, The Oval and Trent Bridge. My first ever day at cricket saw Aussie Ross Edwards score 99 in an Ashes Test. Then in 1976 that glamorous, immensely talented West Indies team toured England. The first two Tests were draws, then they smashed the hosts all over the place. My brother Max and I were taken up to Trent Bridge in the school holidays for the first two days of the Nottingham Test. We saw Viv Richards score a majestic 232.

I never knew what it was like *not* discussing sport at home. My father was a sports journalist – well-established in his career by the time I was born and writing right up to when he died in 2007. He never did anything else. By the time I was going to football regularly he'd long since lost interest, but he was always happy to discuss the past. Brought up in Hampshire, a Bournemouth fan as a boy, he cycled ten miles each way to their home games from the edge of the New Forest. I remember him telling me how he cried the day they missed out on promotion from the old Third Division South just after the war. He told me many stories. One that stood out was when he reported on a Spurs game in Poland in the early 1960s. He was taken on a tour of Auschwitz during that trip, something that deeply affected him.

It was pretty much ingrained in me, this sport thing. In my early teens I would come home from school night midweek games and wear my Arsenal scarf to bed. When Arsenal were at home on a Saturday in the late 1970s, I spent about twenty-four hours from Friday lunchtime onwards in a state of distracted excitement thinking ahead to the game.

Once I started work I began venturing outside London with Arsenal. Then I took an interest in events north of the border, going to my first Old Firm games in the season before Graeme Souness turned up at Rangers to revolutionise Scottish football.

George Graham's arrival at Highbury heralded an exciting new era and I pretty much immersed myself in everything I could relating to Arsenal. Football wasn't then the totally all-consuming *product* that the media pushes on a largely willing public today. Outside the traditional media channels of the day, we had Ceefax (a primitive TV-based text-only information service) and Arsenal Club Call. Club Call was quite good as it happens – a daily recorded message from Bob Wilson, ex-Arsenal player turned sports journo, who spoke for a few minutes about the Arsenal issues of the day.

As a kid I had footballing heroes; the pictures of some adorned my bedroom walls. As I got older the players became the same age as me. The Arsenal team of around 1986 to 1995 (precisely the George Graham era) fell neatly into this category.

On some levels it wasn't that easy being a football fan when I was growing up. Access to top division games was much easier, but there was plenty to put you off. It was an era of rampant hooliganism, with some kind of aggro at just about every game.

I remember the reaction of people I worked with.

"You *go* to games?"

To some, the thought of actually *attending* a football match was quite radical. And as for going to *away* matches…

"You drive up and down the country just to watch a game?"

"Yes. Sometimes by train."

I knew what was going through their minds: This young bloke is either a complete fool, or he's up to no good.

But they were often keen to hear on a Monday if there'd been any trouble at the weekend game I'd been to. It was kind of like those on-the-surface straight-laced folks who have a prurient interest in sex crimes.

"Didn't see anything," was always my stock response, true or not.

In 2000 I emigrated to Australia. Understandably this curbed my ability to go to Arsenal regularly. But it opened-up in me a broader sporting outlook. I went to a lot of cricket. Within a few years I'd seen Test cricket at all six regular Test venues, and by the end of 2017 I'd been to thirteen Boxing Day Test first days in a row. I first followed the National Soccer League, and then the A-League. I got into Aussie rules. I steadily became more adventurous in my sporting travels. For a number of years, I travelled a lot for work – regularly to the UK and also North America. It was during this period – and on holidays – that I rattled up a few interesting *mini-adventures*: Football in Vietnam, Argentina, Poland, Latvia, Thailand and Germany. Horse racing in Argentina, the US and Poland. I saw races at many trotting tracks and greyhound stadiums, ice hockey in Toronto and Vancouver, Thai boxing. It got to the point with work trips where I was organising tickets and arrangements for sport *before* planning the work stuff. It was a *joy* to tick off even seemingly mundane events like a night at Swindon dogs, or a midweek Bristol Rovers game.

I committed to a one item 'bucket list' – to see a game at every Major League Baseball (MLB) stadium. Over an eight-year period I extended that list from three to eighteen (there are thirty).

I started getting a bit obsessive about the whole thing. When visiting a town or city for the first time I *needed* to know what sporting events were on. When visiting somewhere for a game or race I checked to see if I could get anything else 'done'.

I get pretty much the same thrill visiting a new stadium for the first time as seeing anything that actually happens there. I keep lists. I keep the tickets. I take photographs. I enjoy the camaraderie and chatting to the locals (language permitting) – who are generally friendly and up for a chat.

I remember sitting next to a lady at Newport County.

"Who are your biggest rivals?"

"Oooh," she said, in that singsong Welsh accent, "Cardiff. It can get very, er, *intense.*"

Some experiences *have* been intense. Some have been fun. Many run-of-the-mill, and some actually just plain boring.

One Saturday in 2014 three of us took an early train out of London Euston and managed to fit-in Airdrieonians, Scotland vs Georgia at Ibrox and the dogs at Shawfield before the day was over. Planning a trip to see England play a Test match in Dunedin, I took a sharp intake of breath when I discovered there was a harness racing meeting on the evening of the second day. In the US I've managed short notice visits to get to Hollywood Park Racetrack in Los Angeles, and a Chicago Fire game. I've lost track of how many times I've been to two sporting events on the same day.

This isn't a book full of match reports – though in some chapters I do go into some detail. It's a collection of fan-spectator experiences.

And it's not just about football – although football dominates because I've been to more football matches than anything else. Neither is it a book about hooligan exploits – I don't have any to relate. As a football fan, particularly a few years ago, aggro was virtually omnipresent and some near misses do get a look-in. This book is about being a fan, a spectator – not just of the game or race unfolding in front of me, but the history of the event, the location and people. This book is about actually *going*. Even as sport has become increasingly commercial it's still a buzz whether you're in a crowd of 60,000 or 90,000 at the Emirates or MCG, or at Accrington Stanley, or one of 200-odd souls at the dogs.

I feel fortunate to have bridged two quite different eras watching sport. The 1970s seems like a bygone age now. Back then sportsmen didn't seem much different to fans; they just happened to be *much better* than average at their chosen sport. Footballers earned more than the average man, but they weren't out of touch with the people who watched them. Many players spent their whole careers at one club. Cricketers had winter jobs and many of them looked borderline *portly* as they jogged around the field. A generation and more later, everything is slicker. Footballers come and go, kissing a succession of badges along the way. Cricketers – the Australians and South Africans started it – field with an athleticism that would've probably sent Colin Cowdrey for a quick lie-down and/or large gin and tonic.

Sport interests or compels people to different degrees – from armchair fan, to casual spectator, to the obsessive. In the case of a World Cup, be it football, rugby or cricket, people take time off work and spend thousands to travel to the other side of the world to watch a *game*. What happened in the evolution of man that travelling around the world to attend a sporting event became *a thing*? The power of sport as a driver – to train, to participate, to compete, to watch, is quite incredible. From a non-participant's point-of-view, the investment of time, money and emotion in following a team – sometimes at great effort and over long distances – seems way out of whack with whatever obvious benefits we might get out of it. Yet, we do it. In forty-odd years I have been to thousands of sporting events. Football heads that list but there are hundreds, if not thousands, of hours of cricket as well. Horse racing, greyhound racing, harness racing, baseball, ice hockey, hockey. I've seen five *other* codes of football. Bullfighting, boxing, Thai boxing, rowing, volleyball, tennis, snooker, polo… It will sound nerd-like, and odd to some, but outside the birth of my two kids, some of my most memorable experiences have been watching sport: Arsenal's Cup Winners' Cup win in Copenhagen is right up there, as is the League Cup semi-final replay against Tottenham in 1987, the 2010-11 Ashes series win and the Western Bulldogs' out-of-the-blue 2016 AFL Premiership. This is *why* we go. Occasionally we experience something memorable, wonderful.

Arsenal was my first sporting passion. When I think of Arsenal I generally think of certain players and specific matches – Brady, Rocastle, Wright, Adams et al, the aforementioned night in Copenhagen, great wins at The Lane, beating Newcastle to secure the 1998 Double, and others. That passion for Arsenal is confined to particular period in my life. I can pinpoint precisely when it started: 1973. But it faded sometime after 2003. I came back from Australia for the end of the 2002 Double season. I went to the 2003 FA Cup Final when Arsenal beat Southampton. I didn't come back for the 2005 FA Cup Final or 2006 Champions League Final. Subsequent UK visits have seen trips to the Emirates become less frequent. It's almost as though I was in a *relationship* with Arsenal – one that burned brightly early on, then solidly for many years before we drifted apart then separated. We're still friends though; not divorced yet.

My affection for Brentford comes from a different place. It isn't player-generated, and I don't often reminisce about particular games. My affection is for the *club* – its trials, tribulations, successes and ethos. And that it is local to where I was born and grew up. Strangely, my real affection for Brentford kicked-in *after* I'd moved to Australia, nearly four decades after I first fell in love with the game. It's like realising in your late forties that the right girl all along was the one you once lived next door to. I'd gone on-and-off to Brentford since the early 1980s, but it was a very *casual thing*. It was on a trip to England in late 2012 when I belatedly fell for my hometown club. Brentford were at home to Sheffield United in a League One game, which they won 2-0. It was a fun day out – a lunchtime pub crawl through old Ealing haunts followed by a couple of hours at Griffin Park. It was like revisiting a simpler time in football. Something *clicked*.

Although Arsenal was my first love, I wasn't one of those totally one-eyed, one-club fans. I always enjoyed going to other games – whether it was north of the border or other games in London; many of my friends followed different teams. I loved seeing Arsenal away at a ground I'd never been to before and I still get a buzz going into a venue for the first time. Market Rasen race course, the banks of the Thames at Henley and the cricket ground in Dunedin, New Zealand are idyllic places to watch sport.

Nowadays I'd regard myself as a more *rounded* fan of football, and sport, in general.

Football has changed considerably. One of the problems with the English Premier League – Leicester City's remarkable title season aside – is the predictability of it. A club's wage bill correlates almost exactly with their position at the end of the season. In August you can look at the twenty Premier League clubs and break them into mini-leagues of their own – the top four, the Europa League 'probables' and 'possibles', the lower mid-table lot and those that are going to struggle.

The Championship is more interesting. At the start of the season there are a few favourites, but it's far more competitive than the Premier League in terms of the number of teams who stand a chance of winning it. Going up – in second place or via the play-offs – is a big prize as well. Going to games is much more affordable – and you usually don't have to bust your arse getting organised with tickets weeks or months ahead. Clubs can also be more flexible with increased away ticket allocations, meaning a better atmosphere at games.

In the past football was a weekend release for largely working-class men. While not advocating a return to rampant hooliganism and the piss-drenched terraces of the past, it has to be said that football has become over-sanitised. There is a difference between feeling in danger at a football match and standing in noisy, partisan crowds. The fake friendliness stuff has gone too far. This lining-up before kick-off and doing the handshake thing… seriously? These kinds of innovations have largely come from newcomers to the game or the TV channels reshaping the game into the experience *they* want.

"We've decided to come along now and watch *your* game. But we're going to change it, to suit *us*."

The relationship between players and fans at top-level clubs has changed. In the 1970s and 1980s top players earned considerably more, but it was more like three-to-five times the average wage, not two hundred times. Consider the final whistle behaviour of players towards their club's fans – particularly away from home. What once struck me as a very genuine interaction – which varied a bit depending on the final score and importance of the game – now usually looks forced, contrived. Much of the time you see coaches and captains cajoling players into acknowledging the fans. If it doesn't come from the right place, why do it at all?

Top-level players now seem untouchable. There are common stories from the 1940s and 1950s about First Division players chatting with fans on buses on their way to games. Or serving fans in their butchers' shops on the Saturday morning of a match. Players largely came from the communities they represented.

Football is more popular than ever, but much has been lost along the way. How many people who obsess about the game they watch on TV will actually ever get to see their heroes play *live*? I wonder if, at the highest level, it will ever again be a game where working-class fathers take their sons on a regular basis. I wonder just how long the 'money bubble' can last – the inflated wages, extortionate admission prices and the control exerted by TV.

Somewhere along the way 'stakeholders' became more important than fans.

For me it isn't just about the game, race or event I go to. It's also about the town or city, the history, culture, rivalries, stadium architecture and quirks, different experiences, the people you go with and the people you meet. That's what fuels the passion; that's why I like to watch.

Simon Wooldridge

I LIKE TO WATCH

Racing Is My Passion!

We're standing outside a bar in La Boca. Three of us: me, Witek and Darryn – an Englishman, a Pole and an Aussie. Darryn lives in the same town as me in Australia and Witold 'Witek' Zdybicki, one of my oldest friends. It's early 2010.

La Boca is a trendy, arty, but dodgy-as-fuck neighbourhood in Buenos Aires. We're in conversation with three blokes: the driver, Carlos, who brought us here (speaks a little English), the Ticket Bloke (no English) and his weasel-looking mate who speaks enough English to make sense of the whole situation for us. They're laughing because we have cameras and phones and we're wearing watches. Our tickets are for the 'Popular' section of the stadium. 'Popular' means cheap, means standing, means being in the livelier part of the ground.

"Don't take these things," Weasel says, pointing at Witek's video camera and other stuff we're holding and wearing, "you will be robbed."

Darryn and I are staying in Palermo, but Witek's hotel in Recoleta is nearer. Carlos drives us there and we dump our valuables in Witek's room. I put thirty pesos in my front pocket, two hundred pesos in my shoe and a credit card and my driving licence in a low-down side pocket on my shorts. Having to cancel one credit card won't be the end of the world if it comes to it. Witek is disappointed that he's not going to be capturing any of the evening for prosperity; Darryn wonders what the hell he's got himself into.

Carlos drives us further south, to Avellaneda.

"Buenos Aires no," he says, "Buenos Aires Province." We've crossed the line out of the city into Buenos Aires Province. It looks the same. I suppose it's like going from a London postcode to a Surrey postcode. Though, this doesn't look much like Surrey, it has to be said.

Carlos's phone rings. He talks animatedly and sounds defensive. A few minutes later we stop. He gets out and talks to four blokes standing around a shabby old car. One of them looks agitated.

"We're late," I say to Witek and Darryn. "The detour back to the hotel."

Carlos comes back and we set off, following the other blokes.

After a few minutes both cars stop and park. We get introduced to the four blokes. We already paid Ticket Bloke back in the bar in La Boca but these blokes have our actual tickets. Everyone shakes hands, says hello, and the one who'd looked agitated has calmed down. We're very near the ground and well in time for kick-off. Tension over.

"Where are you from?"

"England, but I live in Australia."

"Poland," says Witek, proudly. Always proudly.

"Australia," says Darryn.

"Who do you support?" He asks me.

"Arsenal."

"Are you a hooligan?"

"No. Are *you* a hooligan?"

"No." He smiles. "Racing is my passion!" He places his right hand over his heart then we shake hands again.

We get into the ground. Our non-hooligan guides have led us through the throng outside and navigated our entrance. Then we lose them. Once through the ticket barriers I look ahead at the steps going up into the back of the standing enclosure at one end of the ground. But the steps aren't being used as a thoroughfare. The steps are packed with fans facing *outwards* towards the entrance gates. They are singing and jumping up and down. There's still over forty five minutes until kick-off. I've never seen anything like it. We slowly work our way through the bouncing crowd, up the steps and into the open bowl of Estadio Juan Domingo Perón. The singing and jumping up and down is even more full-blooded at pitch-side.

"Let's move over to the side," I say pointing right to a quieter-looking part of the stadium. We edge a bit in that direction but then a massive surge of bodies engulfs us. I look around and immediately see Witek, but Darryn is on the ground. We help him up.

"You alright?"

He smiles. "Yeah."

Clearly from out of town we've been on the end of what was probably just a *welcome-to-our-patch* jostling. It was more spirited and boisterous than outright threatening. Still, probably a good idea to keep moving. So we did, ending up beyond the halfway line, close to a line of armed riot police protecting the expansive no-man's-land separating the Racing fans from the San Lorenzo visitors. The San Lorenzo section is equally lively, holding maybe four or five thousand of their fans. Another massive no-man's-land of seats and terraces separates them on their other side before the Racing section starts again.

***

Ok, a bit about Racing Club. Argentine football's 'big five' comprises River Plate, Boca Juniors, Independiente, Racing and San Lorenzo. The River-Boca rivalry is world famous and widely documented. When River play Boca it's the 'Superclásico'. Far lesser-known, outside Argentina, is the Avellaneda rivalry between Racing and Independiente. But if you delve into the history, it is by all accounts as fierce as River vs Boca. Their respective grounds are within a few hundred yards of each other – think Dundee United and Dundee or Notts County and Nottingham Forest and you have an idea of the distance but not the antipathy. Racing are a big club – a one-time winner of the Intercontinental Cup, they also have seventeen Primera División titles to their name.

A couple of Racing vs Independiente games stand out particularly in the annals of Argentine football aggro history. A November 1961 fixture was stopped for six minutes while players fought. Both teams ended the game (a 1-1 draw) with *seven* players.

In a 2006 match Independiente were 2-0 up at home when Racing fans decided to riot and fight the police. The game was abandoned, with the points ultimately awarded to Independiente. This particular incident led to the Argentine Football Association banning away fans. This game, with some compelling footage, features in the series *Football Factories International*.

Popularly known as 'El Cilindro', Racing's ground once held 100,000 but is now limited to 51,000 to allow for excited surging fans and the two vast no man's land sections required to isolate away fans. It's an unusual ground – the structure is circular, not an oval or traditional rectangle shape. On the sides there is a considerable gap between fans and the pitch – much greater than at either end. Have a look on Google Maps – it's quite different to anything you'd normally see, yet it's not a multi-purpose stadium.

The atmosphere is intoxicating; there's a real edge to it. At no point though, after positioning ourselves right next to the armed riot police, did we feel uncomfortable. The singing and camaraderie took me back to the late 1970s in England, only factor it up three or four times.

The game was no classic, barely entertaining even. But for three out-of-towners, it was fascinating.

I saw a couple of things I'd never seen before in my years going to football. There was a collapsible 'tunnel' which extended out onto the pitch from the changing rooms to protect the away team and officials from missiles. And when a visiting player took a corner he was surrounded and covered by police holding riot shields.

In front of us, on top of the six-foot narrow wall holding on to the fencing throughout the game stood one very passionate Racing fan. He was living every challenge, pass and decision. When he wasn't watching the game, he was directing fierce abuse at the San Lorenzo fans, fifty yards away. Not a day under thirty-five, he was absolutely consumed, frequently cradling his head in frustration when something didn't go Racing's way.

The game was meandering to a 0-0 when fireworks started going off and smoke bombs engulfed the Racing end. Within minutes the smoke had drifted across the pitch. It was as though the game was being played in low-cloud conditions. It seemed to have a galvanising effect. With eighty-two minutes gone and Racing attacking the goal to our right, a cross gets floated in and is met by a centre forward's textbook downward header. The San Lorenzo goalkeeper saves but only pushes it into the path of the offside-looking Gabriel Hauche who pokes it into the top of the net. He wheels away to his left. No flag. 1-0.

One of my questions of the last couple of hours gets answered. I now understand why there is so much space at the front of the terraces. The crowd needs somewhere to go after a goal as the fans erupt, surging forward, bouncing off each other and the wall at the front of the terraces. The ground wasn't full enough for us to be swept up in the celebratory surge when Racing scored. Even so, bodies powered forward into a kind of trough just in front of the wall. A primeval roar engulfed El Cilindro. It looked even livelier to our left where the most demonstrably fanatic of the home fans were. The wall at the front of the terraces was about six feet high and topped by fencing; on the other side there was a moat. However excited they get, they're not getting on the pitch.

It was a dodgy-looking goal at the time and an even dodgier-looking goal on YouTube every time since. But this is Argentina and with the game goalless heading into the last few minutes this is the home team we're talking about; the home team whose fans have just turned the stadium into a fireworks display. We're at a ground where the officials need to be escorted on and off the pitch by armed police. Ok, so it was a *little bit* offside.

"Racing is my passion!"

And about thirty thousand people clearly demonstrated that passion in those couple of minutes after the goal. What we'd been watching – game-wise – didn't compare with what you'd see at an English Premier League ground, but this had something else, something the Premier League has never had, and never will.

In Argentina the fans are part of the fabric of the club. Much has been written about just how much the fans or 'barras bravas' are part of their clubs. Some of it makes uncomfortable reading. From where I was standing that night in Avellaneda, it felt more exciting and inclusive than any top division game I'd been to in England in quarter of a century or more.

As things calmed a little, I looked up at the fan standing on the wall. He was in a crouching position, shaking. He was crying his eyes out.

The final whistle went, followed by the usual sort of *we-were-always-in-control* celebrations amongst Racing players and fans. The teams left the pitch. But the crowd around us didn't move. I looked over to see San Lorenzo fans streaming for the exits. Our section, and the rest of the Racing sections stayed put.

Someone told me the next day what this was all about: "The other supporters…"

"The away fans?" I asked.

"Yes. The away fans. They have fifteen minutes to vacate."

"Vacate? Get away?"

"Yes," I was told. "Get away."

Very sensible, but a little chilling. Follow your team to an away game and at the end you've got fifteen minutes to *get away*.

The gates opened, and we filed out. We stood out like the tourists we were, but no one gave us a second glance. Would it have been different if Racing had lost?

"Can you remember where Carlos dropped us?" I asked.

Darryn was confident he could lead us through the back streets to where Carlos should be waiting. A few minutes later we found our driver.

"Good game?" he asked.

"Absolutely great," I said, "fantastic atmosphere."

We got in and he pulled away through the crowds heading back to the city. His phone rang.

"Si," he said. "Si, si, ok." And then something else. My Spanish was limited but I realised it was the Racing non-hooligans checking we'd got back alright.

We picked up our valuables at Witek's hotel, then Darryn and I went back to Palermo. It was midnight. We went over to Morelia, the street corner bar-restaurant just across from our hotel and ordered pizza and beers.

The following afternoon I pondered the economics of this little adventure while I waited in my hotel lobby. The face value of my ticket was thirty pesos; I'd paid over two hundred. Driver there and back, Ticket Bloke and Weasel in La Boca, the blokes who'd got us into the ground – these were just the involved parties I was aware of. Being Argentina there'd surely be several other people taking some kind of cut as well. It had been interesting and fun though.

I looked up as Carlos walked across the lobby towards me, smiling. I'd been bitten by the Argentinian football bug. He was taking me to that afternoon's River Plate game.

I LIKE TO WATCH

Pamplona

My old man, the Hemingway fan, had been going to Pamplona since the early 1960s. His introduction, like many of his generation, was *The Sun Also Rises*, Ernest Hemingway's 1926 novel about the annual San Fermín festival in the Basque country in Northern Spain.

I don't think the old man had missed a San Fermín in the previous twenty or so by the time I joined him in 1985. I was the first of his three sons to take up an offer that had been on the table and spruiked to us for many years.

He circled that week in July in his diary at the start of each year. It took on annual pilgrimage-like status for about a dozen of them – friends not only from London but Australia, the US and other parts of the world. It was a loose collective of friends that did Pamplona – some of them my old man saw only at this one time of the year.

Pamplona or 'Pamps', as I've since seen it advertised on the *do-Europe-on-the-cheap-and-tick-everything-off* circuit, has turned into a quasi-festival of binge drinking for backpackers. The same backpackers who, a few months later, tick off Oktoberfest while posting more pictures on Facebook than anyone will ever be interested in. Binge drinking at Pamplona didn't start with backpackers however. My old man and his mates had been doing it for a generation, with stories told and retold around the dining table at home as we grew up.

As far as foreign visitors were concerned, when I first went, we were still very much in a previous era. I would've been one of the youngest foreigners in town. There were however, countless big-bearded English-speaking men paying homage to Hemingway.

I flew with my dad and two of his friends into Bilbao. We picked-up a hire car and drove along the coast to San Sebastian, an attractive if a little tired-looking city by the sea. A night's drinking, dinner and visit to the casino were the order of the day. There was something quite classy, even romantic, for me about standing at a roulette table on the Bay of Biscay on a night when a few hundred miles away my mates would be in the North Star in Ealing, speed-drinking pints of piss-weak lager.

Late the following morning we set-off on the seventy-mile or so drive to Pamplona, stopping en route at a remote hillside restaurant. A long lunch ensued; a wonderful fish dish accompanied by several bottles of wine. It was mid-afternoon when we left. As we approached the car my old man chucked me the keys.

"Your turn," he said, simply.

Ok, a bit of background and context. At this point, July 1985, I was still learning to drive. The vast majority of the driving I'd done to that point was during lessons in a BSM car with my instructor sat beside me. Sober, in a right-hand drive, on the left-hand side of the road.

So, on a mountain-side road in Northern Spain after a long lunch with numerous glasses of wine I got behind the wheel of a Renault or Peugeot or some other kind of generic hire car. Officially, I couldn't drive. I had three passengers, ranging in age from about forty to fifty three. They too had all been drinking. I guessed this was the first test of the father-son bonding 'mini-break'.

The road was winding, and initially uphill. I was sitting on the left, driving on the right and more than once on the receiving end of a no-uncertain-terms reminder that I was on the wrong side of the road. I suddenly felt remarkably sober. I kept at it, diligently. No twenty-year-old wants to bottle out of something in front of their dad. I was changing gears with my right-hand for the first time, using the mirrors in a completely different way and watching a different lane on the road in front. Fortunately, there was little in the way of traffic.

After twenty minutes or so the old man told me to "pull over at the next sensible place to stop". I did as instructed, and we changed places. I felt a sense of relief – though there had been a bit of an adrenalin rush about it. Nothing though, like the adrenalin rush I would experience a few mornings later.

The festival of San Fermín has been a fixture of Basque life for several hundred years – first documented as early as the 1300s. It runs from 6 July, commencing at noon, until midnight on 14 July. The first full day of the festival is 7 July, and until relatively recently the bull running event started at 7 a.m. – thus the seventh hour of the seventh day of the seventh month became symbolic. I assume the 1977 festival was celebrated extra-specially.

The bull running ('encierro' if you're a local) and daily afternoon bullfight are just two of the components of San Fermín. There are also processions, fireworks and other traditional Basque sports. The festival attracts over a million visitors each year.

Legend has it that the start time was moved forward an hour due to the number of injuries caused by people staying up all night before heading to the Calle Estafeta for the 7 a.m. start. The 8 a.m. start, apparently, made a significant difference – most people actually going to bed for a while.

Make no mistake, bull running is dangerous. In the last 100 years or so fifteen people have been killed doing it at Pamplona, most recently in 2000. With thousands of people running each day the odds might sound ok, or ok-ish. But several hundred runners are injured as a result of falls, crushing and knocks of various types. It is *packed* in that street, and for a few minutes, absolute mayhem.

I didn't run that first morning. My old man and his friends mixed it up a bit – depending on hangover states I'm guessing – between running and viewing from an apartment window directly over the Calle Estafeta. They had a long-standing arrangement with a little old lady to use her apartment for viewing purposes each morning during San Fermín. Each day some permutation of their group was there if they weren't in the street below psyching themselves up for the run.

Early on the morning of 7 July 1985 I watched my first bull run from that apartment window. The street was teeming with people, young and old. I guessed the make-up was somewhere in the region of eighty per cent locals, or Spanish at least, versus foreigner-tourists. There were no women. The majority of people were wearing an approximation of the customary dress – a red neck scarf or handkerchief with white shirt or white t-shirt and white trousers. It was an impressive sight.

Each day the bulls are brought to a pen about half a mile from the bullring. The traditional 'running' of the bulls is essentially them being taken to the ring in advance of that day's fight. A bullfight typically consists of six separate fights lasting around twenty minutes each. The process and traditions undertaken in a fight, the roles of bandoleros, picadors and matadors, the awarding of ears, tails or whatever are all documented elsewhere in detail, at length and by writers whose knowledge far surpasses mine – so I'll leave it there. I'm focussing on the bull run.

The half-mile or so from the holding pen to the bullring is largely along the one street, the Calle Estafeta. However, the bulls enter this street from an angle.

"They come in from the right," my dad explained, "and generally stay close to the left-hand wall as they head towards the bullring."

"So the right-hand side of the street is the better place to stand before running?"

"Exactly. The other important thing is how far apart they are," he said. "There are six or seven bulls. I think they have a spare in case one doesn't fight, or something happens. And they're about the same number of steers with them, to help guide them – meant to keep them in line basically."

The street below became increasingly busy as eight o'clock approached.

"Listen out for the fireworks," he said. "There are four, but it's the first two that are important. The first is when the first bull is out and running. The second when the last bull is out. The third one is when they're all in the ring. The first two are the important ones. You want them close together. It means the bulls are in a group. It's safer. The longer apart the first two fireworks are, well… the bulls are separated. You don't know which bulls the steers are with. It's much more dangerous, you could get one bull at the back on its own causing problems."

I looked down again at the street. This time the next day I'd be in that crowd.

"Of course, the easiest way to get hurt," he said, "is being trampled by other people."

Eight a.m. arrived, as did the sound of a firecracker going off. And then another.

I watched, fascinated. I gathered that by Pamplona bull run standards I'd seen a good one. It went off smoothly and without any obvious casualties of either the bull-inflicted or human motor skills misjudgement variety. It was over in a matter of minutes and quarter of an hour later we were in a bar having our first drinks of the day. A light morning nap was followed by another long lunch. It went on so long that we had to go direct from the restaurant to the Plaza de Toros for the evening's fight.

The running of the bulls, Pamplona, 1985.

I'd been to bullfights before on family holidays in Gran Canaria, and in Tarragona on Spain's Mediterranean coast. I was about eight when I first went to a bullfight. Hearing about bullfights when I was growing up, I don't think I ever stopped to think about any of the negative aspects.

I never thought of backing-out of the next day's bull run. At the age I was, having had a somewhat stilted relationship with my old man since about the age of twelve, I was never going to lose face over something like this. I was nervous but was never going to show it.

There was no time to nurse a hangover that second morning. It had been another late night and I'd ended-up separated from my dad and his friends somewhere, buying unneeded and soon-to-be-dispensed-with trinkets from a market stall. I had been trying to maintain the pace with seasoned drinkers thirty-odd years older than me. It wasn't just the volume or length of session I found challenging but the changes from beer, to wine, to brandy, to something else, and then something else again.

We found our way into the Calle Estafeta. There was a persistent hum of voices – excitement, anticipation and nerves rolled into one. I hadn't noticed the hum from the window the day before. I followed my old man.

"Ok," he said. "We'll wait about here." We were standing close to the right-hand side of the street, somewhere roughly below the window we'd used the previous day. "Stay with me. When I say run, you run. When you've had enough just pull over to the right, get right against the wall and stay there. Don't run again." Famous last words.

"What's with the newspapers?" I asked. Many people were holding rolled-up newspapers.

"For show," he said, dismissively. "The idea is that if a bull gets too close you can guide it away using the newspaper against its head or horns. It's bullshit though. Very few people get that close to a bull. They're doing it for show."

Bang. The first firecracker went off. Bang. And then the second. My old man nodded to me as if to say, "that's good". The hum of voices went up noticeably, and people started to bounce a bit on the spot. The bulls were *in play*.

The crowd noise built further as the bulls and steers approached; the distinctive sound of the steers' cowbells telegraphing their approach. I too began to bounce a little on the spot, looking around, edging forward. And then there were people running up the street towards us. The noise was coming from all around and above; the spectators as excited or scared as the runners.

"Go!" My dad said. I was off – not quite hugging that right-hand wall as I went, but within touching distance. Howls, whistles, cowbells and the gentle rumble of feet filled the air. I glanced over my left shoulder, then carried on. Glanced again. Then again. I glimpsed horns through a knot of people running frantically in my direction. I didn't know whether the horns belonged to bulls or steers or a combination. I carried on running – another twenty or thirty yards, I'm not sure. Then I pulled up to the right, against the wall. Bulls, steers and people went by just a few feet away. But there was a second group a little further back, so I decided to run again, to do precisely what I'd been told *not* to do – which was pretty much par for the course as far as this particular father-son relationship went.

They got closer this time. In hindsight probably not dangerously close, but close enough to smell. I ran with them to my left and behind me. The street was packed, and I was conscious of potentially going down and being trampled. The wall to my right then finished and we entered an open area with wooden fencing. The wooden fences were built to withstand an angry bull but designed with big enough gaps

At the Plaza de Toros, Pamplona.

for people to get through. That's what I did. With commotion and noise to one side and behind me, I threw myself at the gap between the first and second blocks in the wooden structure. I got through quickly. As I went through my right shin banged and scraped heavily against the underside of the second bar. Then I was flat on my back, and someone landed near me. We were the right side of the fence though. The commotion continued towards the bullring.

I got up and dusted myself down. My leg was pounding so I rolled up my torn right trouser leg to inspect the damage. There was a lot of blood coming out from a cut just below my knee. I watched the tail end of runners heading towards the bullring. After a few minutes, I got back onto the street and walked back in the direction of where I'd started my run earlier.

We went to a bar. Yesterday's 8.30 a.m. beer became a brandy. I was still coming down off a big adrenalin rush as my dad and his friends chatted about the morning's run before moving onto other topics. They'd done it all many times before.

I checked what the lunchtime arrangements were, then headed back to the apartment. I desperately needed a shit. It was the opposite of a nervous shit – a post-nerves shit, I guess. The combination of adrenalin, hangover and much higher than average alcohol intake over the previous few days produced something quite noxious with a seemingly chemical element to it. Then I slept for a couple of hours.

I enjoyed those few days in Pamplona. I didn't run again on that trip, but I did twice the following year. I recall little from those second and third runs in 1986. Over those two trips to Pamplona I went to seven or eight bullfights. Despite numerous trips to Spain since, I've never been to one again.

I LIKE TO WATCH

Chorzów

In May 1997 I went over to Poland for a few days to see my old friend Witold Zdybicki. We lived in the same road and went to school together for a few years in our teens before he returned to Poland in the 1980s. We stayed in touch, meeting up every few years.

The focal point of that visit was the Saturday night Poland vs England World Cup qualifier in Chorzów. I was joined by Owen Francis – who'd met Witek in London the previous year, and John Matthews, a West Ham supporter friend of ours. We had our first beer at Heathrow at about 7.30 a.m. before we flew out. It set the tone.

An eventful, heavy-drinking few days unfolded. We stayed the first night at Witek's Warsaw apartment before travelling up to Gdańsk, 180 miles to the north, by train on the Thursday. We stayed at the Grand Hotel in Sopot, just north of Gdańsk. In 1997 it was a tired old place – albeit one with loads of character. It wasn't difficult to see why it had originally claimed the name 'Grand'. Even the briefest of brief online searches now show that it has been well and truly done up – with prices to match, I imagine. I think we paid about £20 each back then.

On the Friday we went back to Warsaw and a third heavy night on the booze. Saturday was match day. The game was at the Stadion Śląski in Chorzów, in Poland's industrial south. We set off at about noon – the earliest Witek thought he could risk driving – for the four-hour drive.

I'd done pretty much the same journey six years earlier with Witek – although with no sporting event on the agenda. In 1991 we'd gone to Katowice, Krakow and then Zakopane in the mountains on the border with what was then Czechoslovakia. It seemed as though twenty-five years' worth of developments had been crammed in since my previous visit. The B road equivalent of 1991 had been replaced by a shiny new highway. In 1991 we'd stopped for something to eat, parking in a field, then eating in little more than a shack; a delicious, hearty sausage with mustard presented on a piece of cardboard, washed down with a Żywiec beer. In 1997 we stopped at a McDonald's.

Polish football fans have a fearsome reputation. Our tickets were on the side of the ground, in an area reserved for home fans. Witek reckoned the stadium held about thirty thousand and the media had reported that three thousand England fans would be there. I imagined them packed tightly into one corner of the ground. I imagined correctly.

Witek raised something I wasn't expecting. His number plates.

"The W shows the car is registered in Warsaw. This game is in the south. They fucking hate us when it comes to football. They'll want to fight me as much as they want to fight you."

Oh.

"They're all miners and blue-collar workers down there. They hate Legia fans. They will have separate sectors in the stadium."

"Can you just park somewhere discreetly?" Owen suggested.

"I will try."

On we went.

We had to pick-up the match tickets at a PZPN (Polish Football Association) office in nearby Katowice. The *body* of the ticket was printed but the letters and numbers indicating block, row and seat number were *handwritten in pen*. Not everything had moved on at the same pace as the roads in Poland.

Witek drove around a for a while. We briefly thought about trying to get a drink somewhere but there was a heavy atmosphere around the place and we'd already seen one minor skirmish. It was easy to spot the English fans; their clothes gave the game away. It was almost a fashion vs function thing in terms of what the fans of each country were wearing. It would be less obvious these days.

"We might as well go to the game."

"It's early, but I think you're right," said Witek.

We parked in a big car park next to the stadium, close to the section we'd be sitting in. It would've been difficult to get much closer without a media, Polish FA or FIFA pass.

There was nearly two hours to go before kick-off when we entered the ground. We checked out where we'd be sitting, then had a wander around. The Stadion Śląski was a big, uncovered bowl. The seats were like half plastic buckets nailed to a basic metal frame. It looked like some of the seats in other areas of the ground were benches. There were crumbling-looking terraces at each end, with fences dividing the sections.

I thought it was obvious to people around us that three of the four of us were English. I don't think our presence went unnoticed, but it went uncommented upon – to us at least. We were sitting high up on the side of the ground, a bit away from the more boisterous sections perhaps. The England fans, still gathering, were penned-in, away to our left.

Legia fans arrive for Poland vs England, Chorzów, 1997.

Time to kill, we just chatted, surveying the scene. Then from *outside* the stadium we heard a commotion – a crowd singing and that familiar *aggro roar*. Along with many other fans near us we walked to the back of the stand and looked out to see what was happening.

Marching towards the stadium was a large group. There was several hundred of them, singing and chanting. They were surrounded by police.

"Erm…" started Owen, "the main group of England fans have arrived."

"No," said Witek, "they're from Warsaw. Legia fans. The police have to keep them separate from the other Poles or there will be big fights. I think maybe they came by train."

We watched as they were led around the ground, then went back to our seats. Within minutes the Legia Warsaw fans were flowing noisily into their designated section to our right. While their section was still filling up they mounted coordinated attacks on the sections either side of them.

"Fuck me," I said under my breath.

"All the other clubs hate Legia," said Witek.

"Can't say I'm surprised."

We'd been hanging around a long time for kick-off. We'd wandered around our part of the ground a bit, watched fans arrive, sampled some of the local nosebag, quaffed cokes and then kick-off was upon us. The stadium held about thirty thousand and it was all open – no covered enclosures to trap or amplify sound. Yet it got very noisy. The Poles knew how to get behind their team.

England took the lead in the fifth minute. The combative Paul Ince won the ball in midfield before slide rule passing it to Alan Shearer who struck it home emphatically from just inside the box. This didn't exactly silence the boisterous home fans, but it set a tone for the rest of the game. England were in control. Shearer missed a penalty just before half-time, and it was all put to rest very late on when Teddy Sheringham tapped it in to make it 2-0 in injury time. We'd left by then.

Witek drove out of the car park and away from the ground as the main throng of fans were leaving. The traffic built up and we edged along with other cars heading south out of Chorzów. Witek had booked a hotel about forty miles away. The following day we were going to visit Auschwitz and then head on to Zakopane for the night.

"We are very low on petrol," Witek said as we hit the highway. And then a few minutes later when he saw a sign indicating where the next petrol station was: "I don't think we will make it."

"Are you sure?" Owen asked. "It's not that far."

"I set the gauge back to zero every time I fill up. I know exactly how far this car will go on a full tank."

I'd known Witek for twenty years and didn't doubt him for a moment, much as I would've liked him to be wrong this time. He carried on driving.

"We'll get as far as we can."

A few minutes later the car started spluttering and slowed. He drove onto the grass at the side of the road.

"Shit," we pretty much all chorused. Based on how long since we saw the last sign, we couldn't have been more than a few miles from the next petrol station.

The highway was busy with traffic – largely coming from the game. People naturally looked over as they passed.

"I will try to hitch a lift to the next petrol station. Get a can of petrol and get back here somehow. You just wait with the car," said Witek, ever the quick-thinking pragmatist. "Remember we have all our luggage in the car."

John, Owen and I weren't going back to Warsaw – we were going on to Prague and were flying back to London from there on the Tuesday.

Witek stood a little apart from us, trying to flag a car down for a lift. I stood in front of the number plate, obscuring the W for Warsaw.

As gruff and tough-looking as many of the Poles were, it didn't extend to ignoring a bloke in need. Within minutes a car had stopped and Witek was on his way. The traffic kept streaming our way. Cars with flags and scarves out the windows.

"It's obvious we're English." I said.

"Reckon?"

"The clothes give it away. Look at how they're all looking."

"Nah. They're just looking because we're stopped by the side of the road," Owen said.

"Well, they're not looking that friendly!" said John. "The last thing we want is someone to stop and come over."

We agreed to look away from the cars passing us. I carried on leaning against the boot with John and Owen facing me in conversation.

None of us were smoking – another clear indicator, I thought. Car breaks down, blokes waiting by the side of the road on a night that's getting chillier by the minute. And none of us smoking? Dead giveaway in a heavy-smoking country.

Then the coaches started rolling by. Full of Polish fans. Dozens of coaches passed us. Every face along the window side was turned towards us, and just about every face belonged to a male between twenty and forty.

"We're really getting eyeballed here," I said, looking out of the corner of my eye to the right, whilst facing Owen and John.

"All we need is one coach to stop…"

The coaches streamed past. The faces looked out. This carried on for five minutes or more. It just needed one person to tell the driver to stop and we'd be in deep shit. Kicked to death next to a motorway outside Chorzów in Poland didn't seem a very dignified exit. Far too young, and probably very messy.

There's no denying the three of us were anxious. We were sitting ducks and basically at the mercy of hundreds of complete strangers.

The bulk of the coaches passed us, and then it was back to regular traffic and a sporadic flow of coaches. Still they looked, and still we metaphorically shat ourselves.

It had been about twenty minutes since Witek had left when a taxi exited the lane next to us and pulled over. Witek emerged, petrol can in hand. He paid off the driver, exchanging some kind of joke with him.

"Thank fuck you're here. This was starting to get interesting."

As he emptied the petrol can into the tank, we explained what had happened.

"Shit," he said, laughing nervously.

And then we headed off. We filled up at the petrol station Witek had just come from, and then carried on to our hotel. Two or three very slow, low-key beers at the hotel bar and that was it for the night.

I LIKE TO WATCH

The Old Firm

"Going to the game?"

Fuck.

Sunday 31 August 1986. I was standing at the urinal in a Central Glasgow pub toilet. I'm furthest from the door. This bloke has just come in and unzipped himself a few places away from me. He's between me and the door. There's no one else in here. Two hours from now the Old Firm game between Rangers and Celtic will be kicking off at Ibrox a few miles away. He's not wearing a scarf. And there are no other potential giveaway signs; no head of very red hair, or orange shoes with flutes attached. Am I going to the game? I am. But I'm really just an interloper from down south in this most localised, tense and volatile of world football squabbles. Rangers and Celtic hate each other. Dress it up for 21st century sensibilities if you will. Call it the 'Glasgow derby' if you like. It runs deeper than that. It's a cultural, political and religious battle. Football, really, is just the window on this divide; a divide that originates across the sea in Northern Ireland. It's an argument that's been going on for over three hundred years.

He's a bit older than me, about twenty-five probably. My height and kind of build. Not a casual, but not a 'scarfer' type either. A regular bloke.

"Put me on the spot why don't you?" I answered. "That's a tricky question to answer before the big game when you're from out of town." I looked at him with a bit of what I hoped would come across as a wry smile. Not piss-takey, over-friendly or anxious though.

"Where are you from?" he asked, surprised. Direct, but not aggressive, he hadn't anticipated my accent.

"London."

"You here for the game then?"

"Yeah. Biggest game in the world isn't it? Got to be worth seeing."

"That it is."

I couldn't work out whether he kicked with his right or left. Being a Rangers home game, it was a reasonable assumption that there would be more Rangers fans than Celtic around the city centre before the game. The three blokes I'd come with – who were upstairs in the bar – were Rangers fans. They wouldn't have picked this pub if they thought there might be a problem. However, I did want to give the impression that this was my first Old Firm game so I could play the naïve tourist if I needed to. It was actually my fourth Old Firm game in a year.

"You here with mates?"

"Yeah, upstairs." I said.

"Which team?" he asked, a bit of a smile surfacing.

Ah fuck it, I thought, if there's a problem there's a problem. "Rangers."

"Aaaah! Good man!"

We washed our hands and introduced ourselves.

***

My enjoyment of North London derbies and my appreciation of the history (yes, it *is* Arsenal's fault) had me reading up on some of the other big football rivalries around. This was pre-internet so 'Clásicos', 'Superclásicos' and really anything outside of Britain was off my radar. Even Scotland seemed adventurous.

It was late August 1985 when I headed up to Scotland for the first Old Firm game of the season. To put this in some historical context, this was a whole season before Graeme Souness took over at Rangers. The Rangers and Celtic teams were still made up very largely of Scottish players, a smattering of Irish (from both sides of the border) and the occasional Englishman. Scottish football was rarely reported or even mentioned – beyond simple results listings – in the English media.

I was with Carl Prinzel. He'd knocked off work and we were in a pub near Queen Street station. Carl and I worked for the same company, – me in the London head office and he in a Glasgow store. We'd never actually met until that day but had passed many hours on the phone on work-related stuff which had then usually moved quickly onto football and music. He was a big Rangers fan and my visit to Glasgow the result of a throwaway line a few months previously that had developed into a plan.

We left the pub. There *wisnae* taxi to be found. So, it was a train to the East End of Glasgow. I was fairly nonplussed; ignorance being a kind of bliss and all that. Carl was less relaxed.

"We gotta go to the station behind the Rangers end," he said. But he couldn't remember what it was called. He knew there was also a station that Celtic supporters would use for their three sides of the ground. For obvious reasons it was important we get this right. Fortunately, we did, getting off at Camtyne, a ten-minute or so walk to Celtic Park – importantly, the end of Celtic Park where the Rangers fans would be standing.

We got in just before kick-off and took up a position at the back of the massive terraced away end. There must have been about eighteen thousand Rangers fans in there. And it was packed. So packed, that at half-time I realised I'd been pickpocketed. Two twenty-pound notes folded and resting in my front jeans pocket were gone. No giveaway wallet bulge, but some little fucker had managed to get his fingers into my front pocket. Had to admire it in some way really.

One of the things that struck me was the sheer noise. *Everybody* sang. Volume-wise, it was about a North London derby ratcheted up about three levels. I didn't really understand the songs but knew roughly enough what they were about – enough to realise neither set of fans was singing much about football. Prior to that weekend I didn't know that much of the history. I knew it wasn't really the 'Glasgow derby' and it had nothing to do with city geography. And I knew it wasn't just because they were the big two. It was about Ireland, Northern Ireland, Catholics vs Protestants, the establishment vs the immigrants, two different communities. I just didn't realise the complexities and the deep-running hatred that existed. It was scary yet intoxicating. When I later understood what some of the songs were about and read-up more of the history I started to *get* the intensity of it.

I was twenty when I went to that first Old Firm game. I was a middle-class boy from London whose football-going education had largely consisted of visits to Highbury, other London grounds and a few away games outside the capital. Newcastle and Sheffield were the furthest north I'd ever travelled before for football – Arsenal taking just a few hundred supporters in each case. I wasn't prepared for what I was about to experience at Celtic Park.

***

A generation ago in the English First Division there was none of this two teams coming out together like it was an international and going through some respect-paying charade, lining-up and shaking hands. At Highbury the teams would amble onto the pitch separately and have a bit of a kickabout before the start – usually 3 p.m. on a Saturday. The away team would get booed and Arsenal were greeted with cheers. At Celtic Park both teams *ran* onto the pitch with a look of grim intent. I almost felt as though they were speaking to me personally: We might not be as good as the big teams in England, but we *care* more. They looked workmanlike and dour. They were representing communities as well as football clubs, with a sense of duty and a job to do. This wasn't just a game.

It's hard to imagine now, but at that first Old Firm game I went to Rangers were heading for fifth in the league at the end of season – a whopping fifteen points behind champions Celtic. Rangers hadn't won the league since 1978; seven years a virtual lifetime in football for Scotland's big two. That 1985-86 season in Scotland was the tail end of a brief period when the power shifted away from Glasgow to the 'New Firm' of East Coast clubs Aberdeen and Dundee United. Although Celtic won the league that season they did it narrowly and on the final day. Rangers took the title the next season. And no one outside those two has won the Scottish Premier League since.

This little sojourn north of the border wasn't about seeing Scotland's *best* two teams play a game of *fitba*, it was about starting to get an understanding about the most compelling rivalry in British sport.

There were some good teams in England in the 1980s: Liverpool consistently, Nottingham Forest at the start of the decade and Everton for a few years in the middle. Man United picked up a couple of cups and Aston Villa surprisingly won the title in 1981 and even more surprisingly followed it up the next year with the European Cup. Ipswich and Spurs both had good teams at different times. Aberdeen won a European Cup Winners' Cup in the early 1980s, but it wasn't easy to assess how Scottish clubs would fare regularly against English First Division teams. Maybe the Scottish Premier League was on a par with the lower rungs of England's top tier, or something comparable to the then Division Two. It was hard to gauge with only infrequent competitive games between English and Scottish clubs.

But I wasn't there for the football. Well I was, but not from *that* point-of-view. I was there for the experience. I was among a crowd of 58,365 – which was massive for 1980s Britain. In England that weekend the two biggest supported clubs, Manchester United and Liverpool were away from home. Champions Everton mustered 28,066 for their comfortable home win over Birmingham, whilst future moneybags club Chelsea (who eventually finished sixth) attracted just 15,376 to Stamford Bridge. A 58,000 crowd then was *massive* – the highest league crowd anywhere in Britain that season.

It's hard to describe without resorting to clichés. The atmosphere *was* absolutely electrifying. It *was* intoxicating. I defy anyone to avoid an adrenalin rush the first time they attend an Old Firm game.

I stood at the back of the Rangers end. That end of Celtic Park was known as the 'Rangers end' even when Rangers weren't the visitors. Even the ends at Hampden Park were known as Rangers and Celtic ends – regardless of who was playing.

No classic of a game. Rangers took a first-half lead through Ally McCoist. Celtic equalised in the second half. In this already cliché-ridden chapter I'm going to avoid the word 'erupted' to describe what happened when Rangers scored. But you get the idea. And that's my match report.

Somehow, after the game, in our naivety, Carl and I ended-up on a bus full of Celtic fans for the short trip back to the city centre. Heavy traffic prolonged our anxiety. Carl tucked his Rangers scarf under his jacket and I spoke to him only quietly, under my breath. I'm not sure whether my London accent would suggest an alliance with the Crown and thus Rangers or wouldn't have even raised an eyebrow. But I didn't even want any tourist-assuming: "what did ye think of the game?" questions. Carl was nervous. And watching young Celtic fans write IRA slogans in the steamed-up bus windows didn't exactly endear me to my afternoon's hosts.

We joined Glen Skewis, and a few of their other workmates in Sloans pub in Argyle Street after the game. It had been a good introduction to the Old Firm. My interest in this fixture has varied a bit since, but never diminished.

So taken with that afternoon's experience in the East End of Glasgow I came back for the next Old Firm game a couple of months later. This one was at Ibrox and it was an altogether less tense experience. Carl knew his way around that part of Glasgow better.

Rangers' ground was well ahead of its time in terms of design and safety. The 1971 Ibrox disaster had led to a large-scale renovation of the ground. Ibrox Park had been one of those massive bowl-type grounds that catered essentially for standing patrons, with minimal seating. The record crowd in an earlier configuration was 118,567 for a 1939 game against Celtic. By the 1960s the capacity had been reduced to 80,000 for safety reasons. Two people died in a crush on stairway 13 in 1961, and ten years later sixty-six died after a crush at the end of an Old Firm game. Rangers scored a very late equaliser and spectators leaving turned back in a bid to find out what was happening.

The club started rebuilding the ground within a few years. Identical 7,500 all-seater stands went up at the Copland and Broomloan Road ends of the ground. The 10,300-seater Govan Stand was then built along the north side of the ground. These stands were closer to the pitch than those they replaced. The main stand on the south side of the ground stayed as it was with around ten thousand seats in the upper tier and the last remaining standing areas below. The reconfigured Ibrox opened in 1981. This was the ground I first visited in 1985.

I read somewhere that Old Firm crowds up until the 1960s were split roughly evenly – regardless of the venue. The crowd at that November 1985 Ibrox game was 42,045. Celtic fans had the whole of the Broomloan Road stand and nearly half the main stand. Even allowing for segregation and a small no man's land between the two sets of supporters in the main stand, the full Celtic ticket allocation would have been twelve thousand *plus* – generous by modern standards. The Rangers turnout at Parkhead a few months previously would have been more, albeit in a considerably larger ground. This kind of away fan ticket allocation may have given the police more work, but it added significantly to the atmosphere.

Carl and I had standing tickets. The game we saw was probably Rangers' best performance of the season. They beat Celtic 3-0; their only win out of the four Old Firm league games that season.

The atmosphere was again intense, but I felt more relaxed at Ibrox. We didn't have to navigate risky arrivals and getaways from the game. Again, I was amazed at the noise, and how just about *everyone* sang the songs – be they songs of encouragement for their team, or songs celebrating historical conflicts.

A scrambled first-half goal from young midfielder Iain Durrant was met with unbridled joy around nearly three quarters of the ground. Rangers wrapped it up with second half strikes from the late Davie Cooper, and Ted McMinn. Ibrox jumped and jived.

Preparing this chapter, I searched out some footage of this game on

YouTube. I noticed a few things – the speed of the play was markedly slower than now, the accuracy of passing left a little to be desired but most noteworthy were the tackles. The first couple of minutes saw some ferocious tackling by both teams – most of which wouldn't escape the referee's censure in the 21st century. They were flying into each other, whipping up the crowd even more.

I didn't go to the 1986 New Year's Day game at Celtic, but I was back north of the border for their last meeting that season on 22 March. We sat high up in the Govan Stand, somewhere between the halfway line and the Broomloan Road end which housed the bulk of the Celtic support. Again, Celtic fans had been allocated a good chunk of the main stand. It was a misty, rainy second day of spring in Glasgow.

At this stage in the season with seven games to go, Heart of Midlothian were the surprise pace-setters. They were closing-in on their first league title since 1960. It all (in)famously went wrong on the last day.

Rangers ended the season in fifth place – in a ten-team league; their goal difference an embarrassing *minus five*. Out of both cups by then, the final Old Firm game of the season represented a kind of *last hurrah* for Rangers in 1985-86.

We watched a classic. Celtic took an early lead through future Rangers player Mo Johnston (there's another story), before Brian McClair added a second. The 2-0 lead was a bit against the run of play. Down the Rangers left flank an interesting tussle between Ted McMinn and Celtic full back WIllie McStay was developing. Both were booked before another lunge by McStay on McMinn near the corner flag saw him sent off. The game changed. Rangers quickly got one back through a Cammy Fraser header. Half time; 2-1 to Celtic.

Rangers vs Celtic at Ibrox, August 1986.

Celtic made it 3-1 just after the break. But with the second half barely fifteen minutes old, Rangers had pegged their rivals back to 3-3 through McCoist and Fleck. Then they took the lead through another Fraser header. 4-3. A Murdo McLeod drive from well outside the area levelled it for Celtic. Rangers had a late chance, but Bonner saved well from McCoist. It ended 4-4; the only ever 4-4 Old Firm draw in a league game.

'Had it all' is an over-used phrase to describe a football match. In this case it was right. Eight goals, the lead changing hands, a sending-off, near chances, a raucous atmosphere and two teams giving their all on a wet, blustery day on a muddy pitch. A couple of the goals were crackers as well. I'd seen a modern-day Old Firm classic.

***

A few weeks later Graeme Souness was appointed player-manager of Rangers and a football revolution began in Scotland. For a while Rangers were paying wages that the big English clubs wouldn't, or couldn't, match. They became a big club on the European stage for a while.

Back to 31 August 1986. I walked up to the bar from the toilet chatting to Jim from Falkirk, my new Rangers mate. He joined us for a drink before heading off to another pub. That afternoon Rangers beat Celtic 1-0 through a late Iain Durrant goal. We were sitting low-ish in the Copland Road stand just behind where Durrant scored.

I only managed to get to one more Old Firm game in the early Souness era – a 2-0 Rangers win at Ibrox on New Year's Day 1987. Tickets started to get very hard to come by. That day we had to take the Rangers supporters' bus from Livingston into Glasgow. For some strange reason I wore a green and white striped shirt under my jumper, scarf and jacket. I was introduced to a few people on the bus: "Carl's mate from London. He's alright though." I shook some bloke's hand and the green and white of my shirt poked out.

"Nice shirt," he said sarcastically. "You want to keep that covered." A reminder of how seriously they take these things in Scotland.

I LIKE TO WATCH

Wankhede

I enjoyed Bombay once I got used to the smell of piss. There was a vibrancy and energy that alternated between exhilarating and irritating. At the Colaba end of Bombay there was money, and no shortage of it. But adjacent to say a designer clothes shop there would be a food shack and, just around the corner, people lying in the street. There was a bustle everywhere. There was no shortage of Western tourists and backpackers (not necessarily, or usually, the same thing). There were great places to eat, but you had to determine whether the water in the jug or bottle on the table was safe to drink or not.

It was March 2006 and I was staying in this absolute rat-sack of a hotel in Colaba, the southern end of Bombay.

I'll call it Bombay not Mumbai, for two reasons. I only know one person who lives there, Ajay Aggarwal. He calls it Bombay. Of the many books I've read about India the most interesting, by far, is *Maximum City: Bombay Lost and Found* by Suketu Mehta. So, it's Bombay to me. And anyway, 'Bombay' has a more romantic ring to it.

So, this rat-sack of a hotel. Let me describe the room. Door.

Vestibule-cum-ante-room area opening onto a cavernous dark room with two single beds. The noisiest air-conditioning unit this side of the Dyson factory beta-testing lab. A bathroom, of sorts – really a tiled room off the main room with a *kind of* door. A shower to one side of the tiled room with a shitter and a sink.

There was a fridge in the ante-room bit. Why this room needed a separate section for luggage, a fridge and a single wooden chair, I don't know. I opened the fridge. There was a bottle of water on the shelf of the door. I grabbed it, opened it. It wasn't sealed. It was a plastic bottle with a label. Obviously refilled with tap water. No thanks.

I'll also mention, but not labour over, the pale pinky-cream paintwork in the room. It was, perhaps not surprisingly, peeling at all sides and corners. It may well have been older than me.

I'd been travelling for nearly thirty hours. A day at work. The train from Bendigo to Melbourne. The airport bus from Spencer Street to Tullamarine Airport. Drinks. A wait. Check-in. Wait. Flight to Kuala Lumpur. Wait – at the bar. Flight from Kuala Lumpur to Bombay. Passport and customs. Taxi from the airport to Colaba – over an hour in five lanes of traffic on a road marked out with three lanes. Then a laboured, painful check-in process.

I finally got into my room. I was sweaty and grubby and there was the faint aroma of a dying animal about me. I needed a shower, a change of clothes and to scrub the moss off my teeth, but I couldn't use the bathroom tap water, nor could I use the bottled water from the fridge. So, my duty-free Absolut vodka came in handy, and for the first in my life I brushed my teeth with the aid of not water, but vodka. A true *Gonzo* moment.

Showered, fresh outfit on and teeth brushed with a mixture of

Macleans and Absolut, I ventured out of the hotel. I turned right into the main drag of Colaba. I'm not sure what hit me first, the sheer density-intensity of the crowds or the smell of stale piss. I was tired, hungry and anxious. I needed to get to the Wankhede cricket ground to get tickets for the Test match starting the next day between India and England.

I walked a couple of hundred yards, and then past the Leopold Cafe and Bar – a famous tourist hang-out. It features prominently in Gregory David Roberts' book *Shantaram*. Two-and-a-half years later the Leopold was the scene of carnage during the Bombay terrorist attacks. A bit further along there was another bar-cafe on the corner, the Mondegar – touristy but less touristy. I went in.

I had this kind of toasted chicken club sandwich thing. Though I suspect the bread was probably always that texture and didn't need to be toasted. The chicken was *chicken-y*, not sure – think heated-up tofu that'd been in the hands of someone who'd just eaten a packet of chicken crisps. That kind of *chicken-y*. I had a Fanta to wash it down. Always loved that overseas Fanta in glass bottles; not much fizz to it, but much sweeter.

Hunger sated, I had a good idea as to what was in store. I had to get tickets for the cricket, and one way or another it was going to be involved. I was knackered and irritable. I left the Mondegar with the bill paid and a sizeable thirty per cent tip cajoled out of me and jumped into a tuk-tuk. The Wankhede wasn't far away.

There was a little window at the Wankhede Stadium; the ticket office. Around it swarmed hundreds of Englishmen. It was polite mayhem. Because this was cricket, and despite cricket attracting a not entirely different demographic to football in England, the fans somehow chose to behave differently. Like normal, if not always perfect, human beings.

After twenty minutes navigating my way through an over-extended huddle to reach the window, I handed over a fistful of rupees and walked away with three five-day tickets for the third Test. I walked past the makeshift Barmy Army merchandise stalls. I didn't get the Barmy Army thing then, and I still don't – the need to conform to something that by its very nature is, or should be, non-conformist.

The whole idea of the Barmy Army seems more Australian than English to me – that yearning to identify as part of a group. All walking around in the same t-shirt or cheap polo shirt covered with logos, images and writing. There was so much to look at on their shirts you'd have to ask them to stand still if you wanted to read it.

Tickets in hand, then in pocket, I walked away from the Wankhede. I was as tired as fuck and it was really humid. I ambled back slowly to Colaba Causeway via Churchgate and the Oval Maidan. Much of the architecture around me seemed so *British* that if you squinted and blocked-out the fact that it was sunny, you could easily mistake the surrounds for one of those other great British Victorian cities like Bristol, Belfast or Glasgow.

Some boys, playing cricket after school on Oval Maidan accosted me, albeit in the friendliest possible way. Was I here for the cricket? Where did I live? Who was going to win? Which Premier League team did I follow? Three of the four questions generated typical responses which were readily accepted: Yes, England and Arsenal. The answer to question two threw them though. As it has thrown other locals at later games in India on this trip and on visits to Sri Lanka and Barbados.

"Australia?"

"Yes, Australia."

"But you're English. You live in Australia?"

"Yes."

"Why?"

"Well, a number of reasons…"

"So why don't you support Australia?"

"Well I'm English, and…"

"But you *live* in Australia…?"

And so on. I've had this conversation, or variations of it, dozens of times.

Other England cricket fans have also been a bit thrown by my hybrid 65:35 English: Australian accent. In Kandy, eighteen months later, I was talking to a couple of Yorkshiremen. After a minute or two, one of them took half a step back, appraising me.

"Where are you from?"

"London. Live in Australia though."

"I thought you spoke funny."

Back to Colaba. I ambled back to the Mondegar. I had a few beers, read a copy of *Uncut* magazine and sent some text messages. I was due to meet Witek Zdybicki and his Norwegian *travelling companion* that evening. I was tired. But I hadn't seen him in over a year and was looking forward to catching up. They were staying up beyond the airport, a ninety-minute tuk-tuk ride away. They eventually arrived in Colaba during my fourth beer. A low-key, but enjoyable evening was had.

Five days later.

I'd long since given up breakfasting at the Hotel Ratsack. The first day I chose option one: hard-dried eggs on cold white bread toast, accompanied by 150ml of warm orange juice from a carton. On day two I chose the other option: 'toast with the jam'. The toast was as per option one. The jam was bright red. It looked like some kind of nuclear fall-out or something. It wasn't strawberry or raspberry or

Vantage point. India vs England at the Wankhede, Bombay, 2006.

anykindoffuckingberry.

"What flavour is it?" I asked.

"Jam." Came the response.

"Jam's not a flavour." I said. He looked at me vacantly. "But not to worry, eh?"

It was overpoweringly sweet, like a cross between IRN Bru and something sweeter.

Hence, from then on, after sampling both Ratsack breakfasts, I decamped to the Mondegar for toasties, Fanta and a read of the English language *Times of India* of a morning.

On that fifth morning, the game was poised quite delicately. Theoretically it could have gone one of three ways. India were batting last and started the day on 18/1. They needed about three hundred to win. Unlikely, but doable – on other grounds perhaps. A draw, I felt, was the likeliest outcome until I read some of the stats about teams batting last at the Wankhede. No team had won a Wankhede Test chasing more than 163. A kind of shiver went down my spine. It's on, I thought.

I took a tuk-tuk to the Wankhede. Not sure whether he did it on purpose out of mischief or spite or because he was just plain fucking dumb, but the driver dropped me at completely the wrong end of the ground to where my seat was. I had to walk through hordes of pissed-off Indian fans to get to my section. There was a bit of ugliness in the air. Earlier in the Test they'd booed Sachin Tendulkar, India's greatest player and a Bombay native. They were well pissed-off, but not at English fans. It was a bit uncomfortable, but hardly like walking the wrong way around Anfield or Elland Road as an away fan in the 1980s.

At lunch India had progressed – if you like – to 75/3. The run chase – if ever there really was one – now looked out. An England win now looked more likely than a draw. And then India collapsed, England-style. In fifteen overs after lunch England took seven Indian wickets for just 25 runs. It was exhilarating; Test cricket at its most exciting.

It was Shaun Udal's Test. He was a thirty-seven-year-old journeyman English county player who'd made his Test debut just a few months earlier in Pakistan. Bombay was his fourth and final Test match. Udal finished with 4/14 that day off just over nine overs. His had been a somewhat fleeting Test career, but it ended on a big high.

Ok, briefly, let's put the key match details and hyperbole into the hands of Wisden, and specifically Rahul Bhattacharya: "England's first Test win in India in 21 years, and their biggest by runs on Indian soil. It squared the series 1-1, a fine achievement for any party touring here, but a marvellous one for a side missing half their first-choice players. This was the complete performance from England: debutants, comeback kids and ancient journeymen were galvanised in the liquid heat of Mumbai by Flintoff." It would be hard to put it better. "Liquid heat" it certainly was.

That afternoon, walking away from the Wankhede, I knew I'd seen something very special. That victory, by an inexperienced rag-tag England team *in* India, *in* Bombay, was really something.

Being an outsider in Bombay was an interesting experience. Five days at the Wankhede presented challenges – most obviously what to eat and drink. The choices were limited and wouldn't pass any kind of food safety tests anywhere in the Western world. Interaction with the locals had its challenges, mainly because I didn't want to answer questions all day about the same few topics.

The stadium – it wasn't really a 'ground' in the English cricket sense – was built only thirty-two years previously in 1974. But it was like something from a very bygone age – one of the first CCBs (characterless concrete bowls). Unlike say the Gabba, MCG, Eden Park (not Gardens) and some of England's newer football grounds, the Wankhede did have *some* character because it was such a khazi. In stadium architectural terms, 1975 was a lot, lot closer to 1945 than 2005.

Just south of the Wankhede is Brabourne Stadium, Bombay's Test cricket ground from 1948 to 1972 – an altogether more attractive proposition. It really does have some character. Curiously it's not that much smaller than the Wankhede. So why was the Wankhede built? To house a much bigger capacity? Well, bigger, but not much. Because Brabourne was falling apart or the land had been bought by property developers? No, to both. In classic India cricket style (and history) it was built because of a *dispute*, a dispute over the Brabourne ticketing arrangements. The issue couldn't be resolved so the Bombay Cricket Association simply built the Wankhede. End of. And that was it for Test matches at the Brabourne for nearly forty years.

One night in Bombay I traveled up to Witek's hotel near the airport for drinks and dinner. The journey by tuk-tuk took ages, passing through some interesting areas of Bombay.

"Muslims," my driver said at one point, as we drove alongside a throng of people out at a night market. "This is a big Muslim area."

By the time we reached Witek's hotel, I was half an hour late, and felt like I'd breathed in half of the pollution in Bombay. The other half had turned into grime on my forehead.

Absorbed. Indian fan at the Wankhede, Bombay, 2006.

"What time are you leaving?" The driver asked. "You want me to drive you back to Colaba?"

"I dunno," I said, looking at my watch. It was nearly eight. "Ten o'clock?" I said, raised inflection in my voice. Note the question mark, the driver didn't.

I said my hellos to Witek and his *travelling companion*, ordered a beer then excused myself in the direction of the lavish hotel bathrooms. I washed my face and hands. The fluffy little white hand towel was filthy when I'd finished with it.

It was about half-past ten by the time we finished. I walked over to where I'd been dropped-off earlier. From seemingly out-of-nowhere, some bushes perhaps, my driver emerged, arms flailing.

"Where were you?" he asked, in an advanced state of agitation. "The other drivers," he said, gesturing in the direction of men lounging around their cars and tuk-tuks, "were laughing at me. They said they saw you leaving before. In a car!"

I hadn't realised we'd got so close.

"You said ten o'clock," he remonstrated.

"*About* ten o'clock," I replied. "Anyway," I said, paraphrasing Kafka, "whether I'm late or not, here I am." And I jumped in the back of his tuk-tuk, banging my head on the low roof on the way in.

The journey back was slightly quicker, by maybe twenty minutes. I was intrigued to see a funeral cortege by the side of the road – a coffin atop a cart being wheeled through the streets by a group of men, on its way to a cremation I assumed.

I enjoyed Bombay, but it was hard work. I was booked to return two-and-a-half years later at the end of 2008 on the away to the Ahmeddabad Test. But those Lashkar-e-Taiba terrorists came in by boat and attacked the Taj Mahal hotel, Leopold Cafe, Nariman

House, railway station and other Bombay landmarks, killing over 160 people. There were ten of them but somehow it took the Indian security forces *four days* to regain full control. I was at JFK airport waiting to board a flight to London when I read the text from my wife. After a brief, scene-setting preamble she said: "They've attacked the hotel you booked into. I'd be really worried if you go." I cancelled. It was very rare at that time for Carla to raise a concern or objection about anything I planned to do. When she did, I paid heed. She was good like that, even if she did divorce me a few years later.

I never went back to India, but I'd had fun in what had ended-up as a near four-week trip. The Bombay Test was an undoubted highlight. Interaction with the Indians amused and confused me. India seemed a mix of the olde-worlde stereotype of 1970s television sitcoms and an energetic modern world.

A joke, of sorts. Q: For travellers, what do the letters I.N.D.I.A stand for? A: I'd Never Do It Again.

I LIKE TO WATCH

Stockport County

It was the second weekend in May 2010. None of us had done Stockport. It was final game of the league season weekend, which turned out to be problematic. The powers that be had determined Stockport County vs Tranmere Rovers be an all ticket game.

"Shit, I don't believe it," said a shocked Owen.

"Didn't even think about that," I said. "End-of-season game…"

But it wasn't a meaningless end-of-season fixture. Stockport were already relegated, but Tranmere could still stay up if they won and other results went their way. Tranmere, only about fifty miles away, had brought hordes of supporters hoping to see their team do the not quite impossible, but certainly unlikely. Presumably the local Old Bill considered it some kind of risky fixture, hence slapping 'all-ticket' on it.

"We're just three blokes doing the ninety-two grounds," I told a steward, "we're not Tranmere." I showed him my Australian driving licence. To be fair, he was quite sympathetic and called someone over who he thought had a spare ticket. "But there's three of us." Thanks, but no thanks.

We walked around to the club office where people were picking-up pre-ordered tickets.

"It's all ticket. Can't see this working." I said.

"Don't give up yet," Owen said, "this is a small club and they need the money."

Two or three groups picked up their tickets, then it was our turn. The woman behind the counter was one of those attractive, late middle-aged types who you could imagine being quite loud in the pub and not at all bashful about filthy jokes or male strippergrams.

"Er, hello," Owen started, "I ordered some tickets last week but forgot to print off the email confirmation."

"Surname please."

He handed over his credit card. "Spelling on there. Three tickets it was." And then the coded plea: "I checked my credit card statement online and strangely my card hasn't been debited."

"Oh," she said, quickly working out the situation. "Let me see. Maybe I should just run your card details through again then Mr Francis." A knowing smile.

"Thank you."

So off we walked, tickets in hand, just before kick-off and into the main stand – albeit to seats a little too low down for a great view.

A victory for genuine fans, a small financial win for a struggling club and bureaucracy/the Old Bill gently out-manoeuvred.

"Result," I said. "Well done." I gave him a gentle slap on the back.

"Well, yes," he said, looking a bit serious, "bit lucky really. Big lesson though, always get tickets in advance from now on."

I hadn't realised the gravity of the situation for a man getting very close to doing the ninety-two. If we hadn't got in, me and Muttley (aka 'The Tattooed Dwarf', or just 'The Dwarf') would've just found the nearest boozer, sunk a few beers and forgotten about it after gently moaning for maybe fifteen minutes. Owen would've circled the ground until just before the end when they opened the gates and snuck in to 'claim' it. Not sure what our rules are in this situation. We had previously agreed that even if you see just one ball bowled at cricket and then the day's play is called-off it *would* still count as getting the ground done. In 1996 I'd only managed to get into a Celtic vs Arsenal friendly when the gates were opened shortly before the end. I'd been to Celtic Park a few times previously so fortunately hadn't had to wrestle with that particular internal quandary.

We sat down to watch the game with one end and one side of the ground accommodating the travelling Tranmere fans who comfortably made up half of the 7,208 assembled. Stockport, already relegated, were just going through the motions.

Owen and I waited a few minutes before moving a few rows back from our allocated seats to an unoccupied area to get a better view. The Dwarf, in his inimitable happy-go-lucky, cheeky Cockney whippersnapper, auditioning-for-a-comic-light-relief-role in EastEnders, remained where he was, chatting animatedly to some of the locals. As usual most of them seemed nonplussed but vaguely amused by his incessant ADHD-driven chatter. And then he was chucked out. We were barely fifteen minutes into the game when a handful of stewards turned-up and gently manhandled (not a contradiction in terms if you really think about it – he didn't want to go, and it was more a physical coax as opposed to full-on ejection) The Dwarf out of his seat, and out of the ground. Quite how they would have recorded whatever 'offence' they'd decided he'd committed on the ejection rap-sheet would have been interesting:

Talking in an exaggerated London accent whilst up north?

Discussing the merits (or otherwise) of Guns N Roses?

Cheekily helping oneself to someone else's crisps?

Anyway, Muttley got himself flung out of Edgeley Park, Stockport, Greater Manchester for no discernible reason. There was no conceivable way he could have been mistaken for an away fan in the wrong part of the ground. There was a kind of irony to it. Muttley had a Scouse-like approach to getting into games without paying. "Hello missus! How are you love?" He'd once jokingly said to a Barnet FC employee as he strolled past her into Underhill whilst the rest of us were handing over our tickets.

A couple of stewards hung around for a bit, scanning the crowd.

We later found out that one of the stewards who'd seen us looking for tickets outside the ground had then spotted us in the ground. Knowing that if we'd been looking for tickets twenty minutes before kick-off, we clearly hadn't obtained them in advance, we had thus somehow blagged our way in. When I say 'us' I really mean The Dwarf. For a start Owen and I are actually quite generic-looking in terms of blokes going to football in Britain in the early 21st century – balding to bald, mid-forties, bit overweight, jeans, trainers, hooded jackets and somewhere about the six-foot mark. The Dwarf stood out a bit more for reasons that are not only quite obvious from his moniker, but also from his behaviour. He draws attention to himself in an unashamed manner. When we were younger this often involved taking off all his clothes in the pub and climbing onto pub roofs to do the same – often stone-cold sober. He talks loudly and widely on a range of topics to anyone who'll listen. I usually took this as a sign of being bored with having spent the previous three or four hours with us.

The scanning stewards didn't spot The Dwarf's accomplices due to our generic*ness* (I just invented a word.) Post-eviction, The Dwarf retired to a nearby pub for the remainder of the game – a hostelry he later described as "like the pub in that early scene in *An American*

Werewolf in London". The Dwarf, fair play to him, wrote to Stockport County the following week and ended up with a refund on Owen's credit card for his virtually unused ticket.

Back to the game.

Stockport didn't look like they could give a rat's arse. This relegation (they ended the season with five wins from forty-six games) was the start of their virtual freefall down the English Football League pyramid.

Tranmere scored just before half-time through Ian Goodison. They got another through Ian Thomas-Moore not long after half-time. Three thousand and more happy-go-lucky Tranmere fans went mad at one end and down the side opposite to where we're sitting. And why not? The game is going their way, as are the other scores they need. It looks like they're staying up.

"The whites are staying up! The whites are staying up!" They sang.

Fourteen minutes from the end Tranmere scored a third.

As the game drew slowly to a close, stewards started lining-up in front of the Tranmere sections.

"They're dreaming if they think they're going to stop a pitch invasion at the final whistle."

Stockport fans drifted away in large numbers. However magnanimous you might be, no one likes to see their ground virtually taken over by away fans, lose 3-0, get out-sung all afternoon and then watch those away fans dancing all over your pitch. The final whistle went; the other results have gone Tranmere's way and they've stayed up. Their fans erupt – hundreds of them breaking through the stewards lines to celebrate. There is nothing *hooliganistic* (another new word) about this – ok, apart from maybe a broken cross bar. It's celebratory.

We watched them as we edged slowly along our row towards the exit. Then I see him. Everybody and anybody witnessing it had a

Stockport County vs Tranmere Rovers, 2010.

smile on their face. The Tranmere pitch invasion includes a bloke in a wheelchair being pushed around merrily by his mate/carer. They are having a good time. Everyone is. The Stockport fans leave the ground, smiling. This is what football is all about.

The Dwarf is waiting outside the ground for us and his story unravels on the walk to Stockport station. It's only a short trip back into Manchester. We find a small pub not far from Piccadilly station and imbibe a couple of liveners. From there we headed round to the bar of the Malmaison Hotel for a more relaxed drink or two prior to the evening's greyhound racing at Belle Vue.

***

We rounded off the weekend's sporting fixtures the following afternoon at Turf Moor. A meaningless fixture perhaps with Burnley already relegated and Spurs having already qualified for the Champions League. But are there really any meaningless games at this level now in the era of money, TV and media saturation, and more money?

We met some of Owen's Tottenham mates in the bar at Burnley Cricket Club, next door to Turf Moor. It quickly filled-up with a mix of both home and away supporters. One of the barmaids caught the collective eye of the pre-football crowd. Beer-fuelled innuendo progressed to outright lasciviousness before plateauing-out with talk of kidnap and her being taken back to London as a sex slave.

There were plenty of goals with the game ending 4-2 to Burnley – entertaining enough in that end-of-season kind of way.

I LIKE TO WATCH

Palace Away

An inevitable part of going to football in England in the 1970s and 1980s was the potential for aggro. Additionally, there were aggro near-misses, having to make a run for it, and generally just feeling anxious approaching or leaving a ground. Sometimes it just went off during the game.

My early days going regularly to football coincided with the general shift of aggro from inside grounds to mainly outside. I had seen some large-scale battles in grounds in the late 1970s – mainly Spurs, West Ham and Chelsea attacking Arsenal's North Bank. I'd seen Arsenal takeover QPR's Loftus Road where there didn't actually seem to be that much trouble because so few home fans either turned up or made themselves known.

This isn't a book about football hooliganism or 'firms'. There are plenty of books and YouTube videos to gorge on if that's your cup-of-tea. However, a book largely about the experience of going to football over about forty years can't really overlook a very real, often omnipresent aspect of that experience.

***

Selhurst Park was a nightmare pain-in-the-arse to get to. Crystal Palace away may have *technically* been a London derby for Arsenal, but for a public transport-reliant fan from West London it took ages. When I was older I often got to Luton, Coventry and Southampton away quicker by car than I did to Selhurst Park. Palace spent many years outside the top flight but at different times both Charlton Athletic and Wimbledon were tenants. It ended-up being a ground I visited many times.

First time I went there, Crystal Palace were on the cusp of being the 'Team of the Eighties' under Terry Venables. They were pretty good, briefly. It was season 1979-80 and they'd just come up. Arsenal went to Selhurst Park on 10 November, losing 1-0 in front of over forty thousand.

A year, a month and a few days later, on Boxing Day 1980, I went to Crystal Palace again. Arsenal drew 2-2. Selhurst Park was undergoing significant change. The end I'd stood at the previous season was being knocked-down to be replaced by a Sainsbury's supermarket.

The 'Team of the Eighties' tag quickly turned into a millstone. They collapsed in their second season in the top flight and were relegated after finishing bottom.

Apart from the convoluted travel arrangements – walk to Ealing Broadway, District Line to Victoria, hang around at Victoria, a laboured overground train journey to Selhurst, walk to the ground – these were, on-the-surface, seemingly quite innocuous games to go to as a fourteen and then fifteen-year-old. Not so. Teenage naivety reared its predictable head and a couple of useful life lessons were learned.

For the 1979 game we set off from Ealing. Nick Batt, myself and a couple of school friends. Nick and I had been kicking a ball around together since about the age of six in the suburban close we both lived in. Our mutual affection for Arsenal moved on from pretending to be Alan Ball and John Radford in Hanger Hill Park to standing on the Clock End with Nick's older brother, Steve, during Liam Brady's Highbury heyday. Steve was quite a bit older than us and I'd listened intently to his stories about seeing the 1970 Fairs Cup win and the first Arsenal Double.

I'd been paid for my weekly paper round that day so would've been flush with about seven quid in my pocket. I'd been to a few London away games by then at QPR, Tottenham and Chelsea. What I hadn't done was take such a roundabout route to a game. This was a different era. The majority of fans wore colours then – a trend that largely died-out for a while before re-emerging in the Premier League era.

The London Underground and mainline stations often turned into Saturday afternoon battlegrounds. There were more than ten teams based in London of whom around half would be at home on any given Saturday during the season. Additionally, King's Cross, St Pancras and Euston stations were the London entry and exit points for many fans coming down from the north. The Liverpool clubs, Leeds, Newcastle and particularly Man United were all well-supported, regularly bringing thousands.

I thought little then of travelling across London on a Saturday afternoon wearing a red and white scarf. Many people didn't. But it was an invitation. On one level it was an invitation to a conversation about the game – the one you were going to, had been to, or just in general. On another level it was an invitation to hostility – ranging from a verbal dig to outright assault.

As a West London-based Arsenal fan, a home game meant about a forty-stop round-trip to Highbury. Using Ealing Broadway meant a change at Acton Town to and from games, which often meant groups of blokes eyeing each other up (in a decidedly *non*-sexual way) on the station platforms. If Arsenal and Chelsea played at home on the same day, the train journey back to Ealing would see a big influx of Chelsea fans at Earl's Court, resulting in staring contests and sometimes more.

Club colours became a more optional thing for about ten to fifteen years from the early 1980s. Fans stopped wearing colours for two main reasons – either wanting to avoid being singled-out for trouble, or conversely, because they wanted to travel incognito, so they could *cause* trouble.

Despite our relatively tender years we all looked a bit older than we were. We'd been allowed into pubs already. When I say, 'allowed into' I really mean 'not thrown out of' or 'not noticed'. I was nearly fifteen.

"We'll meet Steve at Victoria," said Nick, of his older brother, "and I think he wants to meet someone else in the pub."

I didn't give the plan a second thought; happy to go along with it. With entry to games then around £1.50 to stand, and a pint of lager about fifty pence, I wasn't going to have to worry about the money side of things that day.

"This is the one." Steve said as we walked across from the station to a big Victorian-era pub. He opened the door and we followed him in. It was busy. I was already quite familiar with that rumbling hubbub chit-chat pub sound. But that sound continued only for a matter of seconds before dying out. Dozens of people, blokes in their teens and twenties mainly, a few maybe older, turned to stare as we walked further into the bowels of the pub. It wasn't looking very welcoming.

From a throng by the bar a bloke walked over. Twenty-ish, wearing a v-neck navy jumper and with a Keegan-style curly perm.

"We don't have Scousers in here." He said, menacingly.

"We're not Scousers," said Steve, "we're Arsenal."

"Arsenal!?" Curly Perm guffawed, "that's even worse!" He promptly punched Steve in the face.

As we scrambled for the door, the punches rained down. Luckily there were a lot of them trying to get at us. Half of them would have been on the end of friendly fire and it was too crowded for anyone to get much traction with their punches. We got to the twin doors, burst out and legged it up the street. Their interest in pursuing us was thankfully short-lived.

"Fuck!" I puffed, leaning over as we stopped a couple of hundred yards away. We all needed a breather. Steve, with his hands on his hips, was breathing in and out deeply.

"Guess we won't be meeting Phil and Chris in there then," he said.

We got to the game in good time after deciding not to try another pub around Victoria. We stood at the back of the Whitehorse Lane terrace – a big open, uncovered end that must've housed ten thousand or more that afternoon.

Arsenal lost 1-0 in an atmosphere of ongoing aggro as skirmishes broke-out sporadically all afternoon inside Selhurst Park. I remember leaving through the car park behind the main stand, Arsenal fans jumping up and down on car bonnets and ripping off wing mirrors and windscreen wipers as we exited the ground.

The Boxing Day 1980 game we tackled by tube and then bus, for some reason, from Central London down into SE25. There were four of us. There must have been a closure or reduced overground train service in London that day.

Arsenal fans were jammed into one corner of the Holmesdale Road end, opposite where we'd stood the previous year.

The teams saw-out a 2-2 draw that has long since faded from memory. We left the ground and started walking in the vague direction of Central London. There had been a much smaller crowd than the previous season, and whatever aggro had taken place must've been quite low-key. Both sets of fans mingled without any obvious issues as the crowds moved further away from the ground into the dense South London back streets.

Get onto a main road and find a bus, seemed to be the general idea. Once we were north of the river we'd come across a Tube station before long.

Fifteen minutes or so later the crowds had thinned-out considerably. We'd found ourselves on a wide, busy road. The post-match traffic was moving along at a little faster than walking pace. A car slowed down beside us – a big, dark four-door thing, possibly a Granada.

"You Arsenal?" A bloke from the front passenger seat asked. "D'you want a lift back to Central London?"

Despite our collective youthful naivety, a big alarm bell silently rang and it wasn't because we were wondering how they'd fit all of us in.

"No, it's alright." I said.

The car stayed level with us for a few moments before its occupants started up a low chant: "Tottenham, Tottenham, Tottenham…"

The bloke in the front passenger seat was slapping a meat cleaver against the palm of his left hand. Then he got out, quickly joined by two more of them from the back. "Tottenham, Tottenham, Tottenham…" I was watching the bloke from the front seat, naturally anxious as to where the meat cleaver was. Then bang! I was punched from the side by one of the blokes from the back of the car. They were older and bigger than us. A flurry of punches rained down, accompanied by some predictable verbals: "You Arsenal slags!" And then it was all over. They got back into their car. No real damage done, though my right cheek swelled-up later in the evening. As with many of these types of things it's more the fear of what *might* happen as opposed to what actually does happen. I assumed the meat cleaver was just for show and the bloke left it in the car when they made their move.

Uncomfortably for us, and somewhat bizarrely in hindsight, we carried on walking along the same road with the Tottenham car edging along in traffic just ahead of us.

"What are they doing down here?" Nick asked, incredulously. Tottenham had played at home the same day, but their ground was fifteen miles almost directly north across London – a significant and time-consuming drive at any time on any day of the year.

"Morning kick-off," I said.

"Bloody hell," said Nick. "They watch their game then drive right across London to attack a few Arsenal fans…?"

The car was still up ahead. It had slowed a bit. We watched as someone got in.

"Bloody hell," I muttered. None of us had the front or guts to run-up and shout a warning. Barely a minute later the car door opened, and the bloke was pushed out into the gutter having taken a bit of a hiding.

We walked on, eventually getting a bus that took us to Knightsbridge and from there the Piccadilly and District lines back to Ealing Broadway.

My first two trips to Crystal Palace. Attacked both times, but not by Palace fans.

I LIKE TO WATCH

Deportivo

My honeymoon was a trip to Galicia in Spain to see Arsenal play Deportivo La Coruña in a second leg UEFA Cup tie. Arsenal were 5-1 up from the first game, took the lead again, but ended up losing 2-1 on the night. Deportivo's ground, Estadio Riazor, had changed significantly since my first visit to a *three-sided* Riazor over twenty years earlier.

Saying that I took my wife to a European away game for our honeymoon makes for a good story. Is it entirely accurate though? Yes *and* no. It was certainly the first time Carla and I had been away since we got married. But that year featured four overseas trips – twice to Northern Spain, a week in Cyprus, and two months in Thailand before arriving in Australia just before Christmas.

I regarded Deportivo as *my* Spanish team, so when Arsenal drew them in the UEFA Cup just a few months before I emigrated to Australia, I wasn't going to miss it.

In 1989 I took myself off to Spain for a few months to write a novel. I'd originally planned to go down the coast of Portugal as well, then into Morocco. But I stayed in Spain, in the north-west. I arrived by boat in Santander and then slowly worked my way westwards around to Vigo, twenty miles north of the Portuguese border, via a series of painfully slow trains and smoke-filled buses.

I wrote every day in cafes and in different 'pension' rooms I rented. I read shit-loads as well. By day I ate on the beach or in a park; bread rolls and meat or cheese that I'd bought that morning in a market. Every evening I ate in a cafe or cheap restaurant – pizza, pasta, toasted sandwiches and occasionally trying some local speciality. I drank beer by night and water during the day. I got to know which bars dished out a couple of free tapas with drinks. When I'd read all the books I'd brought with me I bought books from the small English language sections of local bookshops. These sections were largely limited to classics and the extremely popular, or to be more precise, the extremely popular of the 1980s. Thus, I alternated between Dickens or Dostoyevsky and Robert Ludlum or Sidney Sheldon. I managed this on the equivalent of about £100 a week. Before joining the EU, Spain was cheap for visitors.

The football season hadn't started when I was in Santander. By the time I was in Gijón, just along the coast in the Asturias region, the season was underway, and I was subconsciously building my weekend evenings around the live games on TV and the late Sunday night highlights programme.

Sporting Gijón (or to give their official name, Real Sporting de Gijón S.A.D) have been one of those yo-yo clubs. Since their foundation they have played about the same number of seasons in each of the top two divisions.

Their ground, El Molinón, is just a few hundred yards from the end of the city's San Lorenzo beach. It hosted West Germany's group games in the 1982 World Cup. Two of these games went down in

World Cup history – West Germany's 2-1 defeat to Algeria and their final group game – a contrived 1-0 victory over Austria that saw both countries progress to the next round at the expense of Algeria. This game became known as known as the 'Nichtangriffspakt von Gijón' (non-aggression pact of Gijón) or 'Schande von Gijón' (shame of Gijón). The dubious outcome to this game led to a change in World Cup rules with the final games in each group being played at the same time thereafter.

Sitting in a bar on the main road behind the beach, a barman with impeccable English regaled some stories about the Germans stay in Gijón.

"One German guy," he told me, "a big fat man…" and he demonstrated far and wide with his hands, "sat on a stool there," he pointed, "all night and drank beer after beer after beer. He was so depressed after the Algeria game. He drank over a hundred bottles of beer."

"Over a hundred beers!" I was flabbergasted. "How do you know? Did you count them?"

"He was the only man drinking that type of beer. We had some here in the fridge, maybe half a crate, and four crates out back. He drank them all."

"Fuck me."

"Yes!" He said. "Indeed 'Fuck me!' though I don't think he fucked his wife that night."

We both laughed.

Sporting Gijón started 1989-90 away from home with a defeat at eventual champions Real Madrid. On Sunday 10 September Valencia came to Gijón. The team line-ups meant little to me, apart from the familiar face of ex-Man United defender Kevin Moran at the heart of the Sporting defence.

This was my first football match outside the UK. I paid 1,500 pesetas for a terrace ticket, which, converted to pounds, was about double what it cost to stand at a First Division game in England at the time. I got in half an hour or so before kick-off and had a mooch around. The stadium was tired-looking – a washed-out, faded red and white (the colour of Sporting's shirts) dominated the stadium. The terraces and stands seemed steeper than grounds in England.

El Molinón then held about forty thousand. It has since been significantly reduced due to all-seater legislation. Google searches haven't helped determine what the official attendance was that day, but I'd have estimated it at about fifteen thousand. The El Molinón Wikipedia page states the average gate that season was 18,450 – albeit with a surprisingly low high in the mid-twenty thousands. I would've

Sporting Gijón vs Valencia at El Molinón, 1989.

imagined games against Barcelona and Real Madrid getting closer to capacity.

One stand-out memory was the near-miss crowd noise. Used to the English "whoah!" or "oooooh!" kind-of sound, I was somewhere between amused and taken aback at the Spanish equivalent which was an "aieeeee!" sound.

The game was played at a noticeably slower pace than I was used to. Sporting took an early lead. But it was a lead they could only hold onto until ten minutes from the end when Valencia equalised. It actually turned out to be an early season high point for the Asturian side who lost six and drew only this one game in their first seven. They rallied after that, finally finishing lower-mid-table.

That season, Sporting's Asturian neighbours Real Oviedo also played in the Spanish top division. The two clubs alternated weekends for home games. Looking back I don't understand why I didn't just take the train down one weekend (I stayed in Gijón for three weeks) to catch a Real Oviedo game – it was only about twenty miles away.

Later during my trip, I arrived in Oviedo one evening as a game was taking place – the floodlights illuminating the town. I could've easily got an earlier bus if I'd known. These days I'd never miss an easy opportunity like that to get a new ground, race course or stadium added to the list. To be fair though, there was no internet in 1989.

After Gijón I travelled further west and stayed in small scenic port and seaside towns like Luarca, Viveiro and Ortigueira before arriving in La Coruña.

My novel hit a roadblock. I wrote about fifty thousand words and then had a better idea and wrote about fifty thousand words of something else. I came home later that year with two half-finished handwritten first draft novels which I never touched again. For a couple of years,

I lived in a flat near Acton Town. I had all my notebooks on the windowsill above my desk in the bedroom. I didn't realise how damp it was on that windowsill or that rain was getting in. That was the end of those two half-written novels.

La Coruña is a port city of about a quarter of a million people in the region of Galicia, in Spain's north-west. It didn't fit the usual English image of Spain. It rained, a lot. Even in summer, it didn't get that hot. The people didn't fit the Spanish stereotype looks-wise; they were mainly much fairer – some with an almost Celtic-look to them. There was more of an industrious feel and vibe to the place compared to other cities in Spain. It isn't a region heavily reliant on tourism.

I arrived late one evening and took a room close to the bus station. The following day I headed into the Old Town area and got myself a room for the equivalent of about £4 a night. I immediately loved the Old Town. I felt like I'd finally arrived in the place I'd been looking for the previous few weeks. There was a square with mazy, narrow streets running off it where there literally *was* a bar on every corner. Not far from the Old Town was the iconic Torre de Hercules – a lighthouse reportedly in use since the second century.

It was still a surprise though to see a large replica of the Torre de Hercules as a focal point at the back of the terrace at the Estadio Riazor. They must be pretty proud of this lighthouse, I thought. They were. In an era of less uniformity in football grounds than now, Estadio Riazor stood out as an unusual ground. Like Sporting Gijón it was close to the main city beach – the Riazor from which it drew its name. The two stands on either side of the pitch facing each other were very similar. At one end (the furthest from the beach) was a wide terrace that spanned the end of the ground and curved around close to the stands. In the middle at the back of the terrace stood

Deportivo La Coruña vs Salamanca at Estadio Riazor, 1989.

the towering replica of the lighthouse. It was a three-sided stadium. At the other end there was an open space and a big hall; an indoor sporting complex for badminton, basketball and the like.

Deportivo were then in the Segunda División – albeit one of the bigger clubs at that level. They went on to finish fourth that season and second the following year, getting promoted in the process. On Sunday 1 October 1989 I stood on the terrace with the lighthouse to my left towering over the crowd at that end. At half time I found a different vantage point on the other side of the ground as Deportivo coasted to a 3-0 win over Salamanca.

The next week, Deportivo were away. Their reserve team, a regional División 3a team, Fabril Deportivo, played Lemos at the Riazor. I was one of a few hundred hardy souls at the game, which Fabril won 1-0.

The following Sunday I was *still* in La Coruña. Something about the place. Deportivo were at home to Castilla CF, Real Madrid's reserve team. The name Castilla may be familiar to West Ham fans. Like West Ham, second division Castilla reached the final of their domestic cup competition in 1979-80, beating four top division sides along the way. Unlike West Ham they lost (6-1), having had to face their own first team, Real Madrid, in the final. Because Real Madrid also won the league that season – meaning a spot in the European Cup – it meant Castilla got to play in the European Cup Winners' Cup where they met West Ham early on.

Anyway, on Sunday 15 October Castilla CF played at Deportivo and won 1-0 in front of 13,221. It was hard to get official attendance figures in the Spanish papers then. The other games I went to only have estimates in my diary, but for this one I clearly wrote '13,221'. It's obviously not an estimate and must have come from somewhere.

I'd found my Spanish team; the team from the city I'd loved in an instant. I was also pleased not to have latched onto one of the obvious two or gone for one of the fashionable Basque clubs. Deportivo it was for me.

I was back there almost two years to the day since my first visit. Deportivo were now in the Primera División. I'd travelled to Spain with my girlfriend of the time, staying in some of the same places I'd stayed in two years previously. I was disappointed that the woman in the Old Town pension didn't recognise me. I'm not sure why I'd felt the need to do a nostalgia trip so soon.

The relationship was quite a volatile one. I think we spent as much time – in general as well as on that trip – not talking to each other as actually talking. In that two-week trip we spent four days in La Coruña, and I made sure the La Coruña leg of the trip coincided with a Deportivo game. She didn't want to go. She'd been to Arsenal games – home and away. She'd even once made sandwiches that we ate in the car in Moss Side prior to a Man City vs Arsenal game. I can't remember why she didn't want to go to the Deportivo game. They were playing Real Valladolid. The game coincided with Carlos Valderrama's brief spell at the club.

"Valderrama will probably be playing."

"Who?"

"Carlos Valderrama. He's Colombian. One of the best footballers in the world. You'd probably know him by his hair."

She wasn't impressed. She had the arse-ache, but I wanted to go.

"Meet you after the game for dinner."

The main square in the Old Town was inundated with bars. Even in just a few days we'd worked out a couple of favourites – one of which we called 'The Bar of the Promiscuous Daughter'. It was a tired old bar up some steps in the corner of the square. It had character and was a great people-watching spot. The bar was run by a middle-aged couple – stereotypical by working-class Spanish standards: small, dark and aproned. I'd been there a few times two years previously. They had a daughter who in 1989 had been a young teenager and somewhat inconspicuous. By late 1991 she'd blossomed in a number of ways. She'd grown a massive pair of wangers for starters. And on our handful of visits the biggest group of customers were her friends – a mixed group of about the same age who sat around each evening stuffing popcorn, drinking soft drinks and being loud.

Deportivo won 1-0. It was the only time I ever saw Carlos Valderrama play. He ended up only playing about twenty games for Real Valladolid, so I felt kind of lucky. After the game I walked back along the beach and into the Old Town to meet my girlfriend at The Bar of the Promiscuous Daughter. I got a moderately frosty reception but did my best to ignore it and laid into the beers and tapas for the rest of the evening. A day or two later though, in a different argument, she told me that she'd "never felt as alone before" as she had on the Sunday night when I'd been out of her sight at football. For three hours. We split up not long after we got back to England.

In 1994 I found myself back in La Coruña. Same time of year. Same pension in the Old Town – this time the old bird *did* recognise me. Deportivo were now an established top-flight club, having finished third two seasons previously and been runners-up in 1993-94. Deportivo played Espanyol the weekend I was there. It ended 1-1 in front of easily the biggest crowd I'd been in at the Riazor.

It was absolutely bucketing down with rain when I left the stadium. I gradually made my way back to the Old Town via a few bars, reading a few pages of Edward Bunker's *No Beast So Fierce* at each stop. I ended up in an Italian restaurant in the square – the Plaza de María Pita – in the Old Town. It was late – even by Spanish standards; maybe six or seven other people left in the restaurant. I ordered food and a half bottle of red. I read my book and had some wine. I ate the pizza, and then that was it for a while. I woke up some time later slumped in my chair. I was the last customer. Chairs were up on tables all around me and most of the lights had been turned off. I didn't know how long I'd been asleep, but it was no five-minute nap. Two waiters leant on the bar facing out into the restaurant chatting quietly. Realising the situation, I apologised profusely, saying "perdóname" several times, accompanying it with appropriate hand gestures and body language. They took it with cheery good grace. I necked the last glass of wine, and made quick a departure, leaving a good tip when I paid.

By 2000 when Arsenal played Deportivo in La Coruña the Estadio

Riazor had undergone a major transformation. Gone was the terracing and lighthouse at the western end. The other end – where the sports hall complex had been – was now filled-in with a stand identical to the one opposite. The Riazor was now a functional, if unremarkable 32,000 all-seater. Arsenal fans were allocated a section in the south-east corner of the ground.

Going in to the second leg with a 5-1 lead meant it probably wasn't going to be much of a contest. A woman outside jokingly made a 5-0 gesture with her fingers to the entering Arsenal fans and laughed good-naturedly at the response.

Arsenal took the lead through Thierry Henry. Henry was coming to the end of his first season at Arsenal. He'd started quite slowly. I was at The Dell when he scored his first goal in mid-September and he went on to finish the season with twenty-six goals. Deportivo got two goals back and that's how it ended.

For an essentially non-contentious game in front of a modest crowd I was surprised at the reaction of the police after the final whistle. By many accounts some kind of issue with the local plod seems the norm when English clubs play in Spain. Arsenal fans were kept in for a while. They started singing, then they started moving closer to the exits. And then the police moved in with batons out, walloping people over the head. There'd been little in the way of interim-level crowd control action, such as a warning. It seemed like the police went from level zero to level six, skipping levels one to five along the way. We stayed where we were; there was no hurry to get out. I felt less of a potential target having a woman with me. The commotion was all over a few minutes later when the police opened the gates. We walked back to the Old Town.

It will probably appal the football fan purist reader of this book, but I have to confess to that night buying a Deportivo-Arsenal half-

and-half scarf. In the cupboard at home it went to accompany the Lens-Arsenal half-and-half scarf I'd bought at the Champions League opening group game in 1998. I've never worn either or bought one since. Honest.

Arsenal went on to the final of the UEFA Cup that season, losing to Galatasaray in Copenhagen, Despatching Deportivo 6-3 on aggregate on the way was no mean feat. That season Deportivo went on to win the Spanish league for the first, and so far, only, time. They were a top Spanish side for a few years. In addition to their title season they finished second or third eight times between 1993 and 2004.

The last game in Spain I went to on that 1989 trip was at Celta Vigo in a Primera División game against Castellon. I'd been chatting to a couple of locals in a bar in the lead-up to the game. The weekend of the game was the first anniversary of a robbery at the stadium in which a club employee had been killed. I looked at a couple of newspaper articles about it, but my Spanish wasn't good enough to properly digest the stories. I knew what they were talking *about* but couldn't extract the detail.

Vigo was another port city, just north of the border with Portugal – still in the Galicia region. Celta's rivals were Deportivo, but that year they played in different divisions. Celta sounds a bit like Celtic. And that's not just a coincidence. Many people in that part of Spain share their DNA with the Irish. Without wanting to get into physical stereotypes you will come across more than a few redheads and ruddy complexions across Galicia and Asturias. There are some surnames – Lavin for one – which are commonplace in both Ireland and Northern Spain.

It was a dull, rainy Sunday afternoon when I caught a city centre bus a couple of miles to the district of Cola where Celta's Balaidos ground was. It was late October, and while I hadn't yet run out of money, funds were low, and I had a hankering to get back to London. Such was my affection for Deportivo and the city of La Coruña, I felt like a bit of a traitor attending a Celta game. It didn't turn out to be a game or experience that stayed long in the memory. The ground was about a third full. One abiding memory though is of a giant moat that went around the ground, separating the stands and the pitch.

Celta won 1-0. It was one of only five games they won in the league that season (even fewer than Rayo Vallecano who finished below them in the other automatic relegation position). They bounced back a couple of seasons later and by the turn of the millennium they'd qualified for the UEFA Cup five seasons in a row before playing one season of Champions League football.

A few weekends later I was back in the familiar surrounds of Highbury for what turned out to be a memorable 4-3 game against Norwich City.

I LIKE TO WATCH

Hollywood Park

In June 2008 I was on a bit of a 'Californian roll'. I managed to add three new sporting venues to the list in three days. The work conference I was attending in San Diego finished on the Monday. The Padres were at home that night against the Cubs. Nice stadium; practically brand new and right in the heart of the city.

Tuesday, I drove up to Los Angeles, left the hire car at my hotel and cabbed it to Dodger Stadium. It was bumper-to-bumper both ways along the highway, which had up to seven lanes each.

Dodger Stadium was a big, open, cavernous bowl. I learned that it was also a good place to practice your Spanish when you bought a hot dog or beer.

Wednesday, I was booked on the 23.45 out of LAX for Melbourne. I had only one thing planned – a visit to the Warner Bros. Studios, leaving me a free afternoon. A quick search on my laptop over an expensive American breakfast revealed the intriguing prospect of an afternoon meeting at Hollywood Park Racetrack. A slightly more detailed search showed that Hollywood Park was only five miles from the airport and even closer to the car hire drop-off points. With LA traffic to consider though, that might still mean an hour or more. Anyway, my afternoon was sorted.

The Warner Bros. Studio Tour was worthwhile enough, in a predictable way. A visit to Hollywood Park though, set my imagination into overdrive. This was Bukowski territory. In Charles Bukowski's work the racetrack looms like an omnipresent character; a steady, regular constant in Hank's world of drunken carousing, fighting and womanising. Hollywood Park was a place of refuge – for afternoons contemplating the rest of the shit in his life.

Away from my hotel's Wi-Fi, I used a small *Lonely Planet* map to navigate my way around LA. Not the smartest decision I've ever made, but I did get to see quite a bit of LA.

Hollywood Park was in Inglewood, in the south of the city. 'Hollywood Park' *sounded* quite glamorous. I had only vaguely heard of Inglewood and was oblivious to its reputation.

An eye-opening twenty minutes or so started after I turned-off the highway into Inglewood. Waiting at traffic lights I heard a bit of a commotion and some shouting. I looked over. People were looking at *me*. The shouting was *directed* at me. I wasn't welcome in this part of Inglewood. Ok, it was daytime – so theoretically no need to panic, but I locked the car doors nonetheless. When the lights changed, I promptly pulled away.

A few days later I looked Inglewood up online; some interesting statistics. According to Neighbourhoodscout.com the murder rate in Inglewood is 0.18 per thousand people against a national average of 0.04. New York's notorious Bronx district has a murder rate of 0.06 per thousand people – a third of Inglewood's. Blimey.

I drove along a kind of residential-looking street. Crack dens, I quickly assumed, maybe a tad harshly. It was early afternoon, but I didn't see anyone walking around. It was like a ghost town; tired-

Crowd watching the end of a race at Hollywood Park, Los Angeles, 2008.

looking buildings well on their way to decay and then probably empty for years. It wasn't difficult to imagine the future here.

I found the racetrack and parked in a fairly busy car park behind the main stand. Clearly a few diehards enjoyed their Wednesday afternoons at the races.

I went into the general admission section. I'm not sure if Hollywood Park Racetrack ever had any 'family days' or 'family-friendly' events – or anything that involved children or more than the occasional, token woman. Certainly not today. This was bloke central, and a certain type of bloke at that. This was hard-drinking, serious gambling territory. When I say "serious gambling" I don't mean for a lot of money. The people here were taking it very *seriously* – arguing and debating detail, their attention flitting between the live races and the TV screens high up on the walls beaming in races from other meetings. I looked around: poorly-dressed, unhealthy-looking blue and ex-blue-collar workers. Everyone looked to be a kind of generic, run-down, indeterminate middle-age. These weren't men out for an afternoon's socialising at the races with the odd punt thrown in. There were no work groups here *celebrating a success*. No birthdays, or loose-knit bunches of buddies in chinos and polo shirts laughing, joking and backslapping. These were life-hardened, jaded, downbeat men. They were here because that's what they probably always do.

I noticed that although there was a great deal of debate and banter within these groups and while they clearly knew each other, each man was buying his own drinks. These men weren't friends; this wasn't really social.

I ended up having four or five large beers – something very bland with what felt like a pretty low alcohol content. However, I *was* driving. Such was my fascination with the people around me that I'd temporarily lost track of time and forgotten that I'd driven there. I still had to get to the airport and any accident or unscheduled stop in the streets around Hollywood Park would leave me in a potentially tricky situation. I didn't fancy playing out a kind of Sherman McCoy Part Two situation, having to do a metaphorical *runner* from Inglewood.

Hollywood Park was in a state of decay. The seats in front of the grandstand were faded, rickety, and the paint flaked and peeling. Resting a hand on any wooden surface was inviting splinters and probably some kind of infection. Resting a hand on a metal surface would sooner or later mean feeling the sandpapery texture of rust. There was bird-shit everywhere.

After a couple of races I tentatively approached one of the windows to place a bet. I'm not sure being monitored by armed guards while putting on a bet is something to feel comforted by, or nervous about. No one I could see was betting or winning *that much money*. How much cash in your pocket put you at risk of being robbed at

Hollywood Park?

My horse came in. Not much of a win but when I collected, I made a visual display of just how little I was picking up. I didn't want any of the other punters wrongly thinking the slightly-better-dressed-than-the-locals-tourist was flush with much more than a few low denomination bills. Mind you all denominations of US currency look very similar. Drunks or the partially-sighted must get ripped-off all the time.

A visit to the 'bathroom' after the last race meant walking past more armed guards.

I headed out to the car park behind a group of life-weary middle-aged men. Two of them, arms flailing excitedly, passionately debated the outcome of one of the races. Serious stuff.

My drive to the airport was thankfully brief, and incident-free.

Footnote. Hollywood Park Racetrack opened in 1938. The original shareholders and directors included Walt Disney, Samuel Goldwyn, Darryl Zanuck, Al Jolson, Bing Crosby, Ronald Colman, Raoul Walsh and Jack Warner. Any glamour there might have been had long-gone by the time I visited. The decline continued until late 2013 when Hollywood Park finally closed. Initially the talk was of revitalising the area with new housing on the site but that was shelved in place of a planned 70,000 seat NFL stadium scheduled to open in 2019. I wonder what Bukowski would think.

I LIKE TO WATCH

Accrington Stanley

"On my life, you dozy cunt!" Muttley laughed, shaking his head.

Owen shrugged and grinned. He knew he'd dropped a clanger.

"Did you get it mixed up with Altrincham?" I asked.

"Musta done."

Muttley started pacing around, agitated – a not unfamiliar sight to many of us. "Fucking hell, you're normally the most organised bloke in the world."

"Well chaps," Owen said after a short pause, no doubt thinking back to Stockport, "at least I've got us tickets in advance."

"Hardly likely to sell out!" I said.

"I'll get us some more drinks while we all think of a plan." Off he went to the bar, a metaphorical tail halfway, perhaps, between his legs.

The three of us were in the upstairs pub at Manchester Piccadilly station. It was a Saturday and barely eleven o'clock. Owen was getting in the third round of the day. I was pretty fucked already, having only arrived the previous afternoon after the thirty-hour door-to-door journey from Australia.

Owen, Muttley and I met at Euston shortly after 7 a.m. that morning. This particular trip up north was to cover the Accrington Stanley vs Northampton game, and Spurs' Sunday afternoon fixture at Man City.

I didn't go ferreting around in the emails in my phone to labour the point, but the point was that Owen had *definitely* said both games were in Manchester. The Man City vs Tottenham game was definitely in Manchester. Accrington, however, was twenty-five miles and over an hour away, or: "You'd need to get about three trains lads. You'd need to leave now I reckon." This, from the heavily tooled-up copper we'd got chatting to. He'd seen three unfamiliar herberts arrive in the boozer nearly an hour previously and less than discreetly decided to check us out. Upon discovering he was talking to a Spurs, Arsenal and QPR fan who were in his neck of the woods to "get Accrington Stanley on the list" he relaxed. As there were no other obvious herberts around for him to keep an eye on, he sat down for a chat. He was an ex-Man United fan, now following FC United of Manchester and he shared a few stories about following a *real club* again.

"Community, camaraderie, having a laugh with your mates, always being able to get in and it doesn't cost a fortune." He said. "Accrington!?" He laughed again at our unwitting error. "You'll be needing a taxi, I reckon."

There's not a lot in the way of ambience about trains station pubs, so after three drinks we wandered around to the nearby Britannia Hotel on Portland Street which I'd booked online the previous week. Too early to check-in we dumped our overnight bags at reception and walked all of about a hundred yards to the nearest pub.

By 1 p.m., through default, a taxi had become the *only* option. It was going to cost £90 each way. So be it. There were no other realistic options to get to a game that afternoon and living in Australia meant the likelihood of ever getting a chance, or making the effort, to see Accrington Stanley play at home again was pretty slim.

So it was out through the Manc suburbs and up into Lancashire for real. It always *looks* cold in this part of the world. There's something very English-looking about Lancashire towns – the houses, churches, shops and pubs. I like those walls – those slatey-looking thin bricks and odd-shaped bits of stone they put together. I know it's the wrong county, but there was something Bronte-esque about the look of some of these towns.

We booked the same cab for the return trip to Manchester.

There was a large pub near the ground but Owen, organised at least on this score, knew there was a club house-cum-bar in the ground that was open to everyone.

Tickets safely picked-up, we headed into the Accrington Stanley in-ground bar. It was functional – like the social club of an amateur sports club. The décor was tired and the recycled office tables and chairs set the tone. The locals greeted us with muted enthusiasm by way of cursory, dismissive side-long glances before putting their noses back in their beers and continuing their grumbling monologues. It was a mix of predictable old codgers, retired hoolie types and women in unshapely, shiny over-garments that had a 'fire hazard' look to them. The children present all had an air of the Dickensian urchin about them.

More drinks. Owen, understandably in light of his fuck-up, was taking a higher than normal proportion of the responsibility for getting to the bar.

"It's grim up north," I said when Owen sat down. He nodded, a look of home counties disdain on his face. Muttley was already casting his eye around for dysfunctional locals to engage in conversation, annoy or try to line-up later for no-strings sex.

The cab journey had chewed-up valuable drinking time, and the driver's insistence on having the heating on full blast had drained us all a bit. I was flagging and needed a second wind; vodka Red Bulls it was. And then again.

The social club-bar lacked character but wasn't devoid of interest. A series of faded beige-ish head-height office dividers were lined-up from the bar to one corner of the large room. Clearly a no-go area for mere bar punters, we soon worked out that on the other side of the office dividers was the 'corporate hospitality' area. Quite how much more upmarket everything would be just fifteen feet away was open to debate.

We listened as the announcer on the hospitality side of the office dividers thanked sponsors, offered up club and team news and generally jollied along the assembled throng. That the regular bar punters on our side could hear every word – designed for the ears of a different (more upmarket?) audience – felt a bit weird. It was almost as though we were sneakily listening-in on a lovers' tête-à-tête; like we were invading someone's privacy.

One particular statement from the announcer caught our collective ear. The Accrington Stanley chairman would be in the Crown pub after the game for a meet-and-greet Q&A session with supporters. He'd be there from about five o'clock. My initial reaction was a patronising *isn't that quaint* kind of thing. But on quick reflection – and Owen and I talked about it while Muttley was off annoying locals – what a refreshing change it made. Club listens to fans. Sure, scale-wise, it was a more manageable thing to do at say Accrington as opposed to Arsenal or Man United, but even so. Clubs genuinely engaging with their supporter base was an alien concept for many football fans in England. Some clubs though, were starting to listen, though whether that was out of well-intentioned choice or necessity was a different thing.

We took our seats slightly to the left of the middle of the stand closest to the club social rooms. It was bitterly cold. Forty-eight hours earlier I'd been in late spring Australia, with temperatures in the mid-to-high twenties centigrade. Accrington wasn't much above freezing. There was a slow start to the game and we got chatting to a bloke who was on his own.

"You don't sound like you're from around here," he said.

"Neither do you."

He was a Wolves fan, on the same mission as us – to get grounds on the list. We exchanged ground-hopping anecdotes for a while before things petered out.

Northampton Town took the lead through their burly forward Adebayo Akinfenwa. He was a footballer who looked nothing like a footballer; his physique earning him the nickname 'the beast'. He was the heaviest player on the pitch, and probably the heaviest association footballer I'd ever seen, yet his skills on the ball, and in the air, seemed miles ahead of anyone else that day. The much-travelled forward went on to score a hat-trick in a 4-2 win. It turned out to be the only hat-trick of his career.

The two teams put on a thoroughly entertaining game for the 1,441 crowd. Proof, yet again that there is more to footballing life in England than the Premier League. It was an enjoyable trip to see the current incarnation of one of the world's oldest football clubs in one of the game's traditional heartlands. Accrington's ground was overlooked by housing and some imposing hills. A contingent of their supporters behind one goal were just about relentless in their vocal encouragement. I felt almost like I was in a 1960s British kitchen sink drama film. Somewhere in the crowd was an angry Albert Finney who'd soon be going home for his tea before a night out on the ale. Maybe there were several Albert Finneys there.

As planned, our minicab was waiting at 5 p.m. We'd done a detour via the small club shop where I bought a replica home shirt as a souvenir and Muttley, despite his forty-eight years on this planet and a level of maturity you *might* expect to come with that, let off a stink bomb. The shop cleared in seconds.

None of us had the energy or inclination to journey out to Belle Vue dogs that night so we holed-up at the bar in the Malmaison Hotel before ordering more curry than five blokes – let alone three – could eat, back at the Britannia.

I may have been jet-lagged, drunk and practically falling asleep on my feet, but I was on the ball enough to make sure Muttley didn't know my room number. Owen had relaxed his guard though.

I met them for breakfast.

"Do you know what that little fucker did last night?" Owen said, stifling a grin. Muttley was laughing his head off. "He broke into my room at about two o'clock and let off a fucking stink bomb!" Muttley just continued laughing. "It took me hours to get back to sleep. I felt like I was going to be fucking sick."

An hour later we were having a *gay walk around Manchester. We came across the National Football Museum close to the city centre and I made a mental note for a future visit. From there it was a leisurely walk to the Lowry Hotel for pre-match drinks; the match in question being Manchester City vs Tottenham Hotspur. Two days, two new grounds on the list.

We weren't the only people in the bar of the Lowry who were going to the game, but it was a far cry from any other pre-match drinking establishment I'd been to. The atmosphere was somewhere between being in a church and some kind of executive conference. Muttley, under strict instructions, behaved, though he did blurt out louder than necessary, "there's Giggsy!" when Man United legend Ryan Giggs came in with a couple of blokes.

A weekend of contrasts continued at the Etihad, Manchester City's new-ish ground, where we saw a 2-1 home win. Tottenham had taken an early lead, but second-half goals from Agüero and Džeko turned it around for the home side who went on to finish runners-up in the league that season.

*A gay walk is nothing to do with being gay, though you *can* be gay or straight or whatever you like, to go on a gay walk. The phrase slipped into irregular usage a few years ago. A gay walk is basically a hangover-clearing, morning-after-a-heavy-night, all-male walk around a city or town you don't live in. Walks in parks, along canal sides or rivers can also constitute a gay walk. It can be sightseeing without calling it sightseeing. There might be two or five of you (but there's no limit). It can include stops at cafes or museums or shops. It's essentially the *flip side* to how you spent the previous evening (drinking in a pub, bar, club, restaurant – usually indoors). The gay walk ends as soon as one member of the group leads the others into a pub.

I LIKE TO WATCH

The Strange Case of Melbourne Heart

The recent history of club football (soccer) in Australia is a bit messy and littered with ups and downs. More downs.

The outside view is that Australia is a very sporty country. It is. Aside from cricket, tennis, swimming, horse racing and bowls – which are all massively popular – there are four codes of football played to high levels.

Australian rules football. Played nowhere else in the world and not even dominant across Australia's six states and two territories. Definably though *the* national code and easily the most widely-attended. Massively attended in fact, compared to other sports in Australia and other codes of football around the world. Predominant across the southern states (Victoria, Tasmania, South Australia and Western Australia), its making (heavily commercially-backed) inroads into rugby league territory further north. An early or mid-season game between two of Melbourne's big clubs, if both are going even *ok*, can draw a seventy thousand crowd. If Collingwood were one of the two, make that eighty thousand. A hard and often exciting game to watch, it can often be too high-scoring or one-sided to have much drama. The fact that it is 'uniquely Australian' in a country overrun with American and British cultural influences is a key factor in its popularity.

Rugby league. More teams and very much a New South Wales and Queensland thing. There is one Melbourne club – which has generally punched above its weight in the last twenty years. It's played internationally, but despite having a World Cup every few years it's a competition where really only Australia, England and New Zealand seriously compete. League receives widespread media coverage and gets good TV viewing figures but attracts low crowds compared to Aussie rules with twelve to twenty thousand being optimum until the latter stages of the season. I'm not sure why – though with so many Sydney teams involved and Sydneysiders having numerous other activities to address like going to the beach, talking about house prices and how Sydney is the *real* centre-piece of Australia – they probably don't have enough time to attend in big numbers.

Rugby union. Like in England more your posh, private school background game. A strong national team over many years but under-supported and under-appreciated at club level. Australia has five teams (albeit one is based in Tokyo) in the Southern Hemisphere tri-nation Super15 competition. Like rugby league it is more a New South Wales and Queensland thing.

Football (soccer). For the remainder of this chapter, 'football'. Surprisingly, considering global trends, football is a relatively late addition to the suite of codes in Australia popularity-wise. Football only really grew with the post-war influx of mainland European migrants. Unsurprisingly perhaps, many of the clubs that formed were aligned to particular migrant groups. What developed were Greek clubs, Italian clubs, Macedonian clubs, Croatian clubs etc. The club names usually made it clear how they were aligned: Brunswick

Juventus, Melbourne Croatia, St George Budapest and so on. You get the picture.

In time football *will* become more popular. At some point this side of about 2035 average crowds at club football matches in Australia *should* eclipse the rugby codes. (Aussie rules is another story completely.) Australia's easier route to the World Cup since an early 2000s reconfiguring of qualifying groups *should* guarantee a place every four years. But the momentum that was built between about 2005 and 2015 hasn't *kicked-on* – to use the Aussie parlance.

Since 2005 the top of the club structure has undergone a revolution of sorts. Until the early 2000s club football was largely watched by first, second and third generation migrants. They followed their team for cultural and nationalistic reasons. Unsurprisingly there were a few problems with this particular *model*. "Too ethnic" bleated middle Australia. And when middle Australia saw TV news footage of running battles between the fans of Melbourne-based Greek and Macedonian clubs at a pre-season friendly in leafy Albert Park they were understandably appalled.

A typical scene at a South Melbourne game in the early 2000s would see groups of Greek-Australians chattering away, eating Greek snacks from Greek vendors. Anyone over about sixty was likely speaking Greek as well. Those under sixty largely spoke in what Anglo-Aussies charmingly called a 'wog' accent. Amongst a typical crowd of maybe six thousand around this time there would be about fifty British blokes like me, wandering around (usually on their own, sometimes in pairs) in Brighton, Arsenal, Liverpool, Wolves, Bristol City and Man United shirts. We were all a long way from home, trying to latch on to something. I spent many a Sunday afternoon on the terraces at Albert Park looking for something, or a small part of something, I'd left behind in England.

The standard wasn't great, but there were *moments* – like a 3-2 away win at Melbourne Knights in 2002 when a young Massimo Murdocca made a mazy run through the Knights' defence to score his first and only South Melbourne goal.

Growing football in Australia meant making it more palatable for the wider, still largely Anglo-centric Aussie population. This meant reducing the status and appeal of the *ethnic* clubs. So out went the National Soccer League at the end of the 2003-04 season. It was floundering anyway – reducing from sixteen to thirteen clubs in quick succession in the early 2000s. It was drawing smaller and smaller crowds and had a miniscule presence in the media. Describing it as having 'niche appeal' would be exaggerating its impact.

The A-League was launched for the 2005-06 season – a brave-ish new world for the game in Australia. Originally the league featured just eight clubs, five of whom came from the National Soccer League. Three teams were new franchise clubs – Melbourne Victory, Sydney FC and Central Coast Mariners. Later replacement teams and additions – Melbourne Heart, Wellington Phoenix, North Queensland Fury, Gold Coast United and Western Sydney Wanderers were all franchise teams.

The Melbourne franchise club, Melbourne Victory, was granted a five-year 'exclusive' in Melbourne, meaning no other Melbourne club in the A-League until at least 2010-11. It was a great way to build a supporter base.

I never watched any of it that first season – live or on TV. I went to my first A-League game in December 2006. Melbourne Victory played away at Adelaide United on the evening of the first day of the Adelaide Ashes Test. I was in Adelaide for the cricket so ended up ticking off the ground at the end of a long day. My abiding memory of the game was the forty-year-old Romario hovering around Adelaide's attacking third, sporting grey hair and the start of a comfy middle-age spread.

I didn't feel any affinity with Melbourne Victory. Despite generating a reasonable-sized supporter base quite quickly, a lot of football-interested folk in Victoria also struggled to *get* Melbourne Victory. There was an arrogance about them. And there was of course the Kevin Muscat factor; a divisive figure being player, captain, coach and all-round talisman through the early years of the club was always going to alienate some. I went to other Melbourne Victory games including a late season game against Adelaide United which attracted forty-seven thousand to Docklands. I also saw them play friendlies against Boca Juniors and Celtic; in each case facing a curious dilemma in wanting *both* teams to lose the game.

Then in late 2010, along came another franchise club, Melbourne Heart, joining the A-League five years after Victory as the exclusive window closed. I didn't go to any of their games that first season though I did watch them a bit on the box. They wore red and white, like Arsenal. Stripes, like Brentford. There was a flickering of interest and then a definite interest. They were an underdog club. Finally, a few weeks into their second season I went to watch them. They won 3-0 on a sunny afternoon in the best stadium in Australia. I felt a leaning, an empathy, *something*. Maybe I'd finally found a little bit of what I was missing from England.

Just before Christmas 2011 it was derby day at Melbourne's AAMI Park. Derby night to be precise. With 26,579 inside, the stadium was nearly full. The two clubs shared the stadium, but it was a Heart home game. Each club was allocated an end, with a mix of fans down each side. Despite being the away team, Victory navy blue outnumbered Heart red. Well they did have a five-year supporter base-building head start, didn't they?

Melbourne Heart won 3-2. A bit luckily and certainly against the odds. I was sold.

I like an underdog, and I liked the fact that Heart were #2 in a two-team city. I liked that *we* had fewer supporters than *them*. I liked the red and white. I liked the community-based focus and ethos – the club's address was a northern Melbourne suburbs university campus. It was like supporting a kind of cross between Fulham and Millwall, a spirited little fighter; people like us *and* we care.

My support meandered along. I went to about one game in four (I did live over two hours away), usually taking my kids. Mainly home games, away games against *them* and a one-off interstate trip to Newcastle in early 2013. It was fun, and fairly low-key. We mainly lost but I had good chats with many other supporters – Heart or otherwise. There were plenty of odd Brits to be seen wandering around AAMI Park wearing Newcastle, Everton, Reading, Linfield and Stoke City shirts. I think they probably arrived direct from South Melbourne circa 2002.

Melbourne Heart never troubled the upper reaches of the table (*ladder* in Aussie parlance). But there was an honesty about the club. In retrospect I have to admit that one of the most appealing things about Melbourne Heart was that they *weren't* Melbourne Victory. Their form was mostly poor, albeit peppered by the odd glorious short run. In 2013-14 Heart went the first fourteen games without a win, then won six out the next seven. That short undefeated run included a 5-0 win in Wellington, a great 2-1 comeback game against Sydney with only ten men – David Williams slaloming the pitch for a delightful injury-time winner, and a home derby triumph. The 1 March game against a weary and troubled Victory team – a 4-0 hammering – was without doubt the best performance and most memorable occasion in the short, but curious, life of Melbourne Heart. Early goals from

The last Melbourne Heart vs Melbourne Victory derby, March 2014.

Orlando Engelaar and Mate Dugandzic (unintended – even he would admit it was a cross) put Heart in control. Late strikes from David Williams and Harry Kewell wrapped it up. It was the best-ever night to be a Melbourne Heart fan. And that was about it. A few weeks earlier it had been announced that a consortium, which included an eighty per cent Manchester City stake, had bought Melbourne Heart.

There was one more stand-out that season. With four games left Central Coast Mariners were the visitors and won 2-1, but Heart's marquee player scored a remarkable first-half opener – the goal of the season in Australia. Orlando Engelaar, a languid Vieira-esque midfield giant and Dutch total football exponent, quietly took possession of the ball in midfield. After a few rangy paces forward he looked up. The Central Coast keeper was off his line. Engelaar, with supreme judgment, skill and no little arrogance just belted the ball forward and over the keeper's head; probably the best goal a Melbourne Heart player would ever score.

The season fizzled out. Tenth place (out of ten) in the A-League. But we had *that* run. Original coach John van't Schip returned, Harry Kewell was a fizzer (though charmingly) and Orlando Engelaar was probably the best player in the league despite playing only a handful of games. The now mature, twenty-nine-year-old Massimo Murdocca was Heart's most effective player and looked like a future captain.

Heart's season finished on 12 April and it all went quiet for a few weeks. Then, in early June came the announcement, finally. *Fucking finally* because I was bored of waiting around by this time. Melbourne Heart will change its name to Melbourne City. Melbourne City won't wear red and white – it'll be some Man City-style kit. The club badge will change and include a variation of the City of Melbourne flag within it. Clever move, on the surface, because the City of Melbourne flag, while containing odd images of dairy stock, ships and stuff, is essentially the cross of St George. Going after the English expat demographic then.

The news was finally out. It wasn't really that *big* a news story beyond a few thousand people: Melbourne Heart fans, A-League *generalist* die-hards and Man City fans in Australia. In total maybe twenty-five thousand people, probably less.

I was unhappy. This small club, underdog, community-focused – see earlier sentiments, comments etc – now basically ceased to exist. Take away the name, the badge and the shirt and what are you left with? Indignant, I posted a few comments on social media. I was thoroughly shouted down. My argument was essentially that Melbourne Heart had ceased to exist, this was a new club and I wouldn't be following them. I gorged on it online over a few days. A football club, albeit a new one and with a small supporter base, had simply been brushed aside by its new owners. New name, new strip and new club badge (or *logo* to many Melburnians) and the club's fans were… well not up in arms about it. They didn't question it. They *embraced* it. And they embraced it at a ratio of about ten to one by my reckoning – judging by the 'fors' and 'againsts' on various Facebook posts over a week or so. I wasn't quite a lone voice, but I was in a significant minority.

There were positively joyous statements about becoming "the richest team in the league". Someone posted a picture of wagons, as in *jump on the bandwagon*. People invited friends to become members for the following season now that the club had some money. Some of the critical posts were answered by Man City 'fans' in the UK at pains to paint a very rosy picture of life under City's still relatively new owners. The way some of these things were written it was hard to believe they came from anywhere other than the Man City marketing dept.

I was totally gobsmacked – not that there was this kind of reaction, but the scale of it. Fans of the club were overwhelmingly in favour of their club being taken over and its identity completely transformed. Just like that. Fair enough *to a degree*. Melbourne Heart was a young club with no meaningful history or tradition, but even so, how and why would you so readily embrace not just a change, but the complete eradication of what was there before? I simply didn't get it. But then I recalled a comment a few years previously prior to an upcoming Ashes series. I'd been in Australia several years and was asked who I would be supporting.

"England…?" I said, incredulous at the question.

Eyes rolled. "What? When you could back a *winning* team?"

***

After a few days I stopped arguing on Facebook about Melbourne Heart-City. The argument was over. I was so clearly in the minority it wasn't funny. 'Change' understated it. Total metamorphosis more like. Win at all and any cost was clearly the new mantra.

I thought of Cardiff City and Hull City – protesting about strip changes and name variations. People cared. Why did so few people who followed Melbourne Heart care? Is it really so easy to lose sight of something when something much glossier is dangled in front of you? I started getting emails and seeing social media from Melbourne City as opposed to Melbourne Heart. It was clearly assumed my support would just transition over.

I was pretty miffed by the whole thing back in 2014. I didn't understand it. I had wanted a battle, to see some passion. Look at those Hull and Cardiff fans. They weren't going to take it just lying down: name changes, strip changes. For me this was also a bit of a window on the Australian psyche I didn't understand.

I wasn't going to go to any Melbourne City games. Then I was "going to see how I feel about it." But in September that year they sent a squad up to the country town where I lived to play a friendly. I went. They won 4-0 with one-time £17M Damien Duff playing on a pitch my kids have played on.

The season started, and I found myself at the first Melbourne derby. Victory won 5-2 in front of nearly forty-four thousand. I belligerently decked myself and my two sons out in the red and white stripes of Brentford. Melbourne City had relegated Heart's red and white stripes to their reserve kit and were in Man City pale blue tops with white shorts.

***

Over the next few seasons I went to odd games – both Melbourne City *and* Victory, including a few derbies. But my heart (pun fully intended) wasn't in it. Whatever there had been *about* the Melbourne derby match had declined. Crowds were down on previous years, the atmosphere more subdued and the games seemed to lack edge. The only thing that seemed to have been ramped up at the Melbourne derby was the police presence. A little bit of low-level aggro wasn't unknown, but it was hardly Boca-River, Burnley-Blackburn or an Old Firm game. It was as though the police and authorities *wanted it* to seem or feel more dramatic than it actually was.

I'd really lost interest. As had thousands of other people – not just with Melbourne City, but with the A-League overall. What had looked for a few years like healthy growth in A-League attendances and a growing profile was going flat.

Overall A-League crowds in season 2017-18 hit a six-year low as did Melbourne Victory's home average gate. Melbourne City's home average gate was at a five-year low and lower than the last season they played as Heart – a marketing disaster for the City Football Group.

Football in Australia faces some big challenges. By 2018 things had gone decidedly stale. Ten club teams playing each three times in the league, plus a finals series, plus a midweek cup tournament. The same clubs play each other too often. There is no promotion or relegation, so barring the occasional club closure or team getting chucked out, that's it: ten teams – with a planned extension to twelve for season 2019-20. It's beginning to look quite boring. Extending the league significantly or extending it by having two divisions would be very expensive. The A-League would need to be sitting on major cash reserves to prop-up clubs while they get established. Some of the big cities might be able to support a second or third club – probably if that club was already established in a different league – though an established club would likely have the old 'ethnic' baggage. Support-wise, South Melbourne would hold their own in the A-League, but they are a readily identifiable Greek team. Their presence in a reformed A-League would surely also impact on the gates of the other two Melbourne clubs.

It would be great to see some other regional teams in the A-League. A Geelong team, or one from Wollongong, or Ballarat or Darwin or Hobart, but it's difficult to see how these new teams would survive financially. It's a vicious circle; there's not enough serious money to expand the league or attract the players who might increase gates and reignite some wider interest.

It might well be that seasons 2011 to 2015 go down in Australian football history not as the *glory years* but perhaps as the *optimistic years*. It's difficult to envisage where next for the A-League and top-level football in Australia.

I LIKE TO WATCH

The Ashes

My old man loved cricket and was gently trying to steer me in the direction of leather and willow, as opposed to football, when I was a kid. Christmas presents, despite the time of year, included cricket bats and batting gloves, stumps etc. He didn't overlook my growing interest in football, but it was clear what he favoured.

I'm not complaining. A year before taking us to days one and two of England against the then legendary West Indies at Trent Bridge in the first Test of 1976, he'd tried me out at with a day at Lord's. Guess he wanted to see how a ten-year-old would go, watching six hours of cricket.

Day two at Lord's, 1 August 1975. England completed their first innings, reaching a reasonable 315. Australia started, then collapsed in a fashion that England followers got quite used to in the decades to follow. I wasn't old enough then to realise that Dennis Lillee scoring 73 (ultimately his highest Test score) was something special. I do remember clearly the sense of all-round disappointment when Australian batsman Ross Edwards departed one run short of a century. How many Australian cricketers managed to play in an Ashes Test at

Lord's over the years? How many of them scored a century? Not that many – eighteen up to that point to be precise. To go out on 99 was, in the sporting sense, heart-breaking. Australia finished on 268 – which they would've been mightily relieved about considering their 81/7 position earlier in the day. My dad was probably relieved as well; I'd enjoyed the day and cricket was on the agenda.

Between the ages of about ten and fourteen I played a lot of cricket each summer – in the little close where I lived, with friends whacking a tennis ball around, in parks with a cricket ball but no pads, and for my schools – where we at least had *some kind* of protection. I considered myself an all-rounder, though, truth-be-told, my bowling was far more consistent. In a precursor to an adult life keeping lists, I kept a notebook during those years that detailed my cricketing achievements: runs scored, wickets taken and if I'd taken a catch or somehow been involved in a dismissal. My stats-keeping wasn't as sophisticated as to keep a record of the runs scored off my bowling though; or maybe I didn't want to.

I saw odd days of Test and county cricket over the next twenty-five years and always followed the England home matches on TV. I remember going with my dad to the Oval Ashes Test in 1977 during the school holiday. He hadn't got me a ticket, so I had to join him in the press box for the day (no ID in a lanyard around your neck in those days), on the strict proviso that I wouldn't muck around or make any unnecessary noise. With a pen and scorecard, I studiously kept a record of the day's play, and had probably the best view of any twelve-year-old in the ground.

I enjoyed cricket, but I wasn't *driven* to go and watch it the way I was with football. That is until I moved to Australia.

By my previous standards I watched quite a bit of cricket in the

Australian summers of 2000-01 and 2001-02. By the time England arrived for an Ashes series in late 2002 I was thoroughly into it. At that stage my international cricket-watching in Australia had been confined to trips to the MCG. So, one quiet evening in about July or August I sat down at my PC, credit card at the ready, and organised tickets, flights and accommodation for four of the five Ashes Tests.

Perth seemed like a long, long way away, so I gave it a miss. I didn't go to every day of the other four in Brisbane, Adelaide, Melbourne and Sydney but went to eleven days across the four Tests. England lost the series 4-1 which wasn't a major surprise, but I was left with two abiding memories: Michael Vaughan's batting (633 runs in a heavy defeat of a five-match series), and what a lovely place to watch cricket Adelaide Oval was.

Set in parkland close to the Torrens River and a short walk from the city centre, Adelaide Oval was an absolute picture. There was a modern pavilion at the city end, and a grass bank at the other – with its famous scoreboard. Opposite to where I was sitting were these beautiful old, sandy-coloured low stands – the George Giffen stand, Sir Edwin Smith stand and Mostyn Evan stand. All had been built between the 1880s and 1920s. I was sat in the open, in what must have been a temporary stand. I spent two days getting horribly sunburnt watching England struggle. It was so hot that a number of times I just took myself off – during play as well as the breaks – into the shade beneath the stand. Those two days were stifling; so much fluid for so few pisses.

I stayed in a hotel on Hindley Street – thankfully not too far down into the bowels of what the Aussie tabloids had once deemed "the most dangerous street in Australia". It looked pretty rough, but I didn't hang around there in the evenings.

In late 2002 I hadn't yet lived in Australia for two years. In trying to fit in and show that I wasn't a "whingeing Pom" I was prepared to take a lot more stick over the cricket than I would've done in later years. In addition to Australia having possibly their strongest Test team in history at the time, England were playing the kind of stuff that was promising-ish compared to some of their 1990s performances, but still looked far from world-beating.

The first Test in Brisbane ended in a bludgeoning 384-run defeat. The scene was set at the end of day one with Australia on 364/2. Local boy Matthew Hayden got a century in each innings. England's first innings performance wasn't too bad, but what really sticks out from that game was the horrific injury to England bowler Simon Jones when he was fielding close to the boundary on that first day. It was just below where I was sitting.

Adelaide that series I went to days two and three. Another ok England first innings (342, with Michael Vaughan scoring 177) was blasted into almost meaninglessness by Australia's first innings 559/9 declared. Australia won without batting a second time.

It felt a bit strange going to games I felt England had little chance of winning and where I was just making up the crowd numbers. It was the first Ashes series in Australia since I'd lived there so I felt a kind of obligation. I also wanted to get a few new grounds on the list.

I didn't go to Perth. It was another innings defeat. Melbourne was next for me – the fourth Test. I went to the first three days. Australia batted first and amassed 551/6 declared (the same score would haunt England four years later in Adelaide) with the little ninja-like assassin Justin Langer scoring a neat 250 of them. At the time Australia had two openers, Langer and Hayden, who seemed invincible. They hit big scores and scored very quickly. When they were out Australia had Ponting and the Waughs to amass a few more. Then just for fun Gilchrist would come in and hit the ball all over the place like it was a one-dayer. It was daunting for the opposition. England had to follow-on at the MCG and posted a very respectable 387 in their second innings (Vaughan 145). For the first time in the series Australia had to bat again, though they only had to chase down just over a hundred.

For the first time I sat with the Barmy Army on day three of that Melbourne Test. While I respected their collective tendency to behave – relative to their international footballing counterparts – there was still something a bit, er, non-cricketing and pretty basic about most of them. I got the distinct feeling the Ashes was more about the *trip*, the cheap drink (the exchange rate at the time was about £1 to $3) and the opportunity to group together and sing silly songs about the Aussies.

Four Tests; 4-0 down. There was some retrospective fighting talk after the fifth Test in Sydney when England captain Nasser Hussain, discussing the series on TV, said something along the lines of "there was no way I was going to lose 5-0 to Steve Waugh". And he didn't. I went to the first three days. England batted first. Mark Butcher scored a hard-fought century on the first day. We happened to see him in a Darling Harbour restaurant that night. I generally always ignore sporting celebrities when I see them, figuring they get pestered enough as it is. But we were having dinner with my old man and his wife, Sarah. He went over to say hello to Butcher and congratulate him on his century.

"He's absolutely fucking knackered," my old man reported when he returned to our table.

Day two in Sydney saw Steve Waugh get his century off the last ball of the last over. The Australian captain was then thirty-seven and his place in the team under a bit of scrutiny. A broad consensus was that this would be his last Test, and on his home ground at that.

England had again scored one of those *useful-but-not-exceptional* first innings scores, 362, that you can win, draw or even lose from. By mid-afternoon on day two Australia were a bit under-the-pump in addressing that score. Steve Waugh came in with the score on 56/3. He faced his first ball at 3.39. In the next three hours he passed ten thousand Test runs – only the third player to do so. He got to 50 in just 61 balls. Towards the end of the afternoon he was joined by the free-scoring Gilchrist. Steve Waugh clearly wanted to get his hundred that day. The crowd wanted him to get his hundred that day. Statistically-speaking if he'd got there in the second over the next day it wouldn't have mattered, but there was something about the drama and theatre of it as the close of play approached. In all honesty, I think most of the England fans there were willing him to do it. The last over came around. Twenty-two-year-old Richard Dawson, a spinner playing the last of his seven England Tests, took the ball. Waugh was on 95. A couple of dot balls, then Waugh scored a 3, leaving Gilchrist on strike with two balls to face. Battling his natural tendency to go for a boundary, Adam Gilchrist crafted possibly the most notable single of his Test career. Last ball. Ages of fucking around, field placing changes, little chats between captain and bowler etc etc etc. Dawson bowled, and Waugh smashed a 4 out on to the offside. A roar enveloped the Sydney Cricket Ground. Waugh leapt with joy. If I was an Australian cricket fan it would have been one of my most treasured moments watching the game. As a Pom I was happy to settle with having seen something that would go down in the annals of Australian cricket.

Australia had a one run lead at the end of the first innings. England's second innings saw them finally put together a really competitive score, 452/9 declared with opener Michael Vaughan scoring 183.

Australia could only muster 226 by way of reply. England had won but finished the series at 1-4.

It was a crushing series defeat for England, but I don't think anyone was really surprised. It was hard not to think that despite the steeliness with which Steve Waugh led the Australian team, they had to some degree taken their collective foot off the gas a bit at 4-0 going into that last Test. Historically, the SCG was also actually one of England's better hunting grounds in Australia.

Through the series England had shown some glimpses, some passages of play when they genuinely competed with Australia, though just not often enough. Vaughan's series total of 633 runs was something to get excited about from an England perspective and despite being in the team on the end of a thumping series defeat he was named Player of the Series.

I'd enjoyed the series. I'd got to some new Test grounds and seen a bit more of Australia. While there had been no real surprises on the pitch, I was a bit taken aback at the complete lack of spectator etiquette in terms of waiting, or not waiting, to move between overs. Over the years it became a bugbear.

The 2005 Ashes series in England has been written about, talked about, romanticised about and ruminated about at length. I didn't go, because I lived in Australia. It turned out to be England's first Ashes win in sixteen years.

TV viewing on the East Coast of Australia works out well for English cricket times. A 10.30 a.m. or 11 a.m. start means 7.30 p.m. or 8 p.m. in Australia, with the afternoon session starting at either 10.10 p.m. or 10.40 p.m. It means watching well into the evening session is doable on most days as well. I watched the first two sessions of nearly every day, and a good chunk of the evening session on most days. It was a period when I was also particularly keen on a regular drop of Sauv Blanc. After a few weeks it started to feel quite gruelling.

The series was due to finish at the Oval on Monday 12 September – a late finish to a Test series in England. Cooler, darker evenings were drawing in by then. My first child – and we already knew it was going to be a boy – was due on 1 October. At least there would be a bit of a break between the end of the Ashes and the sprog coming along. I'd be able to catch-up on some sleep and help get a few things sorted around the place in advance of his arrival. Or so I thought.

England were 2-1 up going in to the last match at the Oval. An Australian victory would've drawn the series and they would have retained the Ashes. England had a big lead late in the day by the time Australia went into bat. They faced one over before the teams went off due to bad light. The match was drawn, and England won the series. I watched the presentations, post-match interviews and analysis. It went on well into the early hours.

I wore my England cricket baseball cap to work that Tuesday as I had done throughout the series, but I wasn't going to gloat to my Aussie workmates. The gloating stuff is a bit juvenile for starters and has a habit of coming back to bite you. I was knackered though, and just wanted to get the day out of the way and catch a few early nights before the saucepan arrived.

It was about lunchtime when Carla, my then-wife, phoned me: "He's on his way."

We were at the hospital within an hour. I tried to keep her spirits up over the next twelve hours or so, but I was struggling and fell asleep a few times mid-conversation. I can't think of a time when I had seen another human being in so much pain; it was horrible. At 2.45 a.m. on 14 September our son, Henry *Vaughan* arrived – an Aussie boy-child named after an English Ashes-winning captain.

I nearly pulled it off again when the next Ashes series was held in Australia late the following year. My wife was pregnant again, with the baby due in late January. We didn't know the sex this time, but both instinctively knew it would be a boy. We'd obviously been talking about names, building a mental list of options we liked. In Australia it was easier to rule names *out* than *in*. Some Aussie parents put the Americans to shame with their choice of crap, often made-up names. ("We wanted something *different*, something original.") A once-a-week glance at the baby photos in the local paper was usually a challenge in trying to decipher pronunciation and work-out the thinking behind some of the names. I wanted to keep it simple: Arthur, George, William… something like that. That was a bit *too straight* for Carla, though thankfully she wasn't suggesting the likes of Jarrod, Jarryd, Jarryn or anything that started with a lower-case letter or was hyphenated. Or started with a lower-case letter *and* was hyphenated. At the time Monty Panesar was making a name for himself in the England team and became a bit of a cult figure for a few years. I suggested the name Montgomery.

"No doubt it would get shortened to Monty," I said. I mentioned war heroes, history and suggested that while it was old-fashioned it was also "kind of funky too". She was just about sold on it, though I was hoping she wouldn't remember my mate Lee had a dog called Monty.

But then I blew it. Panesar was playing in that 2006-07 series. Carla clocked that he was a 'Monty' when I started to call-out regularly when he was bowling: "Monty! Come in for your chapati!" in my best-worst self-parodying *It Ain't Half Hot Mum* accent. It wasn't funny. I said it thirty or forty times too often during one particular match, Perth, and it got struck off the potential names list.

***

That 2006-07 Ashes series in Australia was a disaster for England. The Aussies were riled and somewhat indignant that England had managed to sneak a series win fifteen months or so earlier. The team, media and Joe Public were psyched-up for revenge. The hype meant an unprecedented interest in tickets. Tickets went on sale in June. Online queues and frustration reached boiling point and crashing systems. Where had the demand been in 2002-03? I was planning on going to Adelaide, Melbourne and Sydney. Prior to the start of the series I'd managed to get a couple of day one tickets for Melbourne, and Sydney. That was it. As it turned out people were booking-up tickets without necessarily having a buyer for them. I ended up going to three days in Adelaide, and Melbourne and Sydney from start-to-finish (three and four days respectively). In ten days of Ashes cricket that year I paid a whopping *total* of $50 over the collective face value of the tickets I bought. The whole thing wasn't quite as *in demand* as everyone had been thinking.

I flew over to Adelaide with Darryn Mawby, an Aussie mate from Bendigo, to watch the first three days. We didn't have *any* tickets. Now, Darryn's a more outgoing sort than me – he sells houses, you have to be. Seeing that our flight from Melbourne consisted largely of tour groups going to the match, he was up and chatting to people, sniffing out ticket opportunities the moment the seatbelt light went off.

"Bloke over there," he said, "reckons their whole tour group isn't going to get there. He's going to call me later."

We got a bus from the airport to the city centre and found some luggage lockers in the train station not far from Adelaide Oval. We still had the best part of an hour until the first over and there were plenty of people milling around the park outside the ground. Mawby hadn't yet heard back from his bloke on the plane. I got chatting to a young woman, an Irish Barmy Army recruit. She had a spare pair of tickets in the Chappell Stands and wanted $50 each over face value.

"I reckon just buy them," I said. "We don't know if that bloke is going to come through."

We were in. Then just before the start of play Mawby's contact phoned – he had tickets for the following two days, but not that day (I felt better, having so readily paid over the odds for day one.) Mawby's bloke just wanted to recover his costs, so we met him in the lunchtime break and got day two and three tickets off him.

Feeling more relaxed, we watched the morning session. Already one-down in the series after a mauling in Brisbane, England won the toss and batted. It was a slow-ish day's play with England finishing on 266/3 with the two not out batsmen the chalk and cheese of Paul Collingwood and Kevin Pietersen.

Collingwood, the gritty Durham all-rounder (he really was a genuine all-rounder; a few years later I saw him keep wicket for a while in a Test match at Durham) had made the very most of his talents to carve-out a top-class cricket career. He was a kind of *trench warfare* sportsman – tough, resilient, honest, never shirking his responsibilities and always giving his all. Pietersen was different. Masses more natural talent than Collingwood – and any other England batsman of that era – but a suspect temperament and an Everest-sized ego. Pietersen had an unerring talent to attack and play wonderful shots, but there were things about him that didn't sit well. Clearly, he wasn't a team player; the extent to which was made abundantly clear a few years later. When someone as polished, diplomatic, and erudite as Andrew Strauss describes a former teammate as "an absolute cunt" in an off-guard TV studio moment then, well you have to think there's probably something in it. What irked me about Pietersen from very early on was how he walked onto the pitch when he was batting. It spoke volumes. He batted most of his England career at four or five, so with two or three wickets down, Pietersen would be jogging out onto the pitch with the look of an imperialist landowner surveying the peasants. He did that swinging thing with his arms – a kind of swirling warm-up meets muscle-flexing thing. He did a little jog, moving side-to-side. I don't claim any body language analysis expertise but the message I took away every time Pietersen came out to bat was either *I'm here to save the day* (if England were struggling) or *now you're going to see some real batting* (if England were going ok).

There is also the case of Alastair Cook's wedding in 2011. Apparently attended by a significant number, or maybe all, of the then England team, a notable absentee was Kevin Pietersen. The unanswered question that hung in the air was whether he wasn't there because he wasn't invited or because he chose not to attend. The Cook-Pietersen relationship was examined thoroughly years later in books, newspapers and other media. As with Strauss though, to the lay person and even seasoned follower of the game, it was hard to see Alastair Cook as either aggressor or insidious protagonist in a conflict with another teammate. I remember a *Spectator* article which described Cook as the adult equivalent of the boy who would never let the school down. It seemed a fair assessment.

Of course, throughout Pietersen's England career there were media calls and fans who thought he ought to be treated differently. "He has a unique talent, you need to find a place in the team for him. You need to indulge his foibles…etc." Well actually, like many other people, I saw cricket as a team game. And it was hard to think of 'KP' as a real team player during his time with England. Even that nickname, 'KP', made me cringe – it had something of the rapper about it, and something of an ego so big he thought he could be known by initials alone. *Enough already!* And in writing this I'm just playing into what I've said about Collingwood and Pietersen. How many words have I written about each of them?

In 2006 Adelaide Oval, for me, was just about the perfect cricket ground. It was by miles the best ground in Australia. The temporary stand I'd sat in at the 2002-03 Ashes had been replaced by the Chappell Stands – two modest, but comfortable, shady stands which I'd first sat in for the 2003 Test against India. Between the Chappell stands a small temporary stand had been erected to help cope with ticket demand. To the left of the Chappell Stands and behind the bowler's arm at the city end was the modern Sir Donald Bradman Stand. Opposite us were the sandy-coloured George Giffen, Sir Edwin Smith and Mostyn Evan stands. On a sunny day you could have been looking at something in North Africa. At the northern end of the ground was that grass bank, overlooked by trees. In one corner was the famous old manual scoreboard. The ground was a near-perfect mix of new and old, tradition and comfort. In the years since it has been modernised considerably – to the tune of $450M. It's now primarily an Aussie rules football ground.

I'll leave it there.

At the end of that first day we grabbed a taxi for the short journey across the city to Hindmarsh Stadium for the A-League game between Adelaide United and Melbourne Victory. Good idea by the A-League scheduling a football match in the same city on the evening of an Ashes Test. I've seen it happen in Melbourne and Sydney as well; they're always going to pick-up a few hundred from the cricket. This game was notable for a couple of things though. It was a new ground for me, and one I knew I'd unlikely ever go back to. It also saw the then forty-year-old Romario play one of his four Adelaide United games. Yes, *that* Romario. The Romario and Ashes factors prompted a bumper crowd of 15,694 to turn up – considerably higher than that season's (or any season's) average home gate at Hindmarsh.

Hindmarsh wasn't a bad little stadium as it goes. Originally built in 1960 it has been used for a multitude of sports and by a multitude of teams since, including during the 2000 Sydney Olympics. The ground has four distinctive separate stands, albeit only one is covered. We sat high-up in that covered main stand for the first half. The stadium could easily be extended if there was a need.

The game started in quite bizarre fashion with the Adelaide goalkeeper, Robert Bajic, getting sent off after just thirteen minutes for a needless waist-high kick on a Melbourne Victory forward who was simply running past him after Bajic had collected a through ball. Odd.

Unlike in England there is no rule about not taking beer to your seat at football. We took full advantage of the Brazilian beer on special that night – no doubt some marketing link-in to the Romario deal. At half-time we went for a wander and found the bar behind the Melbourne Victory part of the ground. We had to show our Victorian driving licences to get in. It must be said that the A-League authorities really fucked-up when they went down the crowd segregation route in Australian *soccer*. When the league started they had an almost blank canvas. Instead of trying to model crowd make-up and demographics on Australian rules (no segregation, more women supporters, more families) they decided *in advance* of any major crowd issues to segregate supporters along European lines. And as soon as there's an 'us-and-them' thing about where everyone is in the ground, then the 'us-and-them' thing kicks in. You can't easily taunt opposition supporters if they're mixed-up, mixed-in, next to you and all over the place. A major opportunity was lost by the A-League.

We watched the second half from behind the goal Melbourne Victory were attacking as they sealed a 3-1 win, their first at Adelaide United. It was from high up in this stand that we watched the post-match action outside the ground as it kicked-off between the two sets of supporters. Briefly, they really got stuck into each other before the police, including a couple on horseback, intervened. By the time we'd made our way down the steps and onto the street the action was over. We walked away from the ground for a few minutes before we found a pub. It was definitely a locals pub, with a kind of *Snowtown* vibe to it.

"Hillbillies," muttered Mawby as we supped our beers. The South Australia-Victoria relationship is a strained one with a definite resentment element aimed at the more populous state. I didn't get it for a moment, but the undercurrent was often there.

"The hotel closes at midnight," I said, "and we still need to get our luggage from the station."

Ashes hype meant that most hotels in Adelaide that weekend were only taking five-night bookings during the Test. Our hotel was miles away, somewhere out on the way to the Adelaide Hills; the only place we could get for just two nights.

We'd almost finished our second beers when a taxi driver walked in. We were in the front bar, nearest the street.

"Cab for Johnson. Cab for Mr Johnson…"

Mawby and I looked at each other, then walked forward.

"That's me," I said. "Gordon Johnson." We necked the remains of our drinks as we followed him to the door, before the real Mr Johnson appeared from somewhere. Mawby looked at me.

"I don't know either. First name that came into my head."

The next day's play started in the same kind of vein – slow to moderate progress by England, adding about eighty before lunch. Importantly they didn't lose any wickets. The gritty northerner and flamboyant South African both reached their centuries. England were playing sensibly and diligently. Reaching 347/3 at lunch they could conceivably get themselves into a position by the end of the day which they at least couldn't *lose* from. The partnership continued until the last ball before tea when Collingwood was out for 206, becoming only the third Englishman to score a double century in a Test match in Australia. After tea Pietersen went on to score 158 – for the third time in Test matches in just over a year. England played on after tea, before declaring on 551/6 with about an hour to go.

We had decided to stretch our legs and were watching the last session from the grass bank in front of the scoreboard amidst a mixed group of England and Australia fans exchanging some colourful but good-humoured banter.

"Declared too soon," I said. "I don't like it."

Mawby laughed dismissively.

"I've been watching England a long time."

I liked it even less ten minutes later when the teams came out again. Langer and Hayden walked on normally, the England players bounced and swaggered on to the ground with an air of *right, now let's get the job finished.* They need to take twenty Australian wickets, I thought.

I woke up on the Sunday morning in our cheap motel to the sound of a couple shagging in the next room. The walls were cardboard thin. It was almost as if I was in bed *with* them. I reckoned her head was no more than a couple of feet away from mine. I'd like to report that she was howling like a banshee and demanding all sorts of adventurous stuff, but it all sounded fairly conventional from where I was lying. I carried on reading.

On that third morning England had Australia at 65/3 at one stage, and then shortly after Ricky Ponting was dropped on the far boundary. He went on to score 142 in an innings where Australia almost matched the England score. England's captain for the series, Andrew Flintoff, later acknowledged the Ponting drop as the turning point in the match.

We jumped in a cab for the airport about an hour before play finished. We were in the terminal bar to see Australia finish the day on 312/5.

"Still don't like it," I said.

What happened on days four and five of the Adelaide Test destroyed England. They went from some kind of expectation or hope of a victory, to expecting a draw to a confidence-shattering defeat. That defeat fucked the whole series for England. No one was surprised that a 5-0 whitewash was the end result after Adelaide. It must have been soul-destroying for the players. It was bury-your-head-in-your-hands time for fans.

I didn't go to the third Test in Perth, but I went to both Melbourne and Sydney Tests from start to finish – not that either match had to utilise anything remotely approaching near the full time allocation.

As an England fan it was hard to pick any highlights from that series. Collingwood's 206 and his partnership with Pietersen would have been talked about and remembered for a long time if England had won and gone on to get something respectable out of the series. I wonder how Paul Collingwood felt about getting that score and record for it to end as it did? I guess the retirements of Warne, Langer, McGrath and Martyn were some kind of consolation for England fans – but they didn't do England any good that series.

Warne's 700th Test wicket at the MCG during the fourth Test was history to see, as was his 708th and last wicket in the last Test at Sydney. Eleven months later I was in Kandy when Murali took his 709th Test wicket, beating Warne's record. Murali went on to bag exactly 800. Even if you ignore the issue of Murali's bowling action, rule changes and a whole load of other stuff, I would still come in firmly on Warne being the superior Test bowler. Sure, stats don't lie, but have a Google and see who they got their respective wickets against, and where.

Four years and a day later I was again at a Sydney Ashes Test. It was the evening session on day four and I was sitting high up in the Brewongle Stand with Phil Silver. The series was coming to an end. England were 2-1 up after Melbourne and had thus retained the Ashes after their 2009 series win in England. They were closing in on a 3-1 for the series. I'd never seen England as dominant and aggressive as they were in their 644-run first innings. The captain, Andrew Strauss scored an un-Strauss-like 60 off 58 balls whilst his opening partner Alastair Cook went on to amass 189. Ian Bell chipped-in with 115, whilst wicketkeeper Matt Prior coming in at number seven, bludgeoned his way to 100 in just 109 balls. I had seen a number seven wicketkeeper bat like that before in Ashes Tests, but not for England.

On that fourth afternoon England were on the verge of victory. By the time Mitchell Johnson came in with six wickets down Australia still needed nearly two hundred just to make England bat again. These were rare, heady times for England in Australia. After eight-and-a-half years of hurt as a Pom on Australian soil, I was enjoying this. At that point in the game it was really only about whether England could finish the job that night or whether it would go into a fifth day.

England supporters are far more noticeable at Sydney Ashes Tests than in Melbourne. Far more English people live in Sydney than Melbourne, thus boosting the overall England numbers. The Sydney Cricket Ground is roughly half the size of the MCG, so the ratio of England fans is far greater. And for travelling groups from the UK – be it Barmy Army or SAGA Army-types – there weren't many who did Melbourne, but not Sydney. On that fourth day at the SCG the official attendance was 35,622 – probably two thirds of whom were supporting England. And at that stage in the evening, defeat beckoning Australia, it was pretty much only England fans left in the ground.

I don't really know why England fans cast Mitchell Johnson as the pantomime villain in that series but cast him they did. He always seemed ok to me – certainly compared to some of his predecessors and teammates. The treatment he got in that series came back to haunt England horribly three years later. By then David Warner was in the Australian team and there was nothing *pantomime* villain-ish about him.

Anyway, back at the SCG on 6 January 2011. Brad Haddin has just departed and Mitchell Johnson was at the wicket. The very English-looking (he could have stepped out of a Peter Christian menswear catalogue) Chris Tremlett was bowling. Johnson, warming up, played a couple of dummy defensive shots, prodded down the pitch and walked back to his crease. He looked around a bit and then listened to the building wall of noise as Tremlett made his run-up. Johnson was clean-bowled, first ball. The roar that echoed around the SCG is the loudest I've ever heard at a cricket match. It was more like the reaction to a 1980s FA Cup 6th round last-minute winning goal. Tremlett's response was to jog almost nonchalantly down the wicket

England celebrate their 3-1 Ashes series win, Sydney, January 2011.

with one arm gently raised. You could be forgiven for thinking that the towering Tremlett didn't want much fuss. It was Tremlett also who bowled the final ball of the series the following day to dismiss Michael Beer for two, sealing the 3-1 win. The three Tests England won were all won by more than an innings – the first time a touring side had done that in Australia.

Mitchell Johnson's wicket hadn't been meaningful in the context of the game or series, yet it had generated near-wild celebrations. England got an extra half-hour off the umpires that fourth evening but couldn't finish the job. They needed three wickets the following morning as the Australian tail wagged. A very respectable 19,274 spectators turned-up – although it was free to get in.

***

It all started six weeks earlier in Brisbane. Ashes series in Australia have followed a very similar pattern in recent years. Brisbane first, Melbourne on Boxing Day, Sydney very early in January. Adelaide and Perth between first and fourth Tests in early-mid December, though not necessarily in that order. It seems odd that the last Test is over barely a third of the way into summer.

As in 2006-07, England had won the previous series and travelled to Australia as Ashes holders. This was going to be no 5-0 though. I arranged a family holiday in Queensland to coincide with the first Test at the Gabba and went to the first three days. Lee Izzard, one-time of Acton, West London and now resident of Brisbane joined me on day three. I was a bit concerned. Lee's interest in sport (only really football in his case) had declined significantly over the years. He'd never been to a day's Test cricket. I imagined boredom driving him to ripping some of the seats out before the morning drinks break.

By the time we left the Gabba at the end of day three, a Saturday, things were looking pretty grim. Australia led by 221 on the first innings and England had just commenced batting again. A lot more surprising than how the game was poised was that Lee told me he'd enjoyed the day.

"Really?"

"Yeah. I was expecting worse, but that was ok. Bit slow at times." Quite some endorsement.

I didn't go on the Sunday, but something interesting happened. England decided to bat with a degree of determination quite alien to the people who regularly watched them. They were too far behind to win, but they carved out a rear-guard action of 517/1 by the time they declared on Monday. It wasn't just the size of the rear-guard action that necessarily surprised observers, more that it had happened at all. Australia batted again for a while on the Monday afternoon before the game ended in a draw. Getting out of the first Test at Brisbane undefeated was going into recently uncharted waters for England. The second innings score gave us an inkling as to what was possible, and what was to follow.

I went to just the weekend of the second Test in Adelaide; days two and three. An old friend from England, John Matthews was over; I'd seen a bit of him at the Brisbane Test as well.

The alarm went at 4.30 a.m. that Saturday morning. I lived in a Victorian country town which was the right side of the airport from Melbourne. I did that drive to the airport a lot.

Australia toiled a bit on day one to finish on 245 all out – a kind of typical recent years England first innings score in Australia. The Australian captain, Ricky Ponting, was out first ball very early

Self-aware cricket fan? Adelaide Oval, 2010.

Kevin Pietersen on the defensive at Adelaide Oval, 2010.

on, leaving Australia two wickets down at the end of the first over. Michael Clarke followed soon after. Three wickets for two runs in the second over. It was a shame to have missed it. I briefly reconciled my disappointment at not being there for day one with the fact that probably thousands of people who *did* have tickets were still making their way to the ground and hadn't seen this explosive start either.

England had faced one over the previous evening when I took up my seat in the Chappell Stands on day two. They batted solidly, finishing the day on a tidy 317. The real positive was that they'd only lost two wickets and the not out men, Cook and Pietersen, were on big scores and in the form of their careers.

I spent the best part of Saturday evening with John Matthews in a pub on Rundle Mall working our way through the different types of Coopers beers they had on tap. I left with no change to my opinion that the Pale Ale, the green one, was my preferred choice from what the iconic South Australian brewery had to offer.

On a rain-affected Sunday Cook got to 148 and Pietersen finished on 213 not out. It was another day when England only lost two wickets. They were firmly in control. Sitting in the stand late that afternoon watching the rain settle in, the only serious discussion point was if England would get beaten to a draw by the weather. Australia were out of it.

England batted a bit into the Monday, finishing on 620/5 declared. Pietersen and Cook's centuries were ably supplemented by England's middle order, with only the captain, Strauss, not contributing. Australia put up more of a fight when they batted on day four, finishing on 238/4. The following morning the Australian tail collapsed, with the remaining six wickets going in less than twenty overs before lunch. England didn't need to bat again, and for the first time in a generation England were ahead in an Ashes series in Australia.

What the fuck happened in Perth though? I flew over, arriving the day before the third Test started. Owen Francis and his wife, Gill, had arrived from London. Paul Robbins was over as well. We met for drinks and dinner in one of those northern Perth beachside suburbs that looked like it was straight out of a TV soap. I'd been to Perth several times but never really warmed to the place. On a previous visit I'd caught a couple of days of an Australia vs India Test at the WACA, so I had the ground on the list already. I remember entering the WACA, approaching a steward and politely asking where the Inverarity Stand was. "I don't know, sorry," came the dumbfounding response. I'd had several other strange customer service experiences in the Western Australian capital over the years. The city was clean and modern but lacking in character. In fact, the place in Perth that *did* have some character was the WACA. It wasn't a big ground and by 2018 the glossy new, multi-purpose 60,000-seater Optus Stadium had replaced the WACA as the primary cricket ground *and* Subiaco Oval as the home ground of both WA's AFL Aussie rules teams. The Optus Stadium website says it "will host a variety of sports and entertainment events including Australian Football League, International and Big Bash League cricket, soccer, rugby league and union plus concerts" (sic). Yep, another jack-of-all-trades concrete bowl. Not high on my 'to do' list. The Optus Stadium officially opened on 21 January 2018 with England playing an ODI there a week later. I remember watching it on TV and hearing one of the commentators wax lyrical about the fact that no seat in the stadium was further than a certain number of metres away from a food and drink outlet.

In late 2010 the Perth Optus Stadium was still a pipe dream and the WACA still the place to watch cricket. The WACA featured a number of different stands and vantage points, all seemingly put together without any consideration for what was already there. This was what gave it its charm. There was an olde-worlde scoreboard in a similar vein to the one at Adelaide. And two grass bank areas where spectators could get pleasantly pissed in the sun. The aforementioned Inverarity Stand was built at a slight angle that left spectators on its right-hand side (as you faced the pitch) with a slightly longer than ideal sightline to the pitch.

England played very poorly. Looking back at that 2010 Ashes Test in Perth my highlight was probably the evening we went to the Harness Racing meeting at Gloucester Park next door. It was a thirty-second walk from our exit at the WACA to the trotting track. Punters showing their ticket to the cricket were admitted for free. Owen, Gill and I commandeered a table on the grass that just about overlooked the winning line and enjoyed a relaxing evening.

Over dinner on the eve of the third Test we speculated about England retaining the Ashes by the end of this match. A 2-0 lead with two to go would be enough to retain the famous urn. Not that they ever handed it over anyway, but metaphorically speaking...

The following morning, day one, I walked to the WACA. England won the toss and put Australia in to bat. I found it strange when teams did that. It usually takes a while to recall a time when a team put the opposition in and it paid off. But Andrew Strauss's decision looked a good one when Australian only managed 268. It turned out to be a very low-scoring Test. England replied with 187. Australia just about broke three hundred in their second innings, setting England an unlikely 391 to win. The only comfort you could possibly take at that stage was that there was plenty of batting time left in the game. In their fourth innings England collapsed to 81/5 before finally lying down with 123 on the scoreboard. It was shell-shocking; a wonderful response by Australia and a wake-up call that both England players and fans probably needed after the way Brisbane ended and Adelaide unfolded. Fingers were quickly pointed at the presence of the just-arrived England players' wives and girlfriends.

That Perth Test match turned out to be the most expensive England performance I've seen. My tickets for the three and a bit (a very small 'bit' – just ten overs) days of play cost me over $500. England managed a total of 310 runs over two innings. In English money, it worked out at about a pound a run.

Chastened by the situation I brought my return flight forward by about thirty hours and legged it out of Perth back to Victoria and a couple of days back at work before the Christmas break.

Owen and Gill joined us in Bendigo for Christmas Day. The train options to Melbourne the following morning meant arriving with about forty five minutes to spare before the first ball, or about two-and-a-quarter hours before the first ball. This being Owen and I, we got the earlier train. Halfway into the journey at 7 a.m. it was standing room only with people going to the cricket.

This first day was going to be a make-or-break as far as England's Ashes-winning *in* Australia ambitions were concerned. We'd been confident going into Perth only for that confidence to be emphatically shat upon. As always, it was tricky getting good seats for day one of a Boxing Day Ashes Test. The crowd reached just over eighty-four thousand that day. We had seats in a fairly central spot in the Great Southern Stand, directly opposite the somehow-fabled members' stand. I felt a bit edgy, my nerves jangling a bit. Ridiculous really – nothing *I* could do was going to have any impact on the outcome. The feeling was reminiscent of the 1993 FA Cup semi-final between Arsenal and Spurs. It was a feeling defined by the fear of defeat, not the anticipation or hope of victory. To witness the series defeats in 2002-03 and 2006-07 didn't rankle, because there'd been no realistic expectation. After Brisbane and Adelaide in this series expectation had kicked-in but was then ripped asunder at Perth. Defeat in Melbourne was unthinkable. We had a couple of beers to calm our nerves.

England won the toss and again put Australia in to bat. I raised a couple of metaphoric eyebrows.

The lunch break came a little early due to rain with Australia on 58/4. By mid-afternoon, overs-wise, the day's play wasn't even halfway done, but Australia were all out for 98. This was the stuff of dreams. Only five Australians made it into double figures with Clarke top scoring on 20. All the wickets were catches, with six of

The Aussies have left the building. Late on day one, MCG, Boxing Day 2010.

them being caught behind. Premature maybe, but by mid-afternoon every England fan in the ground knew the Ashes were safe. And then England batted. By the end of the day they were 157/0. Any Australian who'd harboured the idea of remarkable turnaround after their first innings 98 had been firmly relieved of that notion. It was quite something sitting in the Great Southern Stand that afternoon as the Members' enclosure opposite emptied long before the end of play. They're not that happy watching their team getting beaten, the Aussies.

We watched days two and three from the Members'. Many locals seemed to feel there was something kind of elitist about sitting in that part of the ground. "I'll be in the Members," or "I was in the Members," gets bandied around a lot by people looking to impress. The pavilion at Lord's it is not. In fact, the only thing I really liked about that part of the ground was the level one bar that offered a nice view across Yarra Park to watch people arriving before the start of play. In any event, an enclosure that includes a Red Rooster franchise is hardly the stuff of elites. The worst part though is the basement-level Bullring bar – a veritable den of obnoxious chest-thumping, pissed-up blokes with barely an eye on the cricket.

England pretty much coasted to their innings and 157-run victory which was confirmed early on day four with the wicket of Hilfenhaus for 0. The Ashes were retained, and the England team celebrated long and hard on the MCG pitch.

I had a ticket to see Public Enemy that night. They were playing at the Corner Hotel, an iconic little venue just a ten-minute or so walk from the MCG. I wasn't sure how to spend the afternoon but thought a celebratory lunch with Owen and Gill along Melbourne's Southbank sounded like a good idea. A few beers turned into a few more with lunch thrown-in sometime mid-afternoon, all washed

The Boxing Day Test ends in an emphatic England win. Melbourne, 2010.

down with several bottles of Sauv Blanc. It was about 8.30 p.m. by the time I left them and gingerly walked around to Crown Casino to grab a taxi to the Corner.

Rap's not really my bag musically, but the opportunity to see a genre-defining outfit like Public Enemy in an almost intimate 800-capacity venue on a relaxed evening during the Christmas holiday was a must-do.

I got to the Sydney Test for day two. Another 4.30 a.m. start eventually got me to the SCG with about a minute to spare before the first ball of the day, but I was just about as far as I could possibly be from my seat. Something was going on. The crowd I was with walking to the ground was stopped and then held back by the police on Driver Avenue at the southern end of the ground. The reason for the delay became apparent as a limo emerged with Australia's Prime Minister du jour, Julia Gillard, in the back. She was smiling, as was her partner, the hairdresser Tim Mathieson. No big deal; but then he *waved*.

I got to my seat in time for the third over.

The Sydney Test turned out to be a third innings*plus* procession for England. Australia scored another England-like 280 in their first innings before England commenced what turned out to be their best-ever Test score in Australia, 644. Cook, predictably, chipped in with 189, bringing his series aggregate to 766 runs – from just *seven* innings. Bell and Prior also notched-up centuries.

The Ashes had not just been retained but won in some style with those three crushing victories in Adelaide, Melbourne and Sydney.

Somehow in that series everything came together for England. It wasn't the strongest Australian side to be fair, but England had some key players in top form and a captain who planned and executed the whole thing expertly. Andrew Strauss is clearly an intelligent bloke who set-out a good game plan. I read somewhere that during his captaincy his reading material was largely management books as opposed to sports books. On the surface this might sound strange, and in other sports it probably would be, but in Test cricket with its strategies, requirements for a mix of stamina and athleticism, playing away in Australia and managing personalities like Pietersen and Swann alongside the more measured likes of Alastair Cook, it made sense.

Phil Silver and I had a few early afternoon celebratory drinks in Paddington after play finished on day five before I got a cab to the airport. As a spectator, a Test series win like this didn't have the drama of a last-minute winning goal, or a one-dayer with a nail-biting run chase. But it was a marathon – for spectators as well as the players. In following that 2010-11 series I travelled something in the region of eight thousand miles by air, a thousand miles by road, spent well over $2,000 on match tickets, stayed seventeen nights in hotels, took twelve days off work and must've done $3,000 in food and drinks. No complaints. That series really was some experience – one I doubt I'll ever repeat.

I LIKE TO WATCH

Rajadamnern Stadium, Bangkok

I spent about two months in Thailand between leaving England and arriving in Australia. It was relaxing, and my then-wife, Carla, and I travelled around quite a bit, taking in Ko Samui, Phuket, Chiang Mai, Sukothai, Pithsanulok, Ayuthaya, Phi Phi Island and other places. We finished up in Bangkok in December, which wasn't quite as relaxing, but it was manic, full-on and fun.

Earlier in the trip I'd managed to get in a couple of football matches at Chiang Mai's 700th Anniversary Stadium, seeing the Peter Withe-managed national team beat Burma and Indonesia 3-1 and 4-1 respectively in the Tiger Cup.

The Tiger Cup (later the AFF Suzuki Cup) is a biannual international tournament organised by the ASEAN Football Federation. It started in 1996 and features a dozen or so teams from Southeast Asia. Japan don't take part. If they did, it might get a bit one-sided. Thailand are the most successful team in the eleven competitions to 2016 with five wins and three runners-up spots.

Carla came along to the first game and we sat in the main stand for something like £1.30 a ticket. I went to the second game on my own, paying about £1 to stand on the terraces, way behind a goal. My presence was clearly a novelty for people around me and I spent most of the match in conversation about the English Premier League, Manchester United, Arsenal and Peter Withe. In each case, for close-to-full crowds of around twenty-five thousand, I can't remember being in more genteel and polite company at football. Goals were met with excited but slightly muted high-pitched cheering – more akin to the reception a boy band support act might get; politely enthusiastic but holding back.

With staying six nights in Bangkok and Muy Thai on four nights each week at one of the city's main two stadiums, I had no excuse for not *ticking off* Thai Boxing. Carla wasn't interested, so I jumped in a tuk-tuk on my own in Khaosan Road to make the short journey to the Rajadamnern Stadium, a mile or two away. Each night's boxing featured eight or nine fights.

I bought a ticket at the stadium. Once inside, I realised I was in a section allocated to tourists – the other spectators were blokes in shorts, recently-purchased fake Lacoste and Ralph Lauren polo shirts and sporting recently-acquired sun tans. It was a mix of Aussies, Americans and Europeans. My immediate feeling was that we were intruding. While we weren't exactly made to feel unwelcome, our presence was more something to be politely tolerated – pretty much how I found the whole Thailand experience. Our tourist money was welcome though.

I found it strange in Thailand that sitting on a pillow was deemed an almost criminal offence – certainly a massive social faux pas. Yet young women – often only in their teens – getting shagged by middle-aged Westerners, often 'playing house' with them for a few months, barely seemed to raise an eyebrow. The human head is sacred to the Thais. You rest your head on a pillow when you sleep. You sit on a pillow with your arse. Your arse is for… well you get the picture. Don't sit on a pillow in Thailand. Well, not when anyone can see you.

The Muy Thai tourist tickets, I later found out, were markedly more expensive. We were in our own, sectioned-off, fenced-in section.

I wasn't and am not a boxing fan, what I'd describe as 'proper' boxing – the noble art of Muhammad Ali, Henry Cooper, Joe Frazier et al, as opposed to Thai Boxing or Muy Thai. My reticence about boxing is not some liberal snowflake kind of thing though. I find the history and social context fascinating and have read many a boxing biography. While there are elements of risk and the potential for injury in many sports, in boxing the *objective* is to club your opponent around the head to the point where he is incapacitated; where his functioning is impaired and where he is unable to carry on. I have trouble thinking of that as a sport. A way to defend yourself, yes. A way to deal with some of life's most obnoxious miscreants, perhaps. But a sport?

But Thai Boxing, or Muy Thai seemed to lack that out-and-out brutality – or so it seemed from my one evening at Rajadamnern Stadium. Aesthetics seemed to be a big part of the overall experience – a strong *visual arts* component with all that bowing in different directions before the fight, little dances and stuff. And keeping with *the-head-is really-important* thing, a fighter has to enter the ring with his head at a higher level than his feet. Sounds simple enough, except it's a tradition for male fighters to jump over the top rope of a ring when they enter. So, keeping your head higher than your feet isn't necessarily a foregone conclusion.

There was a lengthy preamble before each fight. It was interesting, if not quite compelling. I'm not sure it's a sport I could get hooked on.

Rajadamnern Stadium, Bangkok, 2000.

Muay Thai bouts have five rounds of three minutes, with a two-minute break between each round. I wouldn't say I particularly enjoyed it, but there was more artistry than 'proper' boxing. I don't know if the big bouts featured the same kind of pre-fight stoushes for the media that 'proper' boxing had, but there seemed to be a kind of dignity about the whole process.

In the end I watched five bouts. I also watched what was going on in other parts of the stadium. I'd never seen betting like it. It was frenetic; little men running up and down the stands passing bits of paper and banknotes.

It was dark when I left Rajadamnern Stadium. Beers and chicken Pad Thai back in Khaosan Road beckoned. No tuk-tuks around, so I jumped on the back of some bloke's 125 and off we headed. I don't know if he was on speed or just wanted to test this particular tourist's resilience, but he took a few chances with the traffic on the way. Not the first time that happened during my two months in Thailand. I was jaded with the place. In a few days I'd be in Australia. In two weeks, I'd be at the Boxing Day Test.

I LIKE TO WATCH

Scotland vs England; Glasgow, Auckland

Glasgow, 1989.

"I can't believe it," I said to Mark Lavin as we got the Underground across London to Euston station. "I just can't believe it…"

It was a late Friday evening; 26 May 1989. Arsenal had just won the league at Anfield with a last-minute goal from Michael Thomas. It was the most exciting end to a top division title chase in history.

I was in a strange place: combined feelings of elation, disbelief and *guilt*. I'd been to thirty of Arsenal's thirty-seven league games that season prior to the title-decider at Anfield. In the few weeks leading up to Anfield I'd experienced the joy of a sneaky-ish late win at a hostile Ayresome Park, and dismay at the one point taken from the home games against Derby and Wimbledon. I'd given up on Arsenal. Not only did I not go to Anfield that night, I didn't watch it on TV. This is where the guilt kicked-in, and it was a feeling that stayed with me all summer.

This chapter isn't about Anfield 1989 though.

***

We'd decided earlier that week to go to the Scotland vs England game on Saturday at Hampden Park. It was to be the last-ever regular annual fixture played by the two countries. The Rous Cup was a kind of carry-on from the Home Internationals which had been a mini-competition between England, Scotland, Wales and Northern Ireland for decades. The Rous Cup though excluded Wales and Northern Ireland – not enough of a commercial draw.

Growing up, the Home Internationals had usually been an end-of-season competition spread over eight days, culminating in a face-off between the big two. The competition had been tinkered with over the years. Two of the three England vs Scotland games I'd been to at Wembley were played midweek. For a number of years Northern Ireland didn't play a home fixture due to security concerns. For them, the Scots and Welsh it was a great opportunity to get one over on their bigger, imperious neighbour. For many Scots it was the highlight of the season. Games at Wembley saw a massive influx of Scots who largely took over the stadium and made their presence felt around London for days. These games rarely passed-off peacefully. This constant threat of trouble was one of the reasons the series was wound-down and then discarded; the football authorities deciding they only wanted to deal with it in the future if they *had* to, ie when the two countries met in qualifiers for either the European Championships or World Cup.

This was my first trip north of the border to see England.

Euston station that Friday night was what you would expect in the circumstances – a motley crew of England fans from different clubs meeting up to catch the overnight train to Glasgow. Talk was largely of Arsenal's miraculous title win earlier that evening.

We filled up plastic carrier bags with cans of beer and took our seats on the train. It was pretty much as good as an England football special. The few non-football folks on the train surveyed the scene with a wary eye.

Mark and I chatted. He'd decided to join me for the first couple of weeks of my planned novel-writing trip to Spain later that year, so we discussed some loose plans. All around me I heard people talking about Anfield. I was gutted.

I'm not really sure why Mark went on that little jaunt. He wasn't much into football. Nominally a Spurs fan, I can't remember him ever going to White Hart Lane. In seven or eight years of knocking about with him I could only remember him going to one game, the 1986 Milk Cup Final between QPR and Oxford United. About twenty of us had walked to Wembley from the Plumes pub in North Acton to witness the Rs' implosion. And he didn't even see the whole game; he got thrown out.

The service we were on included a change at Carlisle at around 5 a.m. Who the fuck planned these things? Did the same thing happen in winter? The platform at Carlisle became a virtual sea of English football herberts. The connecting train, when it arrived, was full. The aisles and luggage areas of the regular carriages were soon also full. There was a group of about fifteen of us left at one end of the platform.

"There's no room on the train mate." Someone said to a British Rail employee. Clearly not wanting any restless England football fans hanging around on his station platform much longer he opened the door to the parcel carriage for us. "Jump in here lads," he said. This was most probably against all kinds of rules and regulations, but *idle hands* and all that.

After some grumbles about being treated like cattle, we all found a spare spot to sit on the floor. Attention was soon drawn to the fact that we were in a carriage full of parcels of various shapes and sizes, containing who knew what. We decided to investigate. Every parcel under a certain size – ie, a parcel containing something that could easily be secreted in the ubiquitous weekend sports bags that most of us had – was opened. The spoils were varied. Some of the items went back. The rest of the haul was distributed in a surprisingly egalitarian way. I came away with a pink surfy t-shirt, Mark a green one. Sounds horrendous now, but they were quite funky at the time.

Our train pulled into Glasgow Central at about 7 a.m. It was ridiculously early to be out and about pre-match on a Saturday. We'd arranged to meet a few other Ealing mates in a pub at opening time. Pat Rice, Brian Doran, Muttley, Tony Molloy and Joe Keneally had been in Edinburgh the night before and were making the short journey across Scotland for the game.

Time to kill.

After grabbing what must've been one of the last of the previous day's sandwiches from a stall-cum-window we sat down against a wall on the station concourse, biding our time. Strathclyde police had other ideas, and two of their finest threatened to arrest us for vagrancy. I assume they just wanted as many England fans off the streets as possible before the game. At other times I might have used one of my smart-arse type lines ("Officer, pray tell me what appears to be the problem?"), but they weren't in the mood, and I didn't want to come four hundred miles to spend the day in a Glasgow police cell.

We wandered Central Glasgow for a couple of hours. Dozens of England fans were doing the same thing. There was no sign yet of Scottish fans out and about. The only locals to be seen were shoppers and *civilians*. Mark took advantage of our free time to get a haircut while I flicked through the Saturday edition of the *Daily Record* in the waiting area. The sports pages featured a preview of the game, but the paper, all the papers that day, focused on the potential trouble between England and Scotland fans. The narrative was essentially that England fans coming up for the game were *all* hooligans. England fans were travelling to Glasgow for this game in bigger numbers than ever before. There were the usual interview grabs and insights. There was a big mob coming from Carlisle, and Chelsea would, as ever, be well-represented amongst the England firm. Leeds were coming in big numbers. Apparently, all police leave was cancelled in Glasgow that weekend.

After Mark's haircut we sat out in a park for a while.

Glasgow is renowned as a tough town. *No Mean City* is a famous mid-20th century novel about Glasgow slum life and the title a phrase that later worked itself into regular usage when the city was talked about in the media. To many, south of the border, Glasgow was the city of razor gangs, Jimmy Boyle, sectarianism and the Old Firm. I'd been to Glasgow many times previously, mostly for football, and while I'd *felt* the edge, I'd never witnessed any real violence first-hand. Two years previously I'd come up to Glasgow for Arsenal's pre-season friendly at Celtic. Steve Batt and I had stood with some Celtic fans he knew in a home area of the ground. Arsenal won 5-1 and we'd cheered every goal; no one as much as giving us a second look. What *had* been an eye-opener was afterwards when we'd found ourselves in an old school-style pub on the Gallowgate – no women's toilets – a relic from a previous age when expectations and roles were, er, more clearly defined.

There were only a couple of other people in the Vale pub on Dundas Street near Queen Street station when we walked in. I knew this pub, and the one next door, from those previous trips to Glasgow. The others from Ealing soon joined us, after arriving on the Edinburgh train.

A quiet drink with a few Scots before the game, Glasgow, 1989.

We drank like fish as the pub filled-up. We were the only England fans in there and stayed at the bar near the front door – you never know when you might need to get out in a hurry. The atmosphere was fine though. It actually took a while for the other punters to work out we were English. I would've thought it was obvious; none of us was wearing any colours in a pub where nearly everyone had a navy-blue Scotland shirt on or was draped in a St Andrew's Cross or Royal Banner of Scotland.

We exchanged chat, jokes and banter with a few of the Scots and drinks were even bought on both sides. It was going fine for about an hour or so until one younger Scottish fan walked over brandishing a bottle. None of us had to do anything because a couple of the Scots we were talking to quickly disarmed him and told him not to be an arsehole. It invariably changed the mood a bit though.

Six or seven pints and a few whisky chasers out the way it was time to head to Mount Florida. We went in two cabs, arranging to meet outside the England section of the 'Celtic end' at Hampden.

Hampden Park in 1989 was very much pre-renovation Hampden. There was a stand along one side of the ground that seated maybe five or six thousand with what looked like a press box on top. The press box looked like it could fall off at any moment. The rest of the ground was near-crumbling concrete bowl terracing. One end, the 'Rangers end' was partially covered, the rest of the ground open to the elements. Such was the ubiquity of big Old Firm games played at Hampden that the two ends of the ground that so often housed Rangers and Celtic fans became known as such for all games. Even at a time, pre-Taylor Report, when grounds in England weren't exactly in prime condition, Hampden Park was a bit *rugged*.

The rivalry between England and Scotland is the oldest in international football. They first played each other in 1872. The early games were friendlies before the British Home Championships formally commenced in 1884. There have been some memorable victories for both sides; Scotland winning 5-1 at Wembley – the new home of English football – in 1928, some high-scoring wins for England in the 1950s which prefaced the famous 9-3 mauling they meted out to their northern neighbours in 1961. In 1967 just nine months after England won the World Cup, Scotland came to Wembley and won 3-2. Naturally they then claimed to be the number one team in the world.

Up to 2018 the wins tally was quite close with forty-eight for England and forty-one for Scotland, and twenty-five draws. The difference is far greater if you only consider games post World War II; 29-12. The first one I remember was 1975 when England won 5-1. They'd been 2-0 up after just seven minutes. My abiding memory of that game – and I'm sure I'm not alone – was Scottish goalkeeper, Stuart Kennedy, who was at fault for England's first four goals. England's second, a header from defender Kevin Beattie, saw Kennedy run into the post instead of putting a hand out to try and save it. It was comical, and something we mimicked at primary school in the weeks after.

In the 1970s and early 1980s live football on TV was a rarity. We saw the FA Cup Final, England internationals and European Cup Finals involving English teams. Little else. This led to England vs Scotland games taking on a higher status than they probably warranted

A crowd of 63,282 filled, if not quite packed-out, Hampden Park that afternoon, with England fans numbering maybe five thousand. The English FA hadn't taken any tickets in advance, but they were readily available at the turnstiles on the day and England fans allocated their own section.

Both teams were depleted to a degree as a result of the Liverpool vs Arsenal title decider the night before. (In illustrating how things have changed, twelve of the thirteen in the Arsenal squad at Anfield was English, and the thirteenth, David O'Leary, an Ireland international, was born in London.)

Hampden Park wasn't quite the cauldron I'd been expecting for a game against the Auld Enemy. The atmosphere at Old Firm games was significantly more intense. Hampden wasn't helped by the distance between pitch and spectators and that most of the terraced areas had no cover at all – the chants and cheers drifting away more easily.

Although this book isn't really about match reports or describing passages of play, I do like to chuck in the occasional bit of game commentary or analysis. Not this game though. I can't because I was asleep on the terraces for the start of the game. Almost zero sleep the night before combined with a good lunchtime *bevvie* had temporarily wiped me out. Initially I just sat down for a while before kick-off, but one thing led to another and by the time Chris Waddle headed England into the lead after twenty minutes, I was asleep. I won't describe the goal. It was a good move and aside from anything it's worth looking up on YouTube just for Waddle's hair – a mullet of truly epic proportions. England fans celebrating that goal woke me up.

Absent Arsenal and Liverpool players meant we saw some less likely lads in the England squad that day. Big bruising John Fashanu of Wimbledon got his second and last cap, and Tony Cottee made a rare start. A young Paul Gascoigne, on his birthday, came on as a substitute for Cottee. But it was the other England substitute who made the headlines – Steve Bull of Wolves, making his England debut. This fixture was at the end of the 1988-89 season meaning Bull was *technically, officially,* making his England debut as a Third Division player. If that wasn't *Roy of the Rovers* enough, Steve Bull had scored fifty goals for Wolves that season, including thirty-seven in the league as they won the Third Division. Bull was almost a one-club man, but never got to play in the English top division for Wolves. He was one of those players fans easily identified with, because along with the likes of say David Rocastle or Paul Merson at Arsenal at the time, he felt like *one of us.* He was prolific for Wolves and his four goals in thirteen games for England was none-too-shabby either. Bull's goal, England's second, a low, hard close-range shot came just ten minutes from the end. The ground immediately began to empty.

We were kept in for ages after the final whistle – it must have been forty-five minutes while the police got the Scottish fans away from Hampden. Despite the Scots' revised reputation for good behaviour,

England fans kept in at Hampden Park after the final whistle, 1989.

this *was* a game against England. And an England that had turned-up in serious numbers at Hampden Park for the first time. The Scottish media was full of stuff about the English fans that day being pretty much all hooligans out for aggro. Word-of-mouth, TV and radio news fuelled what happened that day.

This game, or rather what happened before and afterwards has gone down in football folklore. It *went off everywhere*. There were over a hundred arrests before the game as a large group of England supporters walked from the city centre to Hampden Park, clashing with locals on the way. Two pubs were attacked in the process. This was the pre-internet, pre-mobile phone era so news didn't spread as fast, but word had filtered through the Scottish ranks about what was going on.

However the hour or two after the game was going to unfold, it was difficult not to envisage a tricky moment or two as we made our way across Glasgow and then on to Edinburgh.

The walk to Mount Florida station wasn't a big deal. Plenty of England fans broke away from the escort though, intent on doing their own thing. We made the short train journey from Mount Florida to Glasgow Central without a hitch. But we had to get across Glasgow to Queen Street station, to catch the Edinburgh train. Google Maps now tells me that the walk between those stations is 493 yards or between six and seven minutes. It's fair to say it felt a bit longer that particular afternoon.

Scottish fans were everywhere around Glasgow Central and there was a huge police presence. The consensus was: mingle and walk. We were close enough to each other to be seen as a group, but with hundreds of people milling around and walking in the same direction, we wouldn't necessarily have been a seen as a group. There was a temptation to walk briskly, but that would have attracted attention. None of the seven of us was wearing any colours, which was a good thing. But to a keen eye, seven blokes *without* colours should have stood out that day.

It was a nervy walk. The further we got away from Glasgow Central, the closer we were to Queen Street. But the further we were away from Glasgow Central the fewer people were around, fewer Old Bill and more chances of getting ambushed. There was a nasty atmosphere about the place and we knew it could go off at any moment. We'd agreed to stick close to buildings, which were mainly shops anyway, and not go walking down the middle of the road or make any big demonstrative thing of crossing a road. Buildings on one side cut-off a route of potential attack whilst providing a potential escape route. This may all sound quite alarmist, defeatist or whatever but the fact was there was just seven of us – a not *un*handy seven as it happens, but the odds would have been ridiculous. Scottish fans were on the look-out. They may only have wanted a row with an equally up-for-it little firm, but it wasn't worth taking any risks by advertising our identity. All communication amongst us was reduced to a series of grunts and nods. I was half-expecting someone to ask me the time; that old one.

We reached Queen Street station unscathed. With the amount of Old Bill around the chances of any aggro on the concourse was minimal. Edinburgh trains were frequent, and it was only a matter of minutes before we were ensconced around two tables at one end of a carriage heading to the Scottish capital. Time to relax. The forty-five-minute journey passed without incident, though there'd been a few sniping comments from Scottish fans passing though the carriage. A long night ahead in Rose Street beckoned.

Auckland, 2011

The 2011 Rugby World Cup was played in New Zealand. That sporting punches-well-above-its-weight nation of about four million embraced it with enthusiasm. I'm sure they would've embraced it just as much even if they weren't favourites and it wasn't their national sport. They're like that the Kiwis – so far from anywhere that visitors and human contact is a joy.

Not a massive rugby union fan, I nevertheless watched the big games on TV and had seen both England and the British Lions play in Australia. The 2003 Rugby World Cup had been a great time to be an expat Down Under.

I'd been tempted to go over to New Zealand for one of England's early pool games in Dunedin, when they'd played Argentina, Georgia and Romania over three weekends. I'd long fancied a trip to what was meant to be the Edinburgh of the Southern Hemisphere, but I knew accommodation there would be a nightmare during the World Cup.

During the early stages of the tournament I happened to be on the phone to an Auckland-based work contact, Ross Fodie. We were exploring ways of getting our respective companies to work more effectively together. Work stuff out of the way, we discussed the World Cup.

"I'm really tempted by the Scotland game." I told him.

"Do it. I can get tickets. There are still some available."

After we hung-up I went online to check flights and hotels. All reasonably-priced, although not the best flight times. I sent Ross a one-line email: "Flights and hotel booked. Speak soon."

New Zealand is two hours ahead of Australia. Auckland is an almost four-hour flight from Melbourne. Even an early evening flight means a very late arrival. I'd done a very late one once before when I went over to see a couple of days of the Hamilton Test match in 2008. (England lost but Ryan Sidebottom took a hat-trick.) But this was even later. I eventually got to my Auckland city centre motel after 4 a.m. The motel was basic, but it would do the job.

I like New Zealand, but there are some strange quirks about the place, and the people. I visited Auckland a lot for work over a few years and have holidayed there several times. The first time I went there was in 2001 for a quick break prior to starting a new job. The bloke on the immigration desk saw my Australian residency visa in my British passport.

"Did you know you can live and work here with that visa?"

"No, I didn't actually." I replied politely.

"You can. See that doorway over there," he turned slightly and pointed to his left and behind him, "you can talk to someone in there and get all the information."

"Ok, er, thanks."

Must be short of people, I thought, walking through to baggage collection.

On that same trip a few days later, I was driving across what seemed like the middle of nowhere on the North Island on the road from Paihia to Cape Reinga. I'd been determined to get to the northernmost point of New Zealand, however much driving I had to do in one day. Having skipped breakfast, I was hungry by late morning. On a windswept hill, that seemed like something out of a Thomas Hardy novel, I came across a small petrol station with shop attached. I went into the shop and surveyed the limited food options.

I took a can of room temperature Diet Coke from the fridge, then addressed the proprietor.

"Sausage roll and a ham sandwich please." I said, keeping it simple.

"Sauce?"

"No thanks."

"How many sandwiches?"

"One please."

After a bit of rustling she handed everything over, I paid, left and set off straight away. The can went in the drink holder and I knocked-off the sausage roll quickly. Sandwich time. I opened the brown bag she'd given me, then laughed. One sandwich *literally* meant one sandwich. Not one *round* of sandwiches, or one *packet* of sandwiches. The ham sandwich I'd seen under glass a few minutes earlier was how you normally saw pre-packaged or pre-wrapped sandwiches presented – two pieces of bread, with sandwich filling(s), then cut in half and placed together to show four triangles of bread with filling between pieces one and two, and three and four of the bread. They fit in sandwich boxes like this, or as I'd seen earlier, they get wrapped in cling film like this. The sandwich I took out of the bag and looked at disconsolately on the passenger seat was just two pieces of triangular-cut bread with filling, hastily re-wrapped in the same cling film that had once held *double* the amount of ham sandwich. The old bird in the shop must've made this adjustment while I was getting my money out. Clearly one sandwich in this neck of the woods literally meant *one* sandwich. Or *half* of one sandwich, if you thought about it.

I'd been to a bit of sport in New Zealand prior to Rugby World Cup 2011. I'd seen Super 14 rugby at both Eden Park and Hamilton, cricket Test matches in Wellington and Hamilton, and an NRL game between the Warriors and Manly at Mt Smart Stadium. There were two notable differences in attending sport in New Zealand that Australia needed to catch up on: sushi options in the food outlets, and free sunscreen at cricket. Not only was the sunscreen free at the Hamilton Test, but it was dispensed by a couple of not unattractive young women who wandered amongst the crowd with containers of the stuff strapped to their backs.

I met Ross Fodie at the Britomart Transport Centre in downtown Auckland, near the harbour. It was lunchtime, so we adjourned to a local pub for a few drinks and lunch. We chatted work for an hour or so, recapping things we'd covered by phone and email in recent weeks, before relaxing into sport and general blokey chit-chat.

"Auckland has really embraced the World Cup. Each suburb in the city has adopted a different country and is flying flags and stuff for that country from pubs, offices, homes and other buildings. It's so much bigger than 1987."

The pub filled-up with rugby folk. Kick-off was still about six hours away. England fans, Scotland fans and locals mixed happily. Conversations got loud, there was a bit of backslapping and lots of laughter.

"Bit different to football," I said, "as in soccer."

"Yeah, I can imagine." We talked football for a bit and I retold tales from years and decades before, including England vs Scotland games I'd been to.

"Bloody hell," Ross laughed when I told him about Hampden Park in 1989, "it won't be anything like that today, I'm sure." So was I. I wondered why this pub seemed to have far more Scottish than English supporters imbibing though.

Ross had managed to get good seats, roughly on halfway and about a third of the way down the stand.

"There'll be a great atmosphere there tonight."

"I've been to Eden Park once," I told him. "Super 14 a few years ago. Would've been maybe twenty thousand there."

"Will be different tonight."

We left the pub and walked to the Queens Wharf 'fanzone'. I would have been happy in the pub, but Ross had arranged to meet people and assured me that despite the contrived sound of the whole thing, the 'fanzone' would be fun. He was right. Despite the cool mist coming off the harbour and on-off spitting rain, there was a relaxed, fun vibe going on. And it got even *funner* as people got drunker as the afternoon progressed. The 'fanzone' was a mix of undercover and outdoor drinking areas. There was a security presence there – as no doubt the competition's insurers, the city council and several other *stakeholders* had insisted upon. But they kept a low profile, as good security people do. It got busier later that afternoon, and again I noticed that Scottish fans were outnumbering the English.

We took the train from Britomart to Kingsland station, which served Eden Park. The game was still over an hour away. The train was full of rugby-goers, a significant proportion of whom, unlike me, had travelled from the UK. Sure, most hadn't travelled just for this game, and many were watching games that didn't even feature Scotland or England. Even so, many people were well over ten thousand miles from home.

England vs Scotland in the Rugby World Cup in New Zealand was going to be a big occasion and maybe just a great one. In the long rivalry between the two countries, this was to be the first time they'd played each other outside Britain.

Ross found an odd little bar near Eden Park and the six of us crammed in. Milling around the ground it seemed as though England fans were again in the minority which surprised me. But by the time we found our seats about fifteen minutes before the start the tide had changed in terms of supporter demographics. By kick-off I reckoned the English fans outnumbered the Scots by about two to one. Where had they all been?

I don't ever remember going to a sporting event where so many people, such a large proportion of the crowd, were as drunk as they were at Eden Park that Saturday night. The 8.30 p.m. start time had obviously been a factor – giving fans ample time to get hammered. Despite this, the atmosphere was totally relaxed, with not the remotest sense whatsoever of any aggro in the air. The bonhomie between the two sets of supporters and the locals was genuine.

Eden Park is a big, but not massive stadium which housed just over fifty-eight thousand that night. I have never heard the British national anthem so loudly and heartily sung as I did that night. It was spine-tingling and truly rousing. The odd but well-documented anomaly here is that although it is the *British* national anthem, thus technically covering both English and Scottish teams, in sporting contests such as this it's used by the English only. The Scots sang

'Flower of Scotland'. Both anthems were impeccably respected.

The game was brutal and hard; a tug of war. It wasn't pretty. I was reminded of that old maxim: "Football is a game played by gentlemen and watched by hooligans; rugby is played by hooligans and watched by gentlemen." The two teams were relentless. With just three minutes to go Scotland had a 12-9 lead. A line-out on the left side of the pitch saw some strong-arm play before the ball made its way across the pitch via series of passes to England's right flank. Chris Ashton broke to score the only try of the game. It was converted by Toby Flood and within moments it was all over. 16-12 to England and Scotland were out of the World Cup.

It was about 4 a.m. when I finally got back to my room that night. Two nights in Auckland; twice into the motel at 4 a.m. After the game we ended-up back down at the harbour in a bar – well more a kind of ante-room to a nightclub; the place divided along age demographic lines. Again, a mix of different supporters, mostly drunk and all good-natured.

At some point before getting back to the motel I found myself standing in the street eating pizza and chatting to some South Africans who'd also been to the game. South Africa had played Samoa the night before in another Auckland stadium. The conversation rambled on and on. Rugby, cricket, football. If there's anything that blokes will fall easily into conversation about, it's sport.

I slept late-ish on Sunday morning before hitting Father Ted's pub in the city centre – a boozer I'd been in on several previous trips to Auckland. Every city in the world seems to have an 'Irish pub' – many of which are so fake as to be embarrassing. This one had some kind of feel of authenticity at least. Over a couple of pints of

Guinness, I pondered the previous day. No classic game in a sport I didn't follow that closely, but as an experience it was right up there. The contrast with a Saturday, twenty-two-and-a-half years earlier in Glasgow when these two countries played a football match couldn't have been starker.

I LIKE TO WATCH

A Baseball Odyssey (and Miami Interlude)

I'll start in Oakland.

Oakland Athletics was actually the fifteenth Major League Baseball stadium (or sixteenth if you count two incarnations of Yankee Stadium) I saw a game in. But I'll start in Oakland because it was here on a cool-ish northern Californian night in May 2012 that I found myself jumping out of my seat for the first time at a baseball game. I'd found *my* team.

I was in and out of the US on a short work trip to Denver. Flying from Australia meant travelling through Los Angeles. After a bit of research, I worked out that a detour via San Francisco before and after Denver would enable me to add both San Francisco Giants and Oakland Athletics to my MLB bucket list. There was an added bonus in that the Colorado Rockies were also playing at home during the trip. Three new grounds; a happy camper.

At the start of the trip I stayed in San Francisco in a hotel close to Union Square. The modern, tidy, comfortable and very 21st century home of the Giants was just a twenty-minute walk away. AT&T

Stadium was situated right next to the water with great views and an all-American wholesome family atmosphere. At one point going on a piss call-beer run I left my bag (including camera, iPod, additional clothing, just-purchased Giants merch) on my seat, asking the people next to me if they wouldn't mind keeping an eye on it. They were a Brooks-Brothered young couple, out on what I guessed was an early-ish date.

The game at Denver a few nights later was similar. I went with a workmate, Sandy Harman, and although near-torrential rain wiped-out a big chunk of the game late on and we missed the delayed ending in favour of a local bar, it was another modern, comfortable stadium with a distinctly family vibe.

Oakland Coliseum though, home of the A's, I later described it as "the Millwall of MLB".

After the conference in Denver I went back to San Francisco for two nights. I fell in love with the place. I'd felt a *connection* the previous week, which was reinforced as soon as I was in the cab heading north from the airport to the city.

It's an easy place to get your bearings. Do the open top bus tour and every couple of minutes the guide points out some world-famous landmark – the Golden Gate Bridge, Embarcadero, Alcatraz, Haight-Ashbury, the church where Marilyn Monroe married Joe DiMaggio. San Francisco is also the birthplace of Levi's – a fascinating business start-up story in its own right.

For a city of 850,000 people covering just forty-eight square miles, San Francisco's cultural influence on the Western world has been immense – particularly post-World War II with the advent of the counterculture, beat writers, hippies, popular music and iconic films like *Vertigo*, *Bullitt* and the *Dirty Harry* series.

San Francisco really is *a cool place to hang out.* Top of my 'to visit' list was City Lights Bookstore. The iconic bookshop and publisher was founded in the 1950s by Lawrence Ferlinghetti and Peter Martin. Its history is intertwined with that of the beat writers. City Lights published Allen Ginsberg's controversial poem *Howl* in 1955. It wasn't the last time they challenged the conservative mores of mainstream American culture. The bookshop itself is a kind of quiet but open secret in the heart of this busy, modern city. I *had* to spend some money in there.

The bar next door to City Lights, Vesuvio, was once frequented by Jack Kerouac. Over a couple of beers, I flicked through my newly-acquired copy of *Howl* and then started reading Richard Hell's memoir, *I Dreamed I Was A Very Clean Tramp* which I'd also just bought.

The juxtaposition between cool and trendy, the wealthy and the homeless in San Francisco is quite jarring. My hotel on the return leg from Denver was just on the edge of the city's notorious Tenderloin district. 'Colourful' aptly describes it. It's an anxiety-inducing area to stay, if falling short of actually being scary.

Sixteen miles across San Francisco Bay is the city of Oakland. From downtown San Francisco it's about a forty-minute ride on a BART train to Oakland Coliseum, home of the Oakland Athletics baseball team – the A's. Oakland is very different to San Francisco. The violent crime rate in Oakland is just about double that of its more glamorous neighbour. When the BART train emerges from under San Francisco Bay on the Oakland side a quick look out of the window reveals not just a different city, but a different-looking world. The contrast is stark. Oakland is Glasgow to San Francisco's Edinburgh; a tough-looking town.

Alighting at Oakland Coliseum station I had a New York Yankees moment, making a mental note to make sure that after the game, like in the Bronx after a Yankees game, I needed to be on one of the busier trains back to San Francisco. This wasn't a place to hang around too long after the game.

Navigating the 'scalpers' (ticket touts) outside the station and on the walkway across to the stadium felt like being in a scene from *The Wire*. There must've been twenty people trading in tickets. Yet, while there were a few fans heading for the game, I wouldn't have described the ticket trade as exactly booming. I didn't see anyone stop to negotiate. I guessed maybe the ticket thing was just a ruse to start a conversation around other things for sale.

The walkway to the stadium went over a wide street, car park, industrial area and train tracks. There was a grittier feel here than at any other baseball stadium I'd visited in the US. It was the US of modern urban noir films.

Oakland Coliseum was built in the 1960s and hosted its first American football game in 1966 and its first baseball game two years later. By 2012 though – and compared to the numerous baseball 'new builds' of the previous decade – the Oakland Coliseum was looking decidedly tired. And having been built in the 1960s, it was a far cry from the character or aesthetics of the classic older stadiums like Boston's Fenway Park or Wrigley Field in Chicago. Caught between two worlds.

I felt a sense of anticipation I'd only previously experienced going to my first baseball game at the old Yankee Stadium.

Oakland Coliseum entirely suited the rundown industrial setting it inhabited. It was refreshingly *not* a citadel of glossy, over-marketed 21st century sport. There was something about that initial experience – exiting the station, dodgy characters hanging around, a small-ish crowd, crossing that industrial semi-wasteland to come upon a grotty, predominately concrete stadium – that reminded me of my earliest experiences going to football. There was an *edge*, no question.

Inside, even the family numbers seemed lower than at other baseball games I'd been to – though this was a midweek evening game. I found my seat behind the home plate, quite a few rows back and at a slight angle, giving me a good view of the game. A few rows in front, slightly to the right, three middle-aged men took their seats. They were all wearing Oakland Chapter Hell's Angels' leathers.

There was a completely different feel here compared to my night at the San Francisco Giants game the previous week; a real blue-collar vibe. (Later, I learnt that Oakland Athletics use the term "green-collar baseball" in some of their marketing.) I didn't feel uneasy though. It wasn't like having to sit quietly amongst the home fans at an away game in England. But when I went for a beer, I *did* take my bag.

Oakland Athletics is the poorest club in Major League Baseball. This is evidenced by their spending and player list. It was also abundantly apparent that night looking around a stadium that was a long way off being even a quarter full. The top decks of the stadium are covered during the baseball season. On my first visit there they could have corralled the whole crowd into just a few bays. The facilities – bars, food outlets and merchandise outlets were also from a bygone age, albeit a recent and living memory one. I didn't come across any cheesy-grinned volunteers wandering around holding placards asking if they could help me.

The Toronto Blue Jays were the visitors that night. I don't understand enough about baseball to follow some of the tactical intricacies, let alone pull-off something committed to paper that suggests I know what I'm talking about. I enjoy the game. I understand the rules.

I like the vibe and atmosphere, but I am not an aficionado. To an outsider, understanding the statistics and records seems to require some kind of post-graduate qualification.

A *roomy* Oakland Coliseum provided me with an opportunity for some exploring and to watch the game from some different angles. So, it was at about beer number three that I relocated to a position overlooking first base.

I'd been to East Coast USA several times in May and enjoyed, or suffered, the heat and humidity. I hadn't done my northern California May weather research though. It was like a windy March night at Highbury.

As well as watching what ultimately turned out to be a dramatic game of baseball unfolding in front of me, I was also people-watching keenly. Compared to previous ballpark experiences Oakland Coliseum felt fairly hard core – not many families, or couples on tentative, early dates. Around me sat predominately working-class men, who were clearly very into the game. They watched closely, shouting out their support and showing displeasure in equal measure.

What had been a fairly run-of-the-mill game reached a thrilling climax. The score was 3-3 with the A's batting at the bottom of the ninth inning. With the bases loaded and one out already, Brandon Inge stepped up to the plate – literally and metaphorically. I can't remember how many pitches he faced before BANG! He hit it high and to the left into the sparsely-populated stands. A walk-off grand slam; a perfect connection taking the score from 3-3 to 7-3. Inge did the obligatory jog around bases behind his teammates and then there was joyous carnage as the Oakland team and coaches enjoyed one almighty great celebratory bundle. The crowd went into a fit of woo-hooing and high-fiving. It was an exciting finish, and one hard not to get caught up in.

I loved the gritty, almost anti-corporate feeling of the surrounds. Oakland Athletics were an underdog team, no question. Just a few months short of twenty years since attending my first baseball game and having taken in games in Toronto and right across the US I had finally found *my* team. For the first time at a baseball game I had jumped up and out of my seat in response to a home run. During the game I had felt myself willing the A's on.

The celebrations died down and the small crowd exited the stadium. I walked the short distance back to the station through *The Wire* territory. Despite the game having just finished the station wasn't busy and I was soon on the BART train back to San Francisco, feeling a bit of a buzz about what I'd just seen.

The crowd at Oakland Coliseum that night was officially listed as 10,784.

I was flying back to Australia the next night – an early evening flight out of San Francisco to make my Los Angeles connection to Melbourne. I spent most of the morning stocking up on things that would've cost me twice as much in Melbourne or London: shirts, Levi's, trainers and the like, plus some junior *in-da-hood* type clothes for my then five and six-year old sons.

Shall I? I pondered. Only briefly as it happens. It felt like the *right thing* to do. Late morning and with only a few hours left in San Francisco, I jumped on the BART train again and made my way to Oakland Coliseum for the afternoon game against the Blue Jays.

It was a brighter day and while the stadium and its environs didn't feel quite as Cold Blow Lane-ish as the previous night, it still fell a long way short of glossy or high-tech. The crowd was a bit bigger – officially 14,815, but again, I'd debate whether there were that many actually inside.

I felt like a proper fan now that I'd been to Oakland Coliseum *twice*. The A's went on to lose 2-5 that afternoon but I was gone by then – leaving in the seventh inning to make sure I got to the airport in time. There was a gentler feel to the crowd; still passionate but not the slight edge of the previous night.

It was mid-afternoon when I left Oakland Coliseum. A few other fans were drifting away as well. I walked back across the walkway to the station. As expected, there were a few *Wire* types hanging around. Ahead on my left two people were standing very close. A male and female both with that shapeless clothes look – baggy tops, wide jeans with the arse about eight-to-ten inches below where the arse actually was. They could have been aged anywhere between about eighteen and thirty-five. I base that assessment on their clothes because I couldn't see their faces. They were kissing passionately. When I was about twenty yards away he slammed her up against the wall. They were now side-on to me. His left hand was on her right breast, his right arm pointing downwards. My suspicions were confirmed as I walked past them and saw his right hand down the front of her jeans. Quite a few people walked past them as their embrace heated-up, but no one gave them a second look. Maybe it just wasn't that rare an occurrence mid-afternoon, midweek in Oakland, California.

I'd found *my* team.

Not quite an impoverished student, I was nonetheless not exactly flush with cash during a US holiday in mid-1992. My girlfriend and I were sharing a room with single bunk beds in a Manhattan YMCA with a shared bathroom about half a minute walk down the hallway. Bizarrely, considering my decidedly un-glam wooing techniques, she still agreed to move in with me later that year. Even the deli sandwiches and warm Budweiser we had in our room each night in lieu of an evening meal didn't put her off.

Anyway, with not much wedge between us we were on the look-out for authentic American experiences at little cost. Early one evening we took a subway train north and out of Manhattan. We got off what seemed like several hundred stops later at 161 Street in The Bronx; the Yankee Stadium stop. Long story cut short, we watched a low-scoring game against Kansas City Royals. And then got away from The Bronx on a busy train back to Manhattan. I wasn't quite hooked, but there was definitely *something* about it.

A year or so later I was back in New York with a couple of workmates, Louise Harnby and Breffni O'Connor. We were taking a short *vacation* after a work conference in New Jersey. Still poor, the three of us shared a room. We were work friends – no relationships or anything, so Breffni and I ended up sharing a double bed: in New York in the August heat, in a poorly air-conditioned fleapit. One afternoon the three of us headed up to 161 Street in The Bronx. Again, it was the Kansas City Royals in town.

In August 1995 I managed to get to two games in a few days in Baltimore and Toronto. I really enjoyed them, but then there was a big gap before another US summer trip anywhere near a city with a Major League Baseball team.

Atlanta, 2007, and another work conference. I ended up with some time to spare. The Martin Luther King Memorial took nearly half a day, but I'd already noted the Braves were playing a home series. In a Braves shop in the Turner Centre I got chatting to a bloke who worked there. Asking about the game, I explained I was in town from Australia (yeah, yeah I know I have an English accent though) and how should I go about getting a ticket? Could I just pay on the gate? He asked me to wait a moment while he went into an office. He came back with a complimentary ticket. What a gent, I thought, and thanked him profusely.

"No sir, thanks for your interest in the Braves, sir. Enjoy the game!" The Americans can do that *make-you-feel-special-hospitality* thing very well.

Late that afternoon I walked from my hotel to the ball park. The walk took me through some interesting neighbourhoods; I didn't need to make a mental note to get a taxi back after the game.

Somehow, later that night, I kind of fell a bit in love with baseball in a low-key way. It was more than the actual game. It was the whole event – the colour, the singing of the national anthem, seeing families out enjoying themselves, drinking those very average-tasting beers with names that conjure up blue-collar America, pretzels, hot dogs and the overall friendliness of the people.

"English, but you live in Australia…? Wow!"

Sitting high up in one of the stands that night, reading a baseball magazine I noted there were thirty MLB (Major League Baseball) teams in the two leagues (American and National). Doable? I wondered, looking at which cities they were in. There were a few two team cities, making it more attractive, more achievable. And so that night I resolved to see a game played in every MLB stadium before I died – my one and only 'bucket list' item. Atlanta was stadium number four. I had twenty-six to go. At that point though, I didn't know that Yankee Stadium was just two years from being replaced, so I was kind of on three.

So that was it, my one bucket list item sorted. Work trips to the US from then on involved a bit of logistical juggling and some additional flights so I could start working my way towards the goal.

The 2008 conference was in San Diego. I managed to get the Padres done and a couple of nights later, before heading back to Australia, I went to an LA Dodgers game. There was an added bonus the day after the Dodgers game – a race meeting at Hollywood Park. It was at Dodger Stadium and Hollywood Park in the space of a day that I learnt that not everyone in southern California was sun-tanned and healthy-looking. Six down.

In 2009 work took me to Washington DC. I did a high-scoring Nationals game against the San Francisco Giants. On the same trip I found an excuse for a short trip to New York and ticked-off Citi Field, the new home of the New York Mets. Seven down -– though pegged back one because the new Yankee Stadium had opened, thus voiding my previous visits.

Chicago Cubs at Wrigley Field, 2010.

LA Angels vs Oakland Athletics, Angel Stadium, Anaheim, 2011.

My 2010 US visit was a bonanza trip in terms of baseball stadiums. I did the new Yankee Stadium, Philadelphia Phillies and the architecturally aesthetic delights of Chicago Cubs' Wrigley Field. Ten down. Wrigley Field was an absolute cracker.

The following year saw Fenway Park, Boston ticked off. Rob Woodcock and I went there two nights in a row. The second night was a landmark game against the Chicago Cubs who hadn't played the Red Sox there for something like ninety years. And like Wrigley Field another, dare I say it, *beautiful* stadium. On the way back to Australia I holed-up in an LA Airport hotel for a day and managed to get down to see the LA Angels in Anaheim about twenty miles away. $100 cab ride there. Three hours back by public transport – no wonder they all own cars. Twelve down, eighteen to go.

Outside Fenway Park, Boston – home of the Red Sox, 2011.

The 2012 conference was in Denver. As mentioned, I got San Francisco Giants, Colorado Rockies and Oakland A's all ticked off. Fifteen down.

April 2013 saw another work trip to the US, though things didn't line-up as hoped in terms of new baseball grounds. I went to four games, but they were all at stadiums I'd previously been to. Toronto was interesting though – it being eighteen years since my previous visit and going to a game in temperatures just above freezing. I re-ticked New York Yankees and Oakland A's (twice).

I didn't go to the US in 2014 and then I finished my job. Travel for the foreseeable future was going to be funded by me alone.

***

In April 2015, after months of on-off debate with Owen Francis and Rob Woodcock, I travelled out to Barbados to see England play the third Test against the West Indies. Barbados from Central Victoria in Australia is just about as long a journey you can do in the world without going somewhere *really* obscure. A long way to go for one Test match, I thought it opportune to come back via the US and get some more MLB stadiums ticked off.

Bendigo to Bridgetown, Barbados took the best part of two days. The journey included a brief overnight stay in Miami. Though this wasn't glamorous, or even edgy Miami that comes into our living rooms via *CSI*, *Miami Ink* or Al Pacino's *Scarface*. This was run-down, near-the-airport Miami.

I arrived at my hotel for the one night stop over. The amount I'd paid – not much more than $100 – should've been an indicator as to the salubriousness. At 11.30 p.m., I not unreasonably expected a hotel bar to be open. And possibly some kind of restaurant or diner. It wasn't that sort of hotel though. My arrival at reception went unnoticed until I coughed loudly, prompting an unshaven young bloke to rouse himself from a couch somewhere out of sight. He might not have been fully asleep, but he really wasn't with it for the first ten seconds of our conversation.

The hotel was a Best Western Plus. Not sure what the 'Plus' bit was all about. Maybe a subtle reminder to bring some of your own stuff. There weren't many plusses, but, truth be told, I hadn't paid a rate that suggested there should be. All went smoothly. Though my requirements weren't likely to tax even the most inexperienced of trainee hotel receptionists. I told him what time I wanted to be at the airport in the morning. He gave me my key and confirmed that I'd paid in advance. He gave me the Wi-Fi password, and told me what the arrangements were for food in the morning.

"Is there a bar nearby?"

"Yeah. Just down the street," he said. "Turn right out of the hotel. Carry on walking. Maybe ten minutes or less. It'll be straight in front of you."

I briefly debated a shower and change but decided against it. Despite travelling for something like thirty hours and feeling a little, er, ripe, the truth was I couldn't be bothered. I was nipping out for a couple of drinks in an area I'd unlikely ever return to. It didn't exactly look like a flash neighbourhood anyway.

Three minutes out of the hotel and I was walking along a street with overgrown yards in front of single and two-story dwellings. At different points I could hear chatter and TVs on. Even to my untrained Florida eye, this wasn't a good area; something about all the cars being at least fifteen years old was a bit of a giveaway.

Halfway down the street I sensed a car behind me. It was going quite slowly, then caught up with me but didn't pass. For ten, maybe fifteen quite unnerving seconds the driver just kept pace with me. *Look like you know where you're going*, I thought to myself, not looking over. Then it sped up slightly and drove on.

What the fuck was that all about? I'd only brought thirty dollars out with me. Imagining that wouldn't be enough to appease my would-be muggers in a dodgy Miami back street, I briefly imagined being tortured for my hotel room key, PIN numbers and everything of value in my hotel room, and then left for dead.

Thankfully I got to the end of the street unscathed. I looked over to my right. There was indeed a bar there. It didn't look like it had any windows. Perhaps they were boarded-up?

It was an 'Irish' pub. Quite what that really means is anyone's guess. I've drunk in 'Irish' pubs in a few different countries. None of them are much like any of the pubs I've been to in Ireland. In fact, if I was Irish I think I'd be pretty pissed-off. Contrived, stereotyping and outright 'plastic'. It's a patronising way of aligning a nation's culture so closely with just getting drunk.

I crossed the street. Outside the bar a woman was chugging away enthusiastically on a cigarette. She was white, of an indeterminable age and in the fifteen stone *plus* region. She was wearing very short cut-off denim shorts and some kind of bikini top or 'going-out' bra – something she must've owned since she was about ten stone. She wasn't pregnant – her overhanging gut was the wrong shape; not 'muffin tops' – more a couple of family-size cakes were hanging over the sides. Her thighs looked like a pair of wobbling art deco vases.

I went into the bar. She tossed her cigarette and followed me in. Was our joint entrance a coincidence, or was she coming in now because I was? She walked around the large circular bar, stepped behind it and came up to me.

"Hi there," she said, friendly as, "what're you having?"

I glanced around at what other people were drinking. Beck's in a bottle is a safe bet anywhere.

"I'll have a Beck's please."

"You going to be here for a while?" she asked.

"Er…" Not sure where this question was leading. "Yeah, probably. A little while." Non-committal.

"Beck's is five bucks a bottle or you can get a bucket for thirteen bucks. Five bottles in a bucket." She nodded towards a couple of blokes to my right who were sharing a bucket.

"I put all the bottles in a bucket of ice and come and open them as you need them." ("Need" not "want", I noticed.)

"Sounds good," I said, reaching for some money.

I was thirsty so asked her to open two. The first was gone in a couple of minutes. The second I laboured over for maybe ten. Then I settled. The pub was no more 'Irish' than my living room, but it was ok. From outside it had looked like a cross between a bomb shelter and somewhere Jodie Foster would be advised to avoid playing pool. It was *very* American in terms of layout, décor and knick-knacks. It had a central, circular bar, countless TV screens showing different sports, music and sports pictures on the walls, exposed brickwork and numerous neon signs advertising a range of beers.

I'd imagined I was chancing myself going into some kind of hillbilly bar where I'd be quickly identified as an out-of-towner on an express trip to death via torture and rape. It turned out to be nothing of the kind. I'd drunk in more threatening boozers in the home counties. The hefty barmaid was extremely efficient. No waiting on getting served, kind words, welcoming smiles and quick chats all round. They're good at that in America. Their low basic wages and aggressive tipping culture makes for good service and, for good bar staff, some nice wedge.

The rest of my evening – maybe another hour, hour and ten perhaps, I spent people-watching. The pub karaoke provided a mix of laughs and admiration. Predictably perhaps, the game karaoke singers were well-oiled thirty to forty-year-olds. The blokes chose the likes of Metallica, Rage Against the Machine and Red Hot Chili Peppers. They outnumbered the woman who went for more Sheryl Crow-like, wronged women ballad-type songs. Everyone enjoyed themselves, and no one took the piss.

I'd clocked a couple of blokes sitting at the bar to my left earlier. They were wearing suits with ties that looked long since loosened. Mid-fifties probably, maybe a bit older. One was quite big, with a confident demeanour. The other was a smaller, specky, wispy-haired type. If he got off the stool, I reckoned he might just scrape a bit over five foot. I guessed it was a boss-subordinate-type situation. They were chatting and keeping themselves to themselves. Then they weren't.

"Hi guys!"

A young Latina woman and her equally young black friend approached them. Without a by-your-leave the two women pulled-up stools and sat between alpha male and his subordinate. What unfolded was an interesting yet fairly predictable conversation. Interesting to me in its brazenness, predictable in topics chosen for their chitter-chatter. The Latina woman seemed very adept at the half business-like, half-seductive interaction. She turned on a 'you are *so* interesting' look and did that semi-swooning thing very well.

Whores. I would've put a grand on it.

My interest waned, so I turned my attention back to the TV screens. California was three hours behind Miami, so I settled into watching the latter stages of a baseball game from Los Angeles.

My five bottles of Beck's were nearly done. I needed a piss. It was after 1 a.m. and I needed to be up at six. I made my way out via the toilet in a different part of the bar. It would've been easy to succumb to another bucket of Beck's but that wouldn't have been a good idea.

I went back to my hotel. A few lights were on as I walked along the street, but there was no TV noise or conversations emanating from open windows. And no clapped-out cars monitoring me.

The next day I flew into Barbados and watched England lose a low-scoring Test match. The unused two days of the Test match we spent having a good look around the friendly island nation.

I spent five nights in the US on the way back to Australia. This was the baseball-focused leg of the trip with three new stadiums to do. I'd done all five MLB stadiums in California. I'd done all the East Coast – from Boston to Washington DC. I'd even managed a few of the less obvious ones like Toronto, Atlanta and Colorado. I was going to do three games, three nights in a row in three different stadiums in three different states: Pittsburgh Pirates, Cleveland Indians and Chicago White Sox.

Pittsburgh was interesting, but brief. I spent the afternoon at the Andy Warhol Museum just a baseball's throw or so from the Pirates' stadium.

Cleveland was a quick in and out. Apart from going to the game I had a Subway across the street from my hotel. That was about it for Cleveland.

Chicago is a great city. In addition to a very cold evening at the White Sox game – in what is surely baseball's leading stadium when it comes to characterlessness, I got to a blues club after the game, a punk-death metal gig the next night and visits to a photography museum and the magnificent Art Institute of Chicago.

Chicago came with a surprise bonus soon after arriving. I took the train from O'Hare into the city and found my hotel. After getting to my room I connected to the Wi-Fi. Then something struck me: didn't Chicago have a Major League Soccer team? After a bit of Googling I confirmed that there definitely *was* a Chicago MLS team. Even more interestingly they had a home game kicking off in just over an hour. Some cross-referencing and a look at Google Maps told me the stadium was about fifteen miles away. It looked like a nightmare by train. I quickly gathered up everything I thought I'd need for the rest of the day and headed out to get a cab.

"Toyota Park." I told the driver.

We hit some heavy traffic for a while, and I wondered whether a quiet afternoon reading in my hotel room might have been a better option. But then things cleared a bit and the Nigerian Chelsea fan at the wheel put his foot down. When we got to the stadium there was only one person in front of me at the ticket office. Somehow though,

I ended up with a ticket on the other side of the ground. After a bit of a traipse, grabbing a large beer and hot dog on the way, I reached my seat at the top of the stand. A near-perfect view and the game was only three minutes old. Result.

The game ended with the visitors, Real Salt Lake, inflicting a 2-1 defeat on Chicago Fire. My journey back to the city was a circuitous one. A friendly club official pointed me in the direction of a shuttle bus that would take me to a train station. From there it was a couple more trains to get me to Chicago White Sox's stadium, Cellular Field, for that night's game.

It was a cold night. Cellular Field, which opened in 1990, was effectively the oldest of the new build stadiums.

Eighteen down, twelve to go.

I LIKE TO WATCH

Hull vs Cardiff

A quick glance around Boothferry Park was almost like looking at one of the outdoor sets of some futuristic dystopian film. Crumbling, run-down and an architectural mish-mash it was a ground that had seen better days – a long time ago. We went there in late 2000 for a Third Division game against Cardiff City. I wonder what odds you would have got then that these two teams would play each other in the Premier League in season 2013-14?

Back then neither club was a *sleeping giant*, but they were probably *sleeping-bigger-clubs* and most definitely *sleeping-biggish-clubs-from-large-cities-that-should-be-meeting-at-a-higher-level-than-this*, ie League Division Three, then the fourth tier of professional football in England.

I'd never been to Hull before. It had a reputation for being both insular and pretty rough. In the late 1980s I'd worked with a few people from Hull after a company merger led to a number of them relocating to our London office. They kept largely to themselves.

Hull was more of a rugby league town than football, which would go a long way to explaining why in 2000 Hull was the biggest place in England that had never had a top division football team.

Three years after our visit to Hull, the *Idler* magazine published a book, *Crap Towns – The 50 Worst Places to Live in the UK*. Hull topped the list. The lengthy Kingston upon Hull Wikipedia page doesn't exactly paint a rosy picture of the city either – particular with regard to the performance of its local council and police force.

I was just a few weeks away from emigrating to Australia and Owen was keen for us to get a few new grounds on the list before I departed. We'd recently knocked-off Gillingham in a game against Man City which featured former World Player of the Year (and future President of Liberia), George Weah. Future late-night throwaway trivia line: "I was at Priestfield Stadium the night George Weah graced the pitch..."

That particular weekend we'd managed to tee-up Hull City and Sunderland home games on the Saturday and Sunday. Owen, Horse and I drove up early on the Saturday morning from London. We'd coaxed Bald Peter, an old mate from Scarborough, down to Hull to join us. We met mid-morning at the B&B I'd booked earlier that week, dumped our overnight bags and made our way to the nearest boozer. First in the pub that day and still the only customers after an hour, we were enjoying our third beer.

After a moment's conversational lull, Owen looked up: "Did we ever play in the back four together for Ealing United?"

Horse rolled his eyes "You mean you don't know?"

I joined in. "Mr Statistician, who, aged twenty-four, would sit-up in bed at night poring over his Ealing United spreadsheets whilst your 44DD girlfriend lay in bed beside you? You don't know the answer? Surprised."

"Disappointed," chimed-in Bald Peter.

Owen took it all quite well. "Fuck me, I don't remember everything!"

"Quite possibly did," I said, "though by my reckoning we have three full-backs here and only you as a central defender."

"Horse," asked Owen, "did you ever play any games at centre back? Can you remember?"

Horse shrugged. "I can't remember. Played a lot at left-back or left midfield."

This somewhat inane speculation continued for a while. How important is it really whether or not the four of us lined-up as *the* back four in a Hillingdon and District Sunday League game sometime between 1989 and the mid-1990s?

"We would've played in the same team in some games though. I'm sure," said Owen, quite some time after everyone else's thoughts were already elsewhere.

"Do you remember that game against The Crane?" He asked.

"When we were all actually sober?"

"Yeah, it was January. Practically the whole team was off it after Christmas and the New Year. Played them off the park. 2-0. You hit the bar," he said, gesturing to me.

"About thirty yards out…"

Sunday league reminiscences continued, while we remained the only customers in the pub.

"Need to go somewhere a bit livelier," said Horse. It was now gone 1 p.m. There were now another three customers in the pub.

We phoned a cab and headed to Boothferry Park, telling the driver to drop us at a decent pub near the ground. Well he dropped us at *a* pub near the ground. Decent? Debatable. It was certainly livelier in that there were a lot more people in there, but it wasn't the sort of place you'd go on an early date or for a Mother's Day family lunch. Unless you lived in Hull perhaps.

We got some drinks.

"Eh, have a look," said Bald Peter in his broad North Yorkshire guttural drawl, "we're gettin' fookin eyeballed in 'ere y'know."

He was right. Strangers in town. Strangers in town on the day the notorious Cardiff City were in town. We *were* getting fucking eyeballed – three Londoners and a Yorkshireman.

The locals' interest in us abated after a while. Or more like they just kept half an eye on us and decided that although we were strangers we weren't Cardiff. It's interesting what the Cardiff reputation engenders in places they visit. They seem to trigger a strong defence mechanism in towns and cities across the country.

"Remember Hayes?" I asked. "Hayes-Cardiff at Brentford."

He smiled. "Fuck me, the whole of West London came out that night."

A brief but relevant digression. Ten years earlier one of our local non-league clubs, Hayes, had been drawn away to Cardiff City in an early round of the FA Cup. First or second round proper. Hayes got a draw, earning a relatively lucrative replay. For whatever reason – most likely ground size and facilities – the replay wasn't played at Hayes but moved a few miles east to Griffin Park, Brentford. (For extended details about this particular evening from a Cardiff perspective see Annis Abraham's account in *Diary of the Real Soul Crew*.) Cardiff fans had a big reputation and they were a biggish club punching below their weight – these two factors largely accounting for why they were so disliked.

Off we pottered to Griffin Park for the game. I met Owen in one of the boozers very close to the ground. We were *aware*, let's say, of some of the possibilities of the evening. By the end of the night we'd seen just about every West London hooligan of the last fifteen years in or around Griffin Park. Blokes you'd thought were long-since dead. Chelsea fans, QPR fans, Arsenal fans, Spurs fans, Cockney Reds, Brentford fans. Blokes we knew who weren't even interested in football were there. Cardiff, in the parlance of the subculture, *didn't show*. Well it would be wrong to say there were *no* Cardiff fans there that night; there was a smattering of them at the Ealing Road end – probably just into three figures. At the other end, in the 'Wendy House', stood and sat the Hayes fans; the genuine Hayes fans, about fifteen hundred of them. Along the side of the ground in the seats and terracing of the Braemer Road stand, and disproportionately close to the Cardiff fans, were West London United – assorted blokes numbering about two thousand. Interested, though not actually actively engaged in this kind of thing, I have to say it was a very impressive turn-out.

I didn't see any aggro. There was a big Old Bill presence of course. Hayes won 1-0, deservedly.

In the post-match celebrations, the Hayes players focused their attentions at the 'Wendy House' end where their *real* supporters were. Even the players seemingly knew the score that night and why they'd played a home game in front of over four thousand for possibly the first time in their lives.

Back to Hull. We finished our drinks, left the boozer and strolled over to the ground. Well-lubricated and having eaten only assorted crisps and peanuts in the previous few hours we were all partway to being pissed. Except Horse. Horse wasn't pissed. I don't know where that bloke puts it or why it doesn't affect him, but it doesn't seem to. And he's known to often get in an extra drink between rounds.

At the ticket window Owen put on his best London finance industry accent. "Hello. Four tickets in the main stand please. The best seats you have please." He handed over the bundle of cash he'd collected

Toilets, main stand Boothferry Park, Hull, 2000.

from the rest of us. He leaned into the office window, straining to hear what was being said. He took the tickets, still talking. "And these are the best possible seats you have?" More nodding. "Yes… thank you very much. And a good day to you to madam." Ok, that last sentence I made up, but his side of the conversation had that overall patronising tone, highlighting the good old North-South divide.

"Right lads," he said. "We're in."

After pisses and some bulk-buying from the snack bar, we found our seats and settled into watching a run-of-the-mill fourth tier English league game. Big efficient defenders, traditional pairings up front, snarling midfielders schooled on Terry Hurlock videos and creatively-intentioned but wayward passes. It was entertaining enough in a fourth tier, seven drinks before the game kind of way. Hull won 2-0. One or more of us may have dozed off briefly during the game. Curiously both goals were own goals – early in the first half and midway through the second. It was that kind of game.

Boothferry Park had seen better days. One of those days had obviously been when they built the functional and, at this level, actually quite impressive two-tiered stand to our right behind the goal. It looked 1960s-ish, maybe early 1970s. I seemed to remember as a kid Hull knocking around the old Division Two in the 1970s. Maybe they established themselves there for a while and this stand was the fruits of that particular era of labour. *I suppose I could look it up and find out.* The other stand-out from Boothferry Park that day was the toilets – the blokes' toilets in the main stand. Untended in any conceivable way since the Coronation would have been my guess. Fifteen quid to get in and toilets like this? They were something approaching what I imagined a medieval dungeon to be like.

Game over, but we weren't in much of a hurry. More piss stops. More meandering. It was a good few minutes after the final whistle when we found ourselves wandering across a car park to the main road. We'd reckoned on getting a bus or cab (or fucking horse-drawn cart) into town.

"Ay oop," said Pete. "Fookin 'ell."

Lining the main road on the other side of the car park were several hundred blokes. Just standing, milling about. A Hull City welcoming committee. Only there didn't seem to be any Cardiff fans around to welcome. We carried on walking towards them. They clocked us; got interested.

One of them walked towards us. "Who are you then?"

"Well we ain't Cardiff." I said. I didn't have a strong London accent, but you'd have known I was from the south-east corner of England. Certainly not Wales.

"We're just four blokes doing the ninety-two grounds," said Horse.

That there was only four of us seemed to make a lot of them lose interest. One of them persisted though. "But you were in *their* end," he said. As in: I acknowledge that you're not Cardiff fans, but you wanted to temporarily align yourself with their notorious following and *big it up*.

"We were in your main stand," I said, showing him my ticket. Good move. Things quickly died down. I was half-expecting something along the lines of "let's do these Cockney bastards anyway" but it was never said. The persistent one continued to hover; a heel-bobbing wannabe.

One of them was quite friendly. "Where's next in the ninety-two?"

"Sunderland, tomorrow."

"Who they playing?"

"Leicester."

"Leicester? Surprise package them."

"Won't last."

"No. But it makes a change."

The heat, as it were, was as good as gone. The Hull firm was casting its collective eye further afield. The wannabe was still mooching around trying to look assertive or some such. He was probably one of those blokes whose own mates took the piss out of him.

We wandered off. There was a very small buzz behind us.

"Don't look back."

"Be better if they find some Cardiff and forget about us."

We walked for another maybe fifteen minutes then went into the first pub we came across; a quiet one. We stayed a while; maybe four hours and got comfortable. Then we walked into town. It was a Saturday night – in a seemingly different era.

We found ourselves in a club, well a big house-cum-pub. We bought a round of drinks and stood there chatting, minding our own business. It was apparent though that we'd attracted attention again. Strangers in town. Mind you this was a town of a quarter of a million people. Weren't they used to seeing the occasional different face? Within a few minutes some bloke was standing next to us, openly listening to our conversation.

"Alright lads? Where you from?" He asked. Not aggressive, but enough to set the antenna tweaking a bit.

"Middlesex," replied Horse, which was strictly true. Of the four of us it was only me that actually lived in a London postcode.

"Oh… right-o," he said. I'm not sure he'd necessarily heard of Middlesex or knew where it was. "Just didn't recognise the accent that's all." He walked off, no doubt to report back to whichever motley little local crew he was a part of.

We finished our drinks and left, conscious of the attention. It wasn't that late yet but there was a negative vibe in the air. Walking down a busy street – shops, banks, cafes, cashpoints etc we saw a queue for a club winding along the pavement. It wasn't particularly warm for the time of year, but all the blokes were in just shirts. Not a jacket in sight. Probably too tough for jackets in Hull.

Then we heard a short scream and raised voices. Two blokes peeled away from the queue, fighting. One of them, in a white shirt, was covered in blood. A few haymakers were thrown by both of the combatants – not much in the way of connecting though. Some of the queue turned to watch the fight. More interestingly, most of the people in the queue didn't bother – clearly it wasn't that rare an occurrence.

We stopped off for a couple at a more traditional-looking pub on the way back to the B&B. The demographic was largely people over fifty; lower testosterone levels. At about 11.30 p.m. we called it a day. It had been a long one and the prospect of getting through a few more hours unscathed in late Saturday night Hull seemed unlikely.

There was a takeaway pizza place along the way. We went in and placed our orders. A couple of girls came in; a good few years younger than us. Some chat, banter and gentle PG-rated innuendo ensued.

"Do you come from Hull?" I asked.

"Oh yes," answered the taller one.

"It's a bit rough isn't it? I mean, no offence and all that."

"None taken, it's as rough as fuck."

We briefly outlined our day.

"You're lucky."

Then other one chipped-in. "My boyfriend," she said, "comes from Leeds. He's lived here two years. He won't even go out at the weekend now, it's just not worth the aggro."

The conversation fizzled after that. Our pizzas came, and we ate them at the tables. Their pizzas came, and they left.

"See ya."

"Yeah, take care love," replied Horse.

I LIKE TO WATCH

Warsaw

The focal point of a late 2010 weekend in Warsaw was the Sunday night's Ekstraklasa clash between Legia and Górnik Zabrze. Owen and I arrived on the Friday night and Witek picked us up at the airport. We were in the hotel bar by 10.30 p.m.

"Cheers!" Beers and vodka chasers for the tourists. Witek stuck to Coke. After some brief catch-up chat Witek outlined the weekend's plans. He's organised like that. The following day was to be dedicated to sightseeing and cultural stuff. Sunday was sport. I'd done quite a bit of the sightseeing-cultural stuff with Witek before, both in Poland and other places. He set a punishing pace at times. He also had a near-encyclopaedic knowledge of Poland and Polish history; I sometimes wondered whether he'd missed his vocation in life.

Saturday included a lot of walking and photography, though late afternoon we got to watch Man United vs Spurs in a barn-sized sports bar and had a quiet dinner in a posh kind of restaurant. I ate sweetbreads for the first time in my life.

I'd been to Warsaw twice before, in 1991 and 1997. To say it had changed would be somewhat of an understatement. In 1991

I remember seeing some fairly down-at-heel blokes selling second-hand car parts out of suitcases in the city centre. In 2010 I saw a man in his sixties sitting in the window of a beauty parlour on a cobbled street in the Old Town having his nails manicured.

Sunday morning came around quickly enough. A couple of hours at the races, then football.

"You're not…!?" Owen spluttered when he saw me at the breakfast table.

"What?" Innocent voice.

"You're not wearing that shirt today surely, are you?"

It was a white England football shirt – that one with the little collars they had for a year or two.

"Yeah. Why?"

"Well…"

"It's zero out there. I'll be wearing a couple of layers on top."

He breathed a sigh of relief.

Polish football had for many years struggled with regular, large-scale crowd trouble. The authorities were reining it in though. One measure was the strictly managed sale and distribution of tickets. Ticket sales had to go through club members and someone could only be a member of one club. Members *could* get guest tickets though and that's how Witek got us into Legia. Our names and passport numbers were printed on the tickets and we had to take our passports to the game.

The match was scheduled for early evening, so with some time to kill we headed down to the southern suburbs of Warsaw to Tor Służewiec for the late morning race meeting. It was one of the few race courses left in Poland. There was some confusion and no little angst at the entry gate. Owen got in a flap with one of the old boys on the gate who'd started to rip his ticket in half.

"No, no…!" he pleaded, aghast that a torn ticket from a somewhat obscure race course would sully his carefully assembled collection.

Nonplussed and confused, the old bloke just shrugged. Witek interjected and a quick debate in Polish ensued, ending with us entering with Owen's ticket still intact. He looked palpably relieved. This is, after all, the bloke who once considered *not* entering Tannadice for a Dundee United vs Hearts game because the tickets issued at the gate on game day weren't *proper* tickets, ie they didn't detail the teams, competition and date. "But I need *evidence*!" he'd said incredulously as we took our seats moments after kick-off that afternoon. He spent the rest of the first half with his arms crossed, tutting.

At the races, Warsaw, 2010.

The Tor Służewiec set-up, facilities and vibe was like racecourses the world over on anything other than a major cup day. From Hollywood Park in LA to Caulfield, Randwick, Lingfield, Windsor and Buenos Aires they were much of a muchness; well-catered but barely populated with mainly middle-aged men smoking, drinking and spending money they probably couldn't afford to lose. Looking to escape something, I guessed.

We grabbed a couple of beers and surveyed our surrounds. Like many city race courses and dog tracks you couldn't help wondering how long it could survive before the inevitable *luxury/executive* (delete as applicable) apartment complex was mooted, argued over, appealed, argued over again then finally ok'd and built. There were hundreds of acres of space in a prime location used at most a couple of times a week, attended by ever-dwindling numbers.

The main club rooms were housed in an art deco building. Aesthetically pleasing enough, but let-down by its current condition.

It was a bright, fresh late Autumn morning. Some metaphorical cobwebs were blown away but four races was enough. We'd *ticked it off* so Witek drove us back into Central Warsaw for a bit more sightseeing and a leisurely late lunch before the Legia game.

We parked about half a mile from Legia's Stadion Wojska Polskiego (Polish Army Stadium). It also goes by the somewhat unwieldy Stadion Miejski Legii Warszawa im. Marszałka Józefa Piłsudskiego (Legia Warsaw Municipal Stadium of Marshal Józef Piłsudski).

We were on a bit of wasteland near a flyover. It reminded me of treks up north to watch Arsenal in the 1980s, only this looked and felt much rougher. Groups of fans were streaming towards the stadium. There were few women, children or families to be seen. The air was filled with testosterone. A few blokes took swigs of beer and vodka

Legia fans, Warsaw, 2010.

before discarding the bottles when they got closer to the stadium and the watchful eyes of the police. I wondered what it would've been like in the years before banning orders running into the four figures were implemented.

Legia's Stadion Wojska Polskiego, in October 2010, was being rebuilt. We joined the back of a large but orderly queue on one side of the stadium. The queue moved slowly. Identity cards. It seemed strange that you could then pass between different countries in Europe without showing your passport, but as a *guest* of the club and non-resident of Poland at Legia that night I needed my passport. Despite being unfinished – and thus big open gaps where stands were still under construction – there was no lack of atmosphere amongst the 17,881 in attendance. And despite the Sunday evening kick-off and near four-hundred-mile round-trip, the away section was close to full, and very noisy.

A scrappy game, punctuated by some niggly fouls and a lack of guile or creativity on the part of either team, sparked into life in the fifty-third minute when Daniel Sikorski gave the visitors the lead. More interesting to me than the goal were the Górnik Zabzre fans. After a short, explosive burst of celebrations their massed ranks then stripped down to their bare chests for the next round of songs. It was borderline freezing out there.

But a hard-won away game in the capital was not to be. Legia scored two very late goals through Miroslav Radovic and Bruno Mazenga to win 2-1. Cue the removal of shirts, jumpers and jackets in the Legia ultras section of the stadium. Clearly a Polish thing.

What hadn't been much of a spectacle to watch had been enlivened by two things – the late turnaround by the home team who had still been one-nil down after eighty-seven minutes, and of course the passion of both sets of fans. For me it was a throwback to the headier days of the 1970s when I'd started going to football and watched every possible highlight I could on TV. But the ante looked to have actually been upped here when compared to say the Kop or Stretford End a generation earlier. It was certainly more organised and choreographed than anything in England in the past.

Witek, a Legia fan since boyhood, had seen major changes in Poland and Polish football since the fall of communism in 1990.

"It's much better now. This stadium was old, horrible. Wooden bench seats. Horrible plastic seats. Big fences. All open. Was not a nice place to come for football, for anything. At the end the old stadium only held maybe fifteen thousand." And then a sobering footnote on darker days in Poland: "For a time, speedway was more popular here than football."

I LIKE TO WATCH

Skonto Riga

In late 2011 I visited Riga, Latvia for a weekend. I'd suggested it to Owen and Muttley a couple of months earlier by email and they were keen. It was relatively handy for Witek, who lived in Warsaw, so he joined us. None of us had been to Latvia before so it was a new country on all of our respective lists.

Muttley and Owen met me in Bristol on the Friday afternoon and we flew on one of those cheap airlines where the seats are designed for skinny midgets. It wasn't a comfortable flight for us, or ninety per cent of the other passengers. And a warm can of Heineken was £5.

Thankfully, it wasn't a long flight, and after getting through Riga airport, changing some money and jumping in a cab we arrived at our converted convent hotel in the middle of the Old Town. Witek was waiting for us in reception. It was late evening – eleven or so – but we found a decent pub with a good range of beers and some ok nosebag. Compared to the outer suburbs we saw on the drive in from the airport, Riga's pretty Old Town seemed like a rose stuck in the middle of some cow dung.

This wasn't a sporting weekend away, ie the focal point wasn't sport-related with everything else built around it. However, when travelling I always find out what's on to see if there's anything I can add to the list. Initially I'd thought none of us would have a chance of getting to Skonto Riga's game on the Sunday afternoon. Witek's flight back to Warsaw was early afternoon, Owen and Muttley were returning to Gatwick in the morning, and my flight was early evening. Now that I knew how long it took to get to the airport I worked-out that I could get to at least the first half of their Virsliga game against FK Jurmala. The Virsliga is Latvia's top division and Skonto, then, its most famous club.

Owen sat there, quietly seething, as I outlined my plan to get Skonto's ground done.

"I did also look into tomorrow's games. We have a couple of lower division options that look like short-ish walks from the Old Town."

With a fold-out tourist map, annotated by our friendly hotel receptionist that morning, we set out across Riga in search of the lower division ground. The map didn't seem to be to scale. Eventually we came across a football pitch that was attached to a school or college. As far as we could all tell, this was where one of the day's games was due to be played in about ten minutes. There was no one around. Nothing happening. Our next attempt at finding a game for the afternoon also floundered, and unsurprisingly we soon found ourselves in a bar on the edge of the Old Town.

The TV in the bar was about to show the Chelsea vs Arsenal game from Stamford Bridge, so we settled in for a couple of hours to watch what turned out to be a highly entertaining 5-3 win for The Arse. For some reason that afternoon I drank Margaritas. Reasonably well-engrossed in the game I looked up about every twenty minutes as Muttley delivered another one.

Never before had I ordered a bottle of Sauv Blanc to help me sober up. But that's what I did when we sat down for dinner after the Chelsea vs Arsenal game. The tequila was running riot through me. It was only about 6.30 p.m. Dinner? I think it might be more accurate to call it a very late lunch.

I seem to remember the dinner was quite good. The Sauv Blanc indeed slowed the intoxication process. Any more than three Margaritas was asking for trouble, and I'd had nine or ten. Preceded by beer. Then the wine. I was in bed in my hotel room by 8.30 p.m. Owen, Muttley and Witek soldiered on somewhere.

I woke up at around two – not altogether surprising considering it had been my earliest night in living memory. There was a faint light in the room from somewhere – a mix of hallway light from under the door and from outside. My hotel room was quite big, though sparsely furnished. They could have got two rooms comfortably out of it – or four if the hotel had been within a half-mile of Paddington station. A table ran partway under the window at the end of my bed. To the right-hand end of the table was my faithful navy-blue Fred Perry weekend bag. There was a book or something small-ish and flat just next to it. At the far left-hand end of the table was a cat, curled-up and presumably asleep. A cat!? How the fuck had a cat got in? I didn't move. Was it a hotel cat? Or a stray – that may have brought in any kind of filth or rubbish from outside. I lay there, nursing a punishing headache, wondering how the hell this cat got in. It didn't move.

After a while I got up, tentatively. My head was pounding, so I walked as gingerly as I possibly could over to the cat. I didn't want to wake it in case it got scared and scratched me. I tiptoed over and looked closer. It wasn't a cat. I picked it up, then turned the light on. It was a furry hat with a metal badge on the front – a Soviet soldier's winter hat. It all came back to me. I'd bought it from an old bloke in the street in the Old Town the previous day, sometime between leaving the bar after the Arsenal game and having dinner. He'd had several hats for sale, as well as Soviet Army great coats hung-up on a nearby wall. I'd given him twenty quid for it. It had a certain *something* about it, but it was hard to imagine much of a need for it back in Australia.

Relieved that there wasn't a cat in my room I went back to bed and tried, unsuccessfully, to sleep. Wide awake at four o'clock in the morning can be a lonely place.

Owen and Muttley left on the Sunday morning after breakfast and a gay walk. Witek and I spent an hour or so at the Museum of the Occupation of Latvia. It was easy to understand the lingering resentment towards both Germany and Russia in this part of the world. Many people of our age had grandparents who'd lived through it and even parents who were children at the time.

We had some lunch, then Witek went off to the airport bus on the edge of the Old Town. It was just me for the afternoon's big game between Skonto Riga and FK Jurmala.

I still had the fold-out city map. It came in useful on the half-hour or so walk out to the nine thousand capacity Skonto Stadium. The furry Soviet hat was tucked away in the faithful Fred Perry bag. I got there about thirty minutes before kick-off. A convention centre next to the stadium was hosting a dog show. My knowledge of the state of Latvian football was somewhat limited and I naively wondered whether holding two events in the same complex on the same afternoon might be problematic – crowds and that.

There weren't that many people entering the stadium. In fact, the dog show next door was generating more activity. It cost me one

Latvian Lat (about £1.20) to get into the game. I went into a kind of social club room inside the stadium. With kick-off approaching there were about ten people in there. I bought a bottle of Coke, which was more than getting into the game. This is going to be shit, I thought, before starting to conjure up ideas for the following day's wind-up email to Owen: "Sell-out crowd, stadium heaving, local derby, flares, pitch invasions, unbelievable noise, a mini Rangers-Celtic, 3-3 draw, two sent off…"

By the time the game kicked off there *might* have been three hundred people sitting in one stand along the side of the ground. The two sets of the respective clubs' vocal supporters numbered maybe forty each. The rest of the crowd was made-up of grizzled-looking late middle-aged Latvian blokes, a few families and tourists. Assuming Riga wasn't home to a sizeable Japanese female community who happened to be Skonto fans, then about a hundred or so of the crowd were tourists.

Low-key doesn't begin to get close to describing the atmosphere or game.

Riga – not exactly a hotbed of footballing passions.

The city of Riga forms the top side of a diamond shape if you looked at it in relation to Warsaw, Moscow and Kiev. All of those major footballing cities were only a few hundred miles away. What happened to Riga and Latvia when the passion-for-football *fairy dust* was being handed out? I understood that ice hockey was the real national sport, but then polo was the national sport of Argentina, but that didn't lessen their love of football.

The stadium was in a tightly-packed residential area. Despite its compact size, it wasn't difficult to imagine this stadium rocking with quite an atmosphere, if it was ever full. I left at 2-0 but looking online the following day I saw that it ended 3-0. It had been one of those forgettable ones.

Skonto Riga had once been *the* team in Latvia. From 1992 they won the Virsliga thirteen times in a row. The following eleven seasons included five second-place finishes and another title. This whole period saw seven Latvian cup wins as well. In the late 1990s Skonto played ties against both Barcelona and Chelsea in European competitions. Then in 2016 Skonto went bankrupt and a footballing dynasty, of sorts, was over.

It hadn't been much of a game, but I was pleased to have added a relatively obscure one to the list. In fact, it hadn't been a bad nine days for new grounds with both Peterborough and Bristol Rovers added the previous week. There were worse ways to spend your free time.

I LIKE TO WATCH

Kandy

The Sri Lankan civil war was coming to its bloody conclusion in late 2007 when England toured. An ODI series and a couple of three-day representative games were played before the real business, a Test series, started on 1 December.

The war lasted nearly twenty-six years, with an estimated hundred thousand people killed. Consider that out of a population of twenty million, on an island just a bit smaller than the *Republic* portion of Ireland.

In very simplistic terms the civil war was fought out between the Tamils in the north and the Sinhalese in the south. As with many conflicts it was about territory, statehood and a desire for independence.

I travelled from Melbourne to Sri Lanka via Kuala Lumpur. Waiting for my luggage at Colombo airport, I checked my phone. "Have fun but be careful," said a text from home, "there was a suicide bomb last night. Loads killed."

My taxi ride to the Galle Face Hotel in Colombo took an hour-and-a-half. It was one long, slow-moving traffic jam.

Hallway sign, Galle Face Hotel, Colombo, 2007.

The Galle Face Hotel was an icon, a throwback to a different time with character oozing from every tile, panel and bit of architrave. I'd organised this trip in a roundabout way. Colombo airport is about a third of the way from the city of Colombo to Kandy. Arriving at the airport and then going south to Colombo meant I was adding considerably to the journey. It was like flying into Heathrow, spending the night in Romford before heading to Bath or Bristol.

I was four or five Lion beers ahead of Owen when he arrived from London. It had been nearly a year since I'd seen him – at the Sydney Ashes Test when Australia made it 5-0. It was somewhat predictable then that our evening was shaped around fast drinking, Arsenal-Tottenham banter, some brief speculation about the cricket, and a shit-load of *do you remember?* anecdotes. We'd known each other since primary school.

"This place, Colombo," I told him, "is to within a hundred miles or so, just about equidistant between Melbourne and London. It really *is* the halfway point."

"Yeah, unlike Saigon for your fortieth when you told everyone *that* was meeting halfway between Australia and England."

"Well you should have checked!" I laughed. "Good trip though."

"It was."

The drive to Kandy the following morning took around four hours to cover the seventy-odd miles. It was one small village after another, linked by long lanes. It was very picturesque, but I regretted not being organised enough to have booked the train, which is reportedly a 'must-do' in Sri Lanka. Our driver was chatty and informative, and we topped-up regularly on water and soft drinks in the back. It was humid, and we were both nursing nagging hangovers.

"It's not as poor as India is it?" I said.

"No. No way," said Owen looking out the window. "Not at all."

But, as we discovered later that afternoon at our hotel, logistics and organisation could be kind of India*esque*.

"Ah… Mr Wooldridge," began the receptionist, "our manager will need to speak to you about your booking. Will you and Mr Francis take a seat over there for a moment." She did that little head wobble thing.

"Is there a problem with the reservation?" Owen asked.

"No, no… just an *issue*. Seat. Please take a seat." She gestured to the lounge area in front of reception. We walked over, sharing pained glances.

"This doesn't look good." Owen said. It looked worse thirty seconds later when a waiter came over and enthusiastically asked us what we would like to drink – at pains to point out that the drinks would be complimentary.

"Two beers then please."

The hotel we'd booked was a big complex in the hills just outside Kandy. From the little we'd seen, it looked like a good choice.

Our beers came, quickly followed by a suited bod in his forties. He explained the situation. Overbooked. A wedding party today. Overbooked for today only. He wanted us to stay one night elsewhere in Kandy, "at a hotel of comparable quality to this" so they could accommodate all the wedding guests. Some other guests had been happy to comply etc etc. He would be most grateful. Very grateful.

Assuming his story was legit then fair enough, I thought. Two blokes just here for the cricket should be pleased to help keep a wedding party together under the same roof for an evening. In any event as Owen probably rightfully pointed-out: "It doesn't sound like there's much option anyway."

We headed into Kandy in a hotel car. The driver took us to a place that was at least three stars below where we'd just come from. It was more like one of those backpackers that had a few single and twin rooms as well. Our room was internal with the window overlooking a small courtyard. Consequently, with a few floors above us, the room was in almost complete darkness at four o'clock in the afternoon.

"Comparable quality, eh?"

"I'll take it up with the travel agent when I'm back." I said.

Kandy is picturesque, a mix of colonial, traditional and semi-modern architecture and unlike some other cities in the region there is a feeling of *space* about it. It's very green and has a lake as a centrepiece. Overlooking one corner of the lake we found a heaving pub-slash-hotel called the Queens. It was full of thirsty English folk – a mixture of uniformed Barmy Army-ites and a broad assortment of blokes in different football club shirts.

I tried a Lion Stout.

"Bloody hell!" I said, checking the label. "It's fucking eight per cent!"

To save time we'd ordered large bottles, containing well over a pint in each. By the time I was halfway through mine, the intense humidity had left me holding a potent room temperature beer.

"Think I'll stick to small bottles of lager after this."

Kandy was a bit to the north and east of Colombo, in the centre of Sri Lanka and closer to Tamil Tiger territory. I broached the subject of the Tamil Tigers with a friendly local who'd just sold me a fake Ralph Lauren shirt.

"There is always a little risk in Sri Lanka from this terrorism," he said, "but Kandy is a small place. Everyone knows everyone. If there is a stranger in town, everyone will know."

I nodded.

"And the Tamils," he said, "they are darker-skinned than us. You can spot them."

We got to the Asgiriya International Cricket Stadium just after eight the next morning. There was surprisingly little activity outside the caravan-cum-hut that constituted the ticket office. The tickets ranged from 100 (44p) to 5,000 (£22) rupees, suggesting something ranging from a spot on the grass to a throne with personal attendant. We bought 500-rupee tickets. Even from outside the ground it was evident that this would be no characterless concrete bowl. There was a bit of time to kill so we went for a wander. The area was swarming with armed police and military keeping a protective eye on the hundreds of tourists and smattering of locals milling around.

We found a little cafe and stopped for a Coke. The cafe had a resident three-legged dog that roamed around amiably. Creatures of some degree of habit, we went there before the day's play each morning for the rest of the Test.

Our 500-rupee tickets provided access to a small stand made-up nearly entirely of locals. Two English blokes in their forties sporting Sri Lankan ODI shirts holding in very English beer guts generated no shortage of smiles and hellos that first morning.

The five days that unfolded were exciting, unpredictable, dramatic, but play-wise also boring at times. It's probably the most eventful and enjoyable Test match I've been to.

Sri Lanka batted first. Early on day one they struggled to 42/5. But they settled after that and went on to post 188. Not a great score, but one that *could* be competitive against inconsistent tourists.

It got very windy that first afternoon. To our left, part of the aluminium roof on one of the stands burst out of its shackles and

Keeping score; inside the scoreboard, Kandy, 2007.

started flapping violently in the wind. At this point you might've reasonably expected a break in play, or a temporary evacuation of the stand while it was made safe. This evidently wasn't deemed necessary as a couple of the ground staff simply got on the roof to nail the panels down again. Then at one point a roof panel came loose at *both* ends and blew off completely.

By the end of bad light-affected day one England had reached 49/1, a solid-ish enough start. We retired to the Queens pub for a blast of liquid refreshment.

On day two we took up a position in the Barmy Army section of the ground. Prior to the start of play we wandered over to the old manual scoreboard a few yards away. It was being manned by three boys in their teens. We got chatting and they invited us into the scoreboard. The different steps, ladders and gantries behind the different parts of the scoreboard looked like a major challenge to manage during a game.

Every time I sat in the Barmy Army section at an England match I told myself I'd never do it again. There was something sheep-like about it all. Some of the songs were funny the first, second and even third times. But the fiftieth time? And there was something about the way many of them watched – or *didn't watch* – the game. Instead of sitting comfortably, sharing a comment or two, or having a quiet conversation, there seemed to be a need to *perform*, to attract attention. This often included standing up, turning around away from the play and trying to get a singalong happening, eyes darting around in search of approval. Barmy Army laugh-a-minute antics included shouting loudly across a group of people using a contrived-sounding nickname to draw someone's attention to something minor and of little interest.

"Hey Yellowman! Hey…! Yellowman! Yellowman, up here. Look! Baggychops has got himself an extra-large coke!"

And this might result in a short period of chanting by about six of them: "Extra-large Coke! Extra-large Coke! He's got himself… an extra-large Coke!"

By lunchtime on day two England had reached 145/3. Not spectacular, but up against Sri Lanka's first innings total it looked pretty sound. Not long after lunch the score reached 169/3. But then we witnessed one of those all-too-frequent mini-collapses that England fans are well acquainted with.

Then, in mid-afternoon rain swept in across the Asgiriya Stadium with an almost monsoon-like ferocity. Play was abandoned for the day with England on 186/6.

We gave the Queens Hotel a miss that evening. In addition to the obvious tourist hang-outs, my guidebook had also enticingly mentioned some other "sour back street bars" in Kandy. I think the phrase "air of malevolence" was even used to describe one of them. So, it was into the back streets we headed.

The names of the two establishments we visited have long since escaped me.

We went upstairs in the first bar. It consisted of a rectangular room decked-out with 1960s canteen tables and chairs. At the end of the room was a table a little higher than the rest. This constituted the bar. It was attended by a middle-aged man who looked thoroughly bored with life. So far, on this particular evening at any rate, none of the few thousand England cricket fans in town had found their way here. It was just Owen and I, and a table of locals sitting around a bottle of mean-looking spirits and a two-litre bottle of Coke to mix it with. While our welcome certainly wasn't hostile, there wasn't a great deal of alacrity about the barman as he shuffled over to the fridge to get a couple of Lion lagers. They cost half what we'd paid in the Queens a few hundred yards away, but they were almost room temperature.

Noisily debating something of seemingly great import, the locals paid us little attention as we took our beers to a nearby table.

"It feels like a pub back room in Glasgow in the 1970s." Owen said.

"Or somewhere smaller probably. Port Talbot."

The table top was in turn dusty, gritty *and* sticky.

"Just the one here, I reckon."

"Yep, just the one."

Then we tried another bar a bit off the tourist track. This one looked like a rundown colonial mansion or small hotel; a place that had once seen better days. Those better days were possibly when it offloaded its meeting room furniture to the bar we'd just left. This place was equally grim, but at least the building was interesting from an architectural perspective and there were a few other customers knocking around. The owners of this bar must've bought the same wattage bulbs as the previous place. It was as though someone thought one very low wattage bulb would suffice for a room the size of a school classroom with twenty-foot ceilings. But at least the beers were cold.

"Just the one?"

"Yep, just the one."

And then it was a tuk-tuk back to our hotel, uphill and a bit out of town. This fifteen-minute journey had become something to look forward to. In the mornings it preceded a day spent in one of the most scenic cricket grounds I'd been to, and in the evening it meant a nice bit of breeze and fresh air after a few hours in a busy, sweaty bar.

***

On day three we upgraded to the 2,000-rupee tickets and sat in the Grand Stand. It had the highest-level seats in the ground and a diagonal view across the ground. We were effectively opposite where we'd sat the previous day. This stand housed a different demographic. The best view in the Asgiriya, this stand had obviously been largely commandeered by the English tour companies. Some rows of seats looked like they were housing the cast from *Last of the Summer Wine*.

That morning England added another fifty or so without losing a wicket but then did that England thing again, going from 239/6 to 281 all out in just eleven overs.

It was during the morning session that Muttiah Muralitharan took his 709th Test wicket, thus beating the record Shane Warne set in Sydney eleven months earlier. I'd been with Owen at the game that day as well. In addition to Murali achieving this feat on home soil in Sri Lanka, Kandy was his home club ground. The scenes that followed were predictably delirious amid a very appreciative, if not quite rousing, level of applause from the England fans. It was odds-on that Murali would reach the 709 in this match and the local officials were well-prepared. There was a presentation during the lunch break and a nicely-presented set of commemorative stamps on sale in the ground within an hour.

England had a first innings lead of 93. Useful, or seemingly so. At the end of that third day Sri Lanka had dug-in and sat handsomely on 167/2. The balance of the game had shifted. In the course of the power shifting to Sri Lanka their thirty-eight-year-old opener, Sanath Jayasuriya, became just the second batsman in Test cricket to score six 4s in an over. It turned out to be his last Test match; he announced his retirement at the end of the game.

***

A watchful eye. Soldier outside the Asgiriya Stadium, Kandy, 2007.

On day four we treated ourselves to the most expensive tickets in the ground – the 5,000-rupee tickets in the Old Trinitians Pavilion. The Asgiriya Stadium is actually the private property of Trinity College, a large all-ages private school, founded in the Victorian era by Anglicans. The Pavilion was, as it sounds, an English colonial-style club house. Except on day four of this Test it was jam-packed with English cricket fans, in this case another sub-set of the five thousand or so travelling England contingent in Kandy. They weren't Barmy Army types. They weren't with any organised tours or cricket clubs, but there was no shortage of different English club football shirts on display. Interestingly there were more women in this part of the ground than other areas. However, it was clear this wasn't a pavilion-full of Test cricket aficionados. Over the course of the day the blokes in here went through more beer per head than any of the other sections of the ground we'd sat in, while many of the women ignored the cricket and sunbathed, chatting.

"Northern hooligans and their birds." Owen observed.

It was a different kind of day at the cricket, if not exactly an exciting day's *play*. For the record Sri Lanka turned the screw heavily, batting nearly all day to get to 442/8 declared, leaving England an unlikely 350 to chase down with five overs remaining on day four, and a full day five. The best we could realistically hope for was a draw, but even that was dented somewhat when Alastair Cook was out for just 4 before close of play.

That fourth day left me with some memories – the likes of which I doubt I'll experience again.

On the far side of the ground to the Old Trinitians Pavilion was a steep hill with what looked like an almost sheer drop. Somewhere on or behind the hill was a monastery and for a lengthy period early in the day a couple of Buddhist monks stood there, motionless, watching the game.

In the street behind the pavilion outside the ground were a few offices or municipal buildings a bit taller than average for Kandy. These buildings provided vantage points for looking into the ground to watch play. However, the roofs of these buildings were lined with heavily-armed military, a sobering reminder of the fragile situation in Sri Lanka.

Not long before the innings change with Sri Lanka on 413/5, the crowd looked on confused as suddenly all thirteen players and both umpires threw themselves to the ground and lay still. Thankfully not a terrorist attack, or cause for *major* concern, it later filtered through that a swarm of bees had descended on the pitch. After a couple of minutes, the players dusted themselves down and carried on. Kumar Sangakkara top scored for Sri Lanka with 152, in the process becoming the first player to score 150 in four consecutive Test matches.

At the end of play as we were finishing our last beers and Owen was lamenting that however the next day transpired, he *still* wasn't going to see an England away win in a Test match, we spotted an elderly man walking over from the standing section to our right.

"It's the bloke from this morning!" Owen said as the man approached the wall that separated the 100 and 5,000-rupee a day sections of the ground. Before the day's play at the cafe with the three-legged dog, this same man had tapped us up for money to get into the ground. He'd obviously spotted us during the day and was now over thanking us again for the money we'd given him seven or eight hours earlier.

"He's angling for some more dough for tomorrow!"

Of course he was, and we gave him some more money without a second thought. He was again thankful, and we shook hands. This whole type of thing is uncomfortable when you think about it. And you really don't need to think about it in too much depth.

Day five started with England facing an uphill battle. A win was mathematically possible – they needed 341 runs off (theoretically) 90 overs with nine wickets in hand. A draw from this position would be considered a result, though not if you looked back to the score after an hour's play on day one. Owen was in the unusual position of actually seeing England *play* on the fifth day in an away Test.

We bought Grand Stand seats again. We were all geared-up for a day of batting attrition from England. Could they survive? They had some solid, experienced batsmen in the side.

"They really need to dig in. I can't see us winning, so runs aren't important. None of this "just go out and play your natural game" crap. That will get them in trouble. Most of them need to do the exact opposite of playing their natural game."

He'd summarised the situation and challenge succinctly.

England stuttered to 55/3 by the morning drinks break and a decidedly dangerous-looking 125/5 at lunch. Bell and first Bopara put up some resistance before Bopara went for 34. Wicket-keeper Matt Prior then joined Ian Bell at the crease. They put on 109 for the seventh wicket and for a while we day-dreamt the snatching of a draw. But Prior was out with the score on 249 and the last three wickets went for just 12 runs. Ryan Sidebottom was given out LBW for the ninth after an inside edge that even the monks outside the ground could've seen from their hilltop vantage point. We can and did protest, as did the players, but the game was over and done with by then. Sri Lanka won by 88 runs with about half an hour to spare before the end of play. If they hadn't got that tenth wicket when they did, light may have become a factor. I'm glad that didn't happen. There wouldn't have been much joy in that. A draw with nine wickets down, being saved by bad light wouldn't have been much to celebrate.

We stayed for the presentations then slunk off into the centre of town to drown the sorrows we'd been anticipating most of the day. We went to another pub, The Pub, on that last night. Crammed full of England fans they were at least mainly different faces and we had different conversations and a change of scenery.

I realised then that I'd seen a *good* Test match. It probably took some time, and many other matches, for it to sink in just what a really *great* game we'd seen. Not just the game, but everything around it. We'd seen a match where fortunes had changed dramatically, which went down to the last few overs on day five, with bowling and batting records broken, on and off field dramas involving bees and collapsing stand roofs. All this in the near-idyllic surrounds of a colonial school cricket ground in the highlands of Sri Lanka, ringed by heavily-armed police and military.

That 2007 Test match was the last one played at the Asgiriya Stadium. The Sri Lankan cricket board then moved Test matches to the 22,000 capacity Pallekele International Cricket Stadium ten miles outside Kandy. The Asgiriya still hosts local games, but what the future holds for international cricket there remains to be seen.

Owen hot-footed it very early the next morning to get to the airport and his flight to London. I had another day, albeit back at the Galle Face Hotel in Colombo. I'd already booked a driver to take me back to Colombo via the elephant orphanage at Pinnawala, about a third of the way. I spent a couple of fascinated hours watching those giant, beautiful beasts.

I somehow managed to get a room in the old part of the Galle Face Hotel about the size of two school classrooms. It had a colonial-style living room with couches, chairs, a dining table and desk, and a bedroom, with a four-poster bed, the size of a city centre apartment. It was a shame not to spend much time in there.

I went out the front of the hotel for a bit of a look around, but it was humid, and I didn't stray very far. I took my camera out to get some front-on pictures of the Galle Face Hotel. A bloke approached me and showed me a card.

"No photos allowed," he said.

"Oh, sorry," I replied, "I didn't realise."

"I know," he said politely. "It's security. It's what we have to do. For everyone it's the same."

I put my camera away.

I went back to the hotel and wandered down to the pool, grabbing a beer on the way. A handful of England players were sat at a table on the patio of the hotel. It was time to catch-up on some reading. I'd barely read ten pages or so of *The Woman in White* when an English woman in her thirties walked past me carrying a copy of the same book, albeit a different edition. She turned sharply looking at me, holding up her book.

"Coincidence!" She called out.

"And hardly a current bestseller." I smiled.

I had an early flight out of Colombo. The lights were out everywhere as the taxi headed to the airport. No headlights even. The driver explained: "There was a warning about a bombing. From the air by the Tamils…"

"An air-strike?"

"Yes," he said, mentally adding "air-strike" to his pool of English phrases. "Air-strike. All the lights in this part of the city must be off."

There wasn't much traffic around, and it only took about thirty minutes. There was a security gate at the airport; cars were being let-in one-by-one. I sat quietly in the back as the security blokes talked to the driver, then opened the boot. They shone their torches into the back to check me out. At the time I thought it would have been obvious that a sunburnt Anglo in the back of a taxi wasn't a Tamil Tiger. But of course, they wouldn't have known anything about the taxi driver's background.

I LIKE TO WATCH

Millwall

Millwall might possibly be the only club in English football to have attracted more newspaper column inches and media attention through the actions of their fans than their players. No football-interested teenager in the 1970s could forget the Panorama TV documentary, or the myth of the 'Millwall Brick'. TV footage of the trouble from Millwall's FA Cup tie with Ipswich in 1978 was a reminder to many of us that we were pleased Millwall played in a different division. Millwall were the visitors to Luton in a 1985 FA Cup game – the riot that ensued becoming a watershed moment in British football.

Games against Millwall and trips to The Den by visiting supporters have been extensively documented in the hoolie porn annals of many a well-thumbed paperback knocking around the homes of usually middle-aged, shaven-headed, trainer-wearing men across England. There's a lot to read about aggro with Millwall if you care to look. I'm not revisiting that territory. Other people have covered it in painstaking detail; people who were involved. This is about going to Millwall as a spectator, as a fan.

***

I went to the old Den just the once, in 1990. Millwall were at the end of their two-year stint in the English First Division; when it was the proper First Division, not the second or third. That division was the Premier League before the Premier League *was* the Premier League. But it also wasn't like the Premier League, because it was still a relatively cheap afternoon or evening out. In 1990 a working-class father could still take his kids to games in England's top division on a regular, not it's-your-birthday-special-treat, basis. A lot of the time back then you just decided on the day whether or not you were going to the game. Most games were still played on Saturday afternoons. Standing at a top-level game was still an option, although even in 1990, post-Hillsborough, we knew change was coming. We knew prices would go up in the coming years, but no one then could honestly have envisaged the sheer scale of the commercial maelstrom and level of media attention that would come to envelop football in the decades that followed.

It was Spurs at the Den on Easter Monday, 1990. I went with Owen Francis, his old man, and Brian Doran. Opportunities to get the Den on the list were going to decline with their upcoming departure from the top division, so I took-up Owen's offer of a ticket. All-ticket games or ticketed sections for away fans were quite unusual then. There was none of this membership scheme or loyalty points stuff or applying months in advance. Generally, you just went to the game. Or didn't. But this game *was* all-ticket, so by 1990 standards it actually took *some* organising – like sending off a cheque or queuing up for tickets after a home game. Simpler times and no booking fees.

On that Monday afternoon we stood on a large covered terrace and saw Gary Lineker score the archetypal Lineker goal. There was all of 10,574 there. Italia 90 hadn't happened yet, and this was still officially English football's *dark ages*. However, it wasn't at all the kind of atmosphere or experience I'd been expecting in South East London. I guess Millwall – on all levels – were just jaded and looking to re-group for the following season back in Division Two.

My abiding memory of that day came well before the game. We'd driven over to South London early to have a few drinks before the match but wanted to be a suitable distance from the ground to find a *non-contentious* kind of pub. It was a part of London where you needed to keep your wits about you at the best of times, let alone when Millwall were at home.

The plan was to drive around and when we saw a pub, Brian and I would quickly check it out while Owen and his old man stayed in the car nearby, engine running. After a while we headed down a quiet street and came across a small boozer. It was one of those pubs that was built into a row of terraced houses as opposed to the more common, noticeable, big corner pub. It went with the territory. Owen stopped the car and Brian and I got out and walked over. It was after 11 a.m. but being a public holiday, things varied a bit opening hours-wise. The door was locked, so I peered through the window.

"Fucking hell! Have a look at this."

His head joined mine looking through the glass panel on the door. There were overturned tables and chairs, and broken glass everywhere. The pub has obviously been the scene of some kind of major row, or simply just smashed up. Surely, it can't have happened already today? I wondered.

We walked back to the car.

"Not open yet?"

Brian and I laughed.

"Could say that!"

"What?" Owen asked.

"Place has been smashed-up," Brian said.

"You're joking!"

"Nope. Glass and chairs and crap all over the place."

"Welcome to South London," piped up Owen's old man as we pulled away.

Fifteen minutes later we were nestled around a corner table in a dingy pub a mile or two away. There were only a couple of other customers. We obviously weren't locals, but no one seemed to care. If there'd been any Millwall 'spotters' in there all they would have reported back was a man in his late fifties with a bloke who was obviously his son and two other younger blokes having a quiet drink.

My next visit to Millwall was on a Monday night in January 1994. Arsenal had been drawn away there in the FA Cup. This was the New Den; Millwall moved there at the start of that season. Built for what now seems like a modest £16M, the ground that night hosted its record attendance of 20,093. It was an all-ticket affair, yet surprisingly the tickets were unreserved.

Unless Millwall extend their ground, that attendance is unlikely to be beaten. The official capacity is 20,146, but sections now remain closed in the away end to maintain some kind of distance between home and away supporters.

We met after work and made our way to Whitechapel on the District Line to change trains for the journey south of the river to the *Badlands*. The platform at Whitechapel was comprised largely of males in the twenty to forty age group, with little in the way of team colours on display. Everyone seemed aware of everyone else in a checking-out kind of way but there were no little firms on the prowl and no real sense of aggro in the air. Presumably it had all been prearranged and if you were in the know and you were interested, well, that's where you'd be. I clocked a couple of Arsenal blokes who sat near me at Highbury.

The train journey and walk to the ground from Surrey Quays station passed without incident.

We were in good time and managed to get a couple of seats at the front of the upper tier. Every seat in the Arsenal section was taken. Looking around though, the demographic was quite different to where I sat in Arsenal's then new North Bank Stand. Arsenal's turn-out that night at Millwall was marked by a seeming absence of females and anyone who might still be at school. And it was less multicultural than you'd see in N5; the Millwall reputation clearly putting some people off.

Not much of a game. Below par top division team away to team a division below from the same city who are up for it. Outcome predictable – a tough, scrappy game. I remember the Millwall fans howling constantly at Ray Parlour, giving him a particularly hard time. Whether that was to do with his then flowing golden locks ("what are you, some kinda poof?") or that he was from Romford and thus an assumed West Ham connection, I'm not sure. The flowing locks I think.

Arsenal won 1-0 with a very late Tony Adams goal. A corner was played in below where we were sitting. Paul Merson jumped up and got in a bit of a tangle with mullet-adorned Millwall goalkeeper Kasey Keller. The ball dropped, and Tony Adams poked-bundled-cajoled it into the net. Foul? Possibly. Certainly more chance of it being a foul these days.

It was a typical Arsenal win in that era; scrappy and dogged. They'd won two domestic cups the previous season and in 1994 were on the way to a famous European Cup Winners' Cup triumph in Copenhagen. The football along the way wasn't always that pretty though.

Arsenal fans celebrated wildly. The Millwall fans, already congregating at the ends of the two stands closest to the Arsenal end, became even more abusive and made even more threatening gestures. To be fair it wasn't all one way and was met enthusiastically in kind from the Arsenal end.

And that was it, as far as I could see. We made the train journey home across London without incident.

My third trip to Millwall was in April 2015. Deep in relegation trouble and heading for League One before the season was over, Millwall were facing high-flying Watford. I was on a three-week trip to England with my sons, then aged eight and nine. Despite their half-Australian heritage, they already had a very keen interest in football, or *soccer* as they say Down Under. During our visit I'd sorted tickets for a few games – two at Brentford, Brentford away at Fulham and Arsenal vs Liverpool. I decided also to fill our middle Saturday with a trip to Millwall – a destination a bit off the obvious tourist circuit. I was thinking years ahead though, to when my sons were in their late teens or twenties, talking to their mates about football in Europe. "Yeah, I've been to Millwall, went there when I was eight."

I had to brief my two boys in advance of our visit to The Den.

"Don't mention Arsenal or Brentford when we're there." Receptive nods.

"Don't say 'who are we going for?' at kick-off time." More receptive nods.

"And whatever you do, don't cheer, react or do anything if Watford score. They'll probably be wearing yellow."

"Will Watford score? They're the away team."

"Yeah but they're near the top and Millwall are next to bottom place."

"Ok." Receptive nods again.

I thought back to a game at Melbourne's AAMI Park when I took them to a Melbourne Heart game. The visitors scored and in his excitement at seeing a goal my eldest, Henry, then about six, jumped up and cheered. Why not? He'd seen a goal. It's just that the *wrong* team scored it.

"Millwall's a different kind of place," I started to explain. And then putting it into a localised Australian context they might get, "it's like a bigger, much rougher version of Long Gully".

I think they got it. They'd already experienced crowd segregation and seen an over-the-top police presence at the Fulham vs Brentford game a week earlier. They'd also seen some fighting in the seats at a Melbourne Heart vs Western Sydney game a couple of years previously.

We set-off from our tiny Airbnb 'luxury apartment' near Ealing Common. I was feeling a bit jaded having spent the previous day and night doing the Circle Line pub crawl; twenty-eight drinks in twenty-seven different boozers. We changed onto the overground network at London Bridge and made the eight-minute journey to South Bermondsey. There was a noticeable police presence on the platform and in the train of mixed MIllwall and Watford supporters. It was pretty boisterous in a light-hearted kind of way.

It was a long-ish walk around the houses to pick-up our match tickets. Inside the ground I nursed my moderately nagging hangover with a couple of quick beers.

My kids were buzzing with excitement. It was their fourth game in their fourth different ground in nine days. I told myself they were getting the bug. Time, of course, will tell. Sipping my beer in the tunnel under the Dockers Stand I watched people coming into the ground. At that point it was hard to equate the fearsome reputation this club engendered with the people I saw around me. Saying that, the number of families or dads with kids or women seemed lower compared to say Brentford. Compared to Legia Warsaw though, it looked like a family day out.

The ground was only twenty-two years old; one of the first of the new build generation of grounds that started popping up post-Hillsborough. On my previous visit it had been open less than a year. New grounds were still a novelty then, and in 1994 The Den had a modest state-of-the-art feel to it. Possibly the oldest of the new grounds, the club might have regretted doing it a few years ahead of the stadium 'bowl' becoming *de rigueur* where filled-in corners could accommodate a few more fans. Millwall had retained the more traditional four-separate-stands-and-open-corners look of earlier eras. The stadium lacked character in that it wasn't a Craven Cottage or even a Plough Lane-era Wimbledon, but it was probably the best of the new grounds. The whole thing was a throwback of sorts – an inner-city football ground surrounded by industrial sites and *social housing*.

There was a sizeable Watford following at the game, and on a bright spring day they made themselves heard. The two teams played out an interesting enough, though somewhat predictable game, with the high-flying visitors comfortably winning 2-0.

It was *different* though. Different to watching games in just about every ground I'd been to. And interestingly, this wasn't a particularly contentious or potentially tense fixture. I noticed a few things.

In looking to abuse a linesman or referee, instead of the kind of exasperated "come on lino, that was offside. You wanker!" Or something at that kind of level of intensity, at Millwall it was something altogether more extreme. Despite it being a fairly run-of-the-mill fixture at the fag-end of a poor relegation season, the Fan

Complaint Level was right up there. When refereeing decisions went against them, fierce-looking grown men in their forties, fifties and even sixties charged out of their seats to the front of the stand to scream apoplectically: "Ref, you cunt! You fucking cunt referee! Ref you're shit. You… are… a… cunt! Ref! Cunt! Fucking cunt!"

I noticed a large group of young blokes in their twenties. They'd adopted that almost uniform 21st century football-going casual look quite well: white trainers, designer jeans, hooded jackets (some with furry elements on the collars), a range of different types of headwear on display, patches on the sleeves of their jackets or chunky-looking knitwear. They weren't English, let alone South East London natives. I tried to work out where they were from by snatches of conversation. They weren't French or German and they were all too pale to be from somewhere in Southern Europe. Dutch? Danish? From somewhere further east perhaps? I couldn't tell. Football in England is quite a tourist attraction but at Millwall? A struggling Millwall at that? Clearly Millwall held an appeal for other reasons.

We sat almost directly over the halfway line. It was a good view. The two thousand plus band of Watford supporters were to our right. They sang pretty much right through the game. One of them, a big bloke, was wearing a bright green sweatshirt. He stood out a bit on a couple of levels. He was singing along with the other Watford fans but wasn't doing anything to draw attention to himself. Then a chant from some Millwall fans went up:

"Who's the fat cunt, who's the fat cunt, who's the fat cunt in the green!?"

The chant was pointed, vicious and lacked humour. What was it like when they played West Ham?

***

I wondered also about Millwall and ratios. In seasons around that time their average home gate hovered around twelve thousand. Why were so many London cabbies Millwall fans? Arsenal, a much bigger club with about five times the number of fans at home games and with a sizeable number of fans who can't get to games, are far less represented in the taxi-driving fraternity in London. Same with Chelsea and Spurs – big clubs, but with seemingly far fewer taxi-driving supporters than Millwall. Why were so many taxi drivers Millwall fans? Was it a scare tactic to put people off thinking about doing a runner?

The other ratio that interested me was the fan-to-hooligan ratio. Without doing any scientific analysis or research, I speculated on what proportion of Millwall's fan base were active or second-level hooligans compared to other London clubs. (I can't back these figures up but would welcome some input at: iltw1979@gmail.com.) I'm ball-parking these figures, but it's the *theory* that counts. The smaller number is the hooligan numbers at the club listed. The second number is their average or optimum home gate *less* visiting supporters. I'm guesstimating these figures for the period up to about 2016: Arsenal three hundred out of fifty-seven thousand, Tottenham five hundred out of thirty-three thousand, West Ham five hundred out of thirty-one thousand, Chelsea five hundred out of thirty-eight thousand and Millwall, a thousand out of ten thousand. How, and why is that? Even if my figures are out, you'll get my point. I'm confident the theory stacks up.

After the game we did another kind of walk around the houses exercise for twenty minutes before coming across a minicab office. Part two of our day's sporting activities was scheduled to start an hour or so later across South London at Wimbledon Greyhound Stadium. Off we went.

I went to Millwall again in March 2018, while I was working on the first draft of this book. I was back in London for a two-week visit that coincided with some of the coldest March weather in history. The mildest of the three weekends I was in London saw Brentford away at Millwall. A few days earlier I'd seen an impressive Brentford win at Burton – my first 'new' football ground in some time.

All the signs for this fixture were good; two in-form teams just outside the play-offs with a few weeks to go.

It was twenty-four years since I'd been to The Den as an away fan. Occasional late nights trawling through hoolie footage on YouTube didn't exactly suggest a warm and friendly welcome in SE16. We met in the Shipwrights Arms near London Bridge station before making the short train journey to South Bermondsey. Fans of both clubs mixed, if not merrily, then certainly without incident, on the train.

"Last time I saw Brentford at Millwall," Owen said as we walked up the long alleyway to the away end, "was at the old Den in 1981. I'd only just turned fifteen. Some bloke outside the ground punched me in the face with a knuckleduster! Fully-grown man he was; I was just a kid."

An entertaining game that Brentford dominated somehow ended in a 1-0 home win, with the goal coming in the first minute. It was a bright, sunny but crisp late winter afternoon. Both sets of fans were in full-ish voice.

We may lament some of the changes in football in the last thirty years, but the introduction of the play-offs isn't one of them. Under the old three-up-and-three-down it would've been season over for all but a handful clubs in the second tier by mid-March. In season 2017-18 clubs down as far as eleventh had something to play for until late April.

I'd arranged to meet some friends in Greenwich that night – which seems a reasonable thing to do after a game at The Den. However, a post-match away fans alleyway lock-in by the police followed by three trains meant just two-and-a-half miles (as the crow flies) to Greenwich became a circuitous journey via London Bridge and Canary Wharf taking nearly two hours.

Millwall, that afternoon, was a bit of a throwback – but in a largely positive sense.

Footnote: For eleven years until 2017 Millwall Football Club lived under the threat of ground closure and relocation. Millwall is only a few miles from Central London and within one of the last genuinely working-class areas of inner London yet to be gentrified. So, it was no surprise to learn that Millwall's biggest threat for many years was from property developers. It's an interesting story and again no surprise to learn of the links between those property developers – an offshore registered company called Renewal – and former Lewisham councillors and the current Lewisham council. In the end the local community and football won-out, quashing the developers' plans. However, prime inner-city London real estate (exactly four miles from Trafalgar Square) will no doubt again attract the attention of property sharks before too long. I just hope the local community and Millwall fans are as resistant, resilient and strong as they were for round one. *The Guardian* newspaper followed this story over a number of years. If you're interested in how a football club at the heart of its community was nearly destroyed to serve the ambitions of property developers, *The Guardian* online archive is a great place to start.

I LIKE TO WATCH

Going To The Dogs

Gentrification has steadily engulfed English football – significantly at its most senior level in the Premier League, with a rippling effect to varying degrees down the divisions. A day at the cricket is different. Following rugby union generally delivers up a far more *polished experience* than a generation ago. Rugby league is now a summer game.

One sport that seems to have resisted changed, and perhaps embedded itself even more firmly within British working-class culture is greyhound racing. A night at the dogs is a fun, cheap, and *uncomplicated* way to spend a night out. End-of-the-working-week drunken bonhomie seems to be the default setting for many of the punters. An evening meeting can feel like stepping into one of the lighter scenes of a Ken Loach film.

"Booked out," Owen told me over the phone. "We can't get a table."

We'd decided to do Owlerton dogs in Sheffield on the Saturday evening of Brentford's game at Rotherham in early 2016. Seven of us had driven up in a people carrier on what turned-out to be a gruelling

The scoreboard at Belle Vue Stadium, Manchester.

twenty-hour day out. We'd hoped to round the evening off with a leisurely meal at Owlerton and enjoy the races from a table. Too late, and too popular – we were, and it was. When we got there the place was heaving with down-to-earth Yorkshire folk having a good night out. It was standing room only in the bars and restaurant area. We quaffed pints and ate our sausage, chips and mushy peas standing up as faces around us got redder and voices louder.

Greyhound racing in England is on a steep downward trajectory. Reality TV, Xboxes and online porn in the warmth and comfort of one's own home offer a cheaper, less involved alternative.

Compared to other heavily-attended sports, greyhound racing is a relatively modern phenomenon. The first greyhound race took place in 1926 at Belle Vue in Manchester. The following year, with new tracks popping up all over the country, over five million people attended greyhound meetings. By 1929 that figure was sixteen million. At its peak there were nearly three hundred tracks in Britain – thirty-three of which were in London. In 2017 there were less than thirty tracks left and attendances had slipped to under two million, a decline of nearly forty per cent in the previous decade. It's not a sport that's fashionable in the right quarters, and unlikely to attract much in the way of investment. But for punters, it was still a lot of fun.

Tying in a greyhound meeting with football was becoming almost a tradition. I'd done Romford before a Spurs vs Blackpool game, Crayford after a North London derby and Wimbledon after a Millwall vs Watford game. Wimbledon and Crayford, particularly, had been great nights out. A Saturday morning meeting at Romford hadn't exactly brought the punters out. Apart from Owen and me, and few odd herberts dotted around the place, the only spectators there was a stag party sitting near us. By about 1 p.m. it was evident they'd peaked too early as words were clearly slurred and a drink or two spilt.

Crayford was a memorable night out. Owen, Martin Cross and I headed down there after the November 2012 North London derby. Arsenal won 5-2 and I met the two Spurs fans with some of their other Spurs mates after the game in Charing Cross Road. I didn't turn on the bragging rights though. (I'd actually been very disappointed with elements of that particular North London derby; the whole experience had changed beyond recognition.) We went to a few of those traditional old Central London pubs then grabbed a train from Charing Cross out to Crayford in Kent. Is it really Kent though or outer outer South East London? At Crayford, with the voices around us, it sounded like we were out somewhere on an extended stretch of the Old Kent Road. I noticed that evening, and at other times, that a night at the dogs is largely an *Anglo* night out.

Quietly savouring Arsenal's North London derby win with two Tottenham fans, I enjoyed a 1970s Berni inn-style meal; starter, roast dinner and dessert washed down with a lot of cheap Sauv Blanc. It was a relaxing, little-effort-required evening with a friendly waitress calling us all "darlin" at every given turn and someone coming to our table to take our bets. Quite how I later navigated Crayford-Charing Cross-Paddington and a walk to my hotel, I'm not sure. My head was pounding the following morning; I was due to meet my brother in Hammersmith at noon to go to Fulham vs Sunderland. Thank fuck for Panadol and Red Bull.

Belle Vue in Manchester is another good night at the dogs. We went there after the Stockport vs Tranmere game when Tranmere stayed up. The old scoreboard at Belle Vue is a thing of quite rare beauty; I could look at it for the best part of a whole race meeting. The Mancs know how to have a good time on a low budget.

At Newcastle we stood outside the main bar-restaurant at the back of a small but very steep terrace. Drinking white wine from plastic pint cups didn't seem to raise an eyebrow amongst any of the locals.

Doncaster was also a good one, though you need a decent supply of patience if planning on calling a cab to get back into town after the last race. We went there after another time at Rotherham United.

One night we ended-up at Shawfield Greyhound Stadium in Rutherglen, on the outskirts of Glasgow. It was the third leg in a sporting triple-header that day after Airdrieonians vs Brechin City and Scotland vs Georgia at Ibrox. We knew when we visited Shawfield that it was the last greyhound track in Scotland. What we didn't know was that it had once also been home to Clyde FC. In fact, Clyde were the original owners in 1898 with the greyhound association first becoming tenants in 1930, and then buying the stadium in 1935. Not seeing a ball kicked there and Clyde having not played there for nearly thirty years meant a claim on adding the ground to the football list wasn't allowed.

There was something homely and familiar about all of these greyhound stadiums. The facilities were all pretty basic – even the more supposedly *upmarket* areas like the restaurants. At each stadium the furniture looked like a mix of stuff from a factory canteen and a 1970s steak house on the brink of receivership. To a person though, all the staff I've ever come across at a greyhound stadium – on the gates, in the bars and restaurants, taking bets – have all been friendliness personified. It's an industry that actually treats its customers *like* customers.

I'd done most of these dog tracks with Owen Francis and linked them in with other sporting events nearby. He was thus a little aggrieved when I added Swindon to the list on a work night-out from Bristol.

"Snidey cunt." He moaned the following weekend.

I met Owen at Nottingham Greyhound Stadium late one Tuesday morning in March 2018. We were tying-in Nottingham dogs with the Burton vs Brentford game that night. The 'on-Trent' bit about Burton had suggested, to us at least, that Burton was near Nottingham. But it was actually closer to Birmingham. Owen got the train up there while I drove; I was heading further north the next day while he was heading back to London. I missed the first two races. Owen filled me in on his day to that point.

"I walked from Nottingham station," he began. "This is a really good place for sport. I walked past Forest's ground, Notts County, Trent Bridge and the race course before you get here. Five sporting locations all in a row."

I got us a couple of beers.

"Did the old bird serve you?" He asked. "White hair?"

"Yeah, why?"

"She's worked here since it opened in 1980."

"Thirty-eight years!? That's loyalty. She was probably in her late sixties when she started."

There were perhaps another twenty-five people in the bar area. Every twenty minutes or so we all left the indoor comfort and warmth to stand outside for a little over a minute to watch the dogs going into the starting traps, then bolt around the track.

"See that bloke," Owen pointed out a man in his sixties wearing a grey anorak. "Before you got here he was watching the race, cheering on some dog or other. Must've had a bit of money on it. Anyway, his dog fell away a bit on the last straight. Finished about fourth. He throws the betting slip on the ground. 'Idle cunt,' he says."

I've done a few greyhound tracks in Australia as well. Bendigo is pretty functional, but Wentworth Park in Glebe in Sydney is borderline grandiose. The facilities are positively 21st century at a stadium that's in the equivalent of London's Kensington or Notting Hill. The Hobart track is 'modern Australian' (a term normally used to describe food which is a fusion of different nationalities or styles) – a multi-purpose affair that serves horse racing, the trots and greyhounds. It's multi-purpose usefulness eradicates any chance of it developing an identity or any character.

A night at the dogs is a throwback to a different age and time – a less complex age and time. At face value it's almost bizarre – dogs chasing a fake hare around a track in a race that might last forty seconds. It's not the easiest racing sport to follow with the naked eye. It's a sport for people who enjoyed watching *The Sweeney*, *Minder* or *Auf Wiedersehen Pet* a generation ago. It's the *right* night out after an afternoon at football. It retains a working-class authenticity – also arguably on the decline. Greyhound racing's future clearly isn't bright, but it's worth experiencing before it's too late.

I LIKE TO WATCH

Western Bulldogs

When I arrived in Australia in late 2000 I already knew there was a Premier League-level of media coverage and general obsession with top-level Australian rules football. I didn't know at that stage that they didn't play on a rectangular pitch like other football codes. Aussie rules is played on a cricket pitch – an expansive oval. I knew little about the game, but if I'd wanted it to remain that way, I would've needed to bury my head in the sand.

At this early point for a predominately UK readership I need to offer some background, factual stuff, and some observations and opinions on the game. Apologies at this point to any Aussie rules followers – you can probably skip the next few pages.

- As stated above, Aussie rules is played on a cricket pitch. This presumably came about because most suburbs and towns had an existing cricket oval when the game started. There is also a widely-held belief that Aussie rules started largely as an activity to keep cricketers fit during winter.

- It's an eighteen-a-side game. Teams also get four players on the bench who can interchange with on-field players throughout the game – as long as only eighteen are on the pitch at any one time. There is a limit to the number of changes during a game. (There are some variations to these rules according to which league(s) the teams play in.)

- There are a number of positions, but no goalkeeper or 'stopper'. All players have the same rights in terms of which body parts that can be used to play the ball.

- You can kick the ball – from your hands, or while it's on the ground – to another player or to kick (score) a goal.

- You can hand-ball (ie, punch) the ball to another player but you can't throw it.

- There are four posts at each end of the ground. A clean kick through the middle two is a goal which is six points. A deflected (by the defending team) kick through the middle posts is a point. Any kind of kick, or deflection between either set of outer posts is called a 'behind' which is one point.

- It's high-scoring. Think basketball-type scores.

- The game is played in four quarters with a change of ends at each quarter. The half-time break is longer, and the teams go off the pitch (which they don't at quarter and three-quarter time).

- Each quarter is twenty minutes – of game time. With stoppages added back in, a quarter will usually run to somewhere around thirty minutes.

- There are no yellow cards, sin bins or sendings off – despite the highly physical nature of the game and resultant argy-bargy, player clashes, shoves, punches thrown etc. Here is the first major flaw in the game. A player can commit a serious foul on an opposition player and give away only a free kick. The player who commits the offence will stay on the pitch for the rest of the game. The fouled player – if it's serious enough – may miss the rest of the game or be incapacitated in some way. The offender will face a 'tribunal' early the following week. At the tribunal he will receive some kind of censure – usually a ban of a game or two, maybe more. So, the team offended *against* receives no *benefit* as a result of the sanction. The offending player's team receive no sanction during the game in which he's committed the offence. Assuming the offending player is a first-choice team member (likely – he started the last game) then the *advantage* as such is gained by the teams he is not allowed to play against in subsequent weeks. Meanwhile the team with a potentially seriously injured player has to play out the rest of the game with some degree of disadvantage. Pretty stupid rule, eh?

- It's officially a national game. The top league is the Australian Football League (AFL) which currently comprises eighteen teams – a mix of traditional clubs, a couple of relocated clubs and some franchise clubs.

- The AFL evolved out of the VFL (Victorian Football League). The VFL was twelve Victoria-based clubs which operated for ninety-odd years until 1990 when it was renamed to reflect a broader-based national focus.

- The VFL season consisted of twenty-two games, with teams playing each other home and away. The AFL, with eighteen teams, still sees each team play twenty-two games. Here's the second major flaw. How can the league be a level playing field when teams don't play each other an equal number of times? Who wants to play last year's Premiers twice when some teams only play them once? Who wants to play last year's wooden spooners once when you could get two chances of giving them a flogging?

- The Aussie rules heartlands are the southern states – Victoria, Tasmania, South Australia and Western Australia. It's only really with the expansionist plans of the game's administrators in the last thirty-odd years that Aussie rules has developed a serious following in New South Wales and Queensland – traditionally rugby states. The NRL (rugby league) has one Victorian team, but has remained largely a New South Wales and Queensland game. The AFL's expansion has been markedly more successful, on all levels. Significantly more people attend Aussie rules games than rugby league (or union) games. Since 2000, average NRL crowds have hovered around fifteen thousand through the season. AFL games have averaged more than double that. During that period the AFL also added two franchise teams who effectively started with no supporter base.

- The eighteen teams currently in the AFL are made-up of two teams from Queensland (who don't share a stadium), two teams from Sydney (don't share a stadium), two teams in Adelaide (who share), two teams from Western Australia (who share), nine teams in Melbourne (who share two stadiums), and Geelong near Melbourne who have their own stadium but are obliged/forced to use one of the Melbourne stadiums on occasion and for big season-end games. Thus, the whole concept of home and away games being a *leveller* goes out the window. This is the third major flaw. *Home advantage* is a variable concept, and variable advantage. All the current teams in Victoria are *traditional* teams who were in the VFL. The non-Victorian teams are a mix of traditional teams (who may have moved there or come from a different league in that area), and franchise teams who have been created to fit the AFL's *strategic growth plan*. However you look at it, the teams that don't share their stadiums are at a distinct advantage.

- While *having a beer at the footy* is a big thing, the game is pretty tough, and in general it's a blokey kind of thing, crowds are generally well-behaved – certainly relative to the big attendances. There is no spectator segregation and there is a far higher ratio of women and families at AFL games than rugby league and 'soccer' in Australia.

- There is a player salary cap. Though this can get weighted for various reasons, including how expensive it is to live in Sydney compared to other places. It can also vary to support the foundation and development of a new team.

- Fixtures are not generated at random. Big fixtures are scheduled in line with commercial imperatives. A prime example is Anzac Day, a public holiday and important date in Australia's cultural and military history. The MCG, which holds 100,000, hosts the Anzac Day fixture. It is second – profile and viewing-wise – only to the Grand Final, the season's showcase winner-takes-all season decider. However, the Anzac Day game is only ever played between *two* clubs – Collingwood and Essendon. Both clubs are traditional big Melbourne clubs with large supporter bases and significant influence within the league and media. They alternate, playing home or away each season. While this doesn't actually mean playing at a different ground, it means that over time they will share the financial benefits roughly equally. No other team gets a look-in. So while there is a salary cap across each team for players, varying degrees of revenue is stimulated by each club based on other, easily-identifiable criteria: gate receipts, advertising and merchandise spring most readily to mind. No one can genuinely argue that a club won't get what it deserves through its own commercial endeavours, but why should the same two clubs get a *free kick* from the league in terms of bumper gate receipts every 25 April? Why don't any other clubs get to play that fixture?

- The AFL is not shy about tinkering with the rules in order to make the game more entertaining for spectators. They trial minor rule changes in pre-season non-competitive games.

- The Premiership is not decided using the who finishes top system as per football in Europe. After the twenty-two games have been played the top eight have a mini-tournament of their own, with the last game being the Grand Final to determine who the Premiers will be. This mini-tournament, known generally as 'the finals', is an interesting one. It's weighted to give advantage to the teams who finished first and second. It's very tough to win the competition overall from a fifth to eighth place finish, although the Western Bulldogs won the Premiership after finishing seventh in 2016. You'll need to pay close attention to this bit: In week one fifth plays eighth and the loser is out. Sixth plays seventh and the loser is out. First is at home to fourth. The next week the loser of first vs fourth plays one of the teams that won in the fifth to eighth group. The winner of first vs fourth has a week off. Same happens with the second vs third game. In each case the team who finished first to fourth but lost their first finals game is at home in week two. Two games the second week, with the two losing teams getting eliminated. In the third week it's the winners from that first to fourth group in week one at home to the two teams who won in week two. This week's games are hard for the team playing a third week in a row. Not only has the other team had a week off, but this team may have played away twice in a row already. Week three's two winners then play-off for the Premiership in the Grand Final at the MCG in week four. It sounds a bit involved but it's not. It's a fair and quite exciting system once you get past the notion that finishing top doesn't necessarily mean you're going to be Premiers that year. Only two teams have won the Premiership from a regular season finish outside the top four – the Western Bulldogs from seventh spot in 2016, and Adelaide from fifth in the late 1990s.

- The AFL is the national league. Australian rules football is the *name* of the game. However, the AFL holds such a dominant position in the game and is so often referred to that the terms "AFL" and "Aussie rules" are virtually interchangeable (well, one for the other at any rate). Many people talk about "playing AFL". Some die-hards find this irritating, though most people don't seem to notice or care.

In 2001 there were sixteen teams in the AFL. I wasn't going to be able to avoid it; not that I particularly wanted to. I was interested. Who was I going to follow? Essendon had won the Premiership the season before, losing only one game along the way. Although they haven't won it since and have experienced a range of trials and tribulations along the way, I kind of saw them as the Man United of Aussie rules. I ruled-out following them on these grounds; also, I didn't want to be a bandwagon-jumper. I also ruled-out Richmond, another of the big Melbourne clubs, a bit of a sleeping giant at that point and for many years afterwards until they finally won the Premiership after a thirty-seven-year gap in 2017. I ruled Richmond out because my then father-in-law *barracked for* (supported) them. His persuading and cajoling was too much after a while. Hawthorn I ruled-out purely on the basis of their yellow and brown kit.

In January 2001 I was sitting on the floor of the rented flat I'd just moved into in Melbourne. I was on the phone to an insurance broker, getting quotes.

"You're a Pom," he said. Bit forward, bit brash, I thought. But I didn't say anything, otherwise the "stuck-up" bit could be applied before "Pom".

"That's right. Just arrived."

"Good on ya. No more warm beer, eh?"

I laughed, kind of. Never heard that one before.

"Who do you barrack for? Have you picked a team yet?"

I had this type of conversation numerous times that first half of 2001.

That 2001 Aussie rules season started in early April. I followed it extensively on TV, learning the rules, getting to know who the key players were, who the big clubs were historically, and more. But it wasn't until mid-May that I went to a game. I picked a match at Carlton's Prince Park ground – at that point the last genuine home ground in Melbourne still being used in the AFL. The other Melbourne clubs shared the MCG and the Docklands-based stadium (Colonial, Telstra Dome, Etihad, Marvel – various names over the years).

Carlton played some of their bigger games away from Princes Park. Princes Park (Optus Oval at the time – but with a plethora of sponsors since) was an old-style ground with terraces and a mix of old and new stands. The writing was on the wall in terms of the AFL agenda regarding where clubs played. Princes Park belonged in a different, less shiny, era. My rationale back then was to see a game there before it closed. I got there again in 2004 and Carlton played its last top-level game there in 2005. It remains in use for lower level games and as an administrative and training base for Carlton Football Club.

I don't know why I left it as late as 19 May to go to a game. The MCG and Docklands were only short train rides from where I was living. I'd already been to a Test match and a couple of ODIs at the MCG. To get to Carlton I had to get a train to Flinders Street in the city centre and then a tram north to Parkville, the heart of Melbourne University territory. At the time I was working two days a week for a small publisher at the other end of Carlton, close to the Melbourne

Museum. I felt a low-level affinity, of sorts, to the area. Carlton beat eventual Premiers Brisbane Lions that day by a thumping 142-68 in front of 21,997. It started at 2.10 p.m. and finished about 4.50 p.m. It felt like a long afternoon. That game turned out to be Brisbane's last defeat of the season.

That 2001 season I ended-up going to four Richmond games, though still didn't feel any affinity with the club. One of those Richmond games was on the afternoon of the night that the British Lions played in Melbourne. I went to that as well. The contrast between the two events was stark. The afternoon's Aussie rules game at the MCG saw Richmond comfortably beat Hawthorn in front of a lacklustre 52,189. That's a big crowd by most standards, but at the MCG it still meant just about every other seat was empty. And on a dull, on-off rainy day many fans spent most of the afternoon in the shelter of the numerous bars.

Melburnians were treated to an altogether different experience when Australia played the British Lions at Docklands. The travelling British comfortably made-up over half the 56,105 crowd – a stadium record that stood for twelve years – until the next British Lions game there. The noise was intense and relentless, the atmosphere close to spine-tingling. After a close start to the game the Aussies ran away with it, winning 35-14.

The 2001 AFL finals series rolled around in September with predictable fanfare. I'd been to six games by the end of the regular twenty-two-week season. Grand Final day was traditionally the last Saturday in September. I had tickets that night for Northern Irish pop-punk outfit Ash at the Corner Hotel, about three stones' throws from the MCG. An afternoon in front of the TV to watch my first

Grand Final beckoned. Then I changed my mind.

"I'm going to see if I can get in," I told Carla.

"What? The Granny?"

"Yep."

I left at about noon, getting the train from Bentleigh to Richmond, then walking the seven or eight minutes to the MCG. The place was buzzing. Essendon – equal leading historical winners with sixteen wins – had reached their second Grand Final in a row. They were playing Brisbane Lions, who were in their first as a Brisbane-based team. In a previous incarnation as Fitzroy they'd played in and won a war-time trophy in 1944, and a regular peace-time flag in 1922.

Part of my rationale in reckoning I might be able to get a ticket was that there was a non-Melbourne team playing, a team with a more modest supporter base. There may have been something in that because it turned out to be the lowest MCG Grand Final crowd since 1955.

I had $200 in my pocket and some change. There were a few people milling about but no obvious touts or 'scalpers'. And they'd be asking too much. The only way I reckoned I was going to get in was through a no-show in group. A single ticket wouldn't get too appealing an offer from a tout. A group with a spare might look kinder upon someone on their own, who was genuine about seeing the game.

By chance I saw a bloke I knew, and we got chatting. He had a ticket. He started canvassing on my behalf and within five minutes I was negotiating a price with two blokes and a girl from Brisbane. The ticket was $98 face value. They said they'd bought four tickets at $400 each as part of a corporate package.

"$180 is all I have," I said, leaving a $20 note and change in my pocket. "Here, take $170. Leave me enough to get a beer inside."

They looked at each other.

"Look, there's cash. Deal done." I was holding out my hand. "You might get more, but there's not a lot going on around here."

First bounce (kick-off) was still an hour or so away but there was a big preamble to these games, a lot of which was worth watching.

One of the blokes nodded, and they took the money. Moments later I was inside the MCG making my way up to the third tier of the Great Southern Stand.

I left a message on Carla's voicemail. "I'm in."

I was excited about getting to a Grand Final in my first year in Australia. Along with the Melbourne Cup and the Ashes it's one of the real icon events in the Aussie sporting calendar. I knew enough about the game by then to follow it properly. Listening to people from Brisbane beside me I realised I knew more about the game than them. In fact, I seemed to be surrounded by people who were there for the occasion as opposed to fans *barracking hard* for one team or the other.

I wanted Brisbane to win; Essendon being the Man United of the AFL to me. They were favourites and their supporters outnumbered their counterparts from Queensland. It was a fairly even game until the last quarter with the lead changing hands several times. Brisbane led at the end of the first and third quarters, whilst Essendon were up by 14 at half-time. Brisbane pulled away strongly towards the end to win by 26 points.

I stayed for the presentations and speeches, though they seemed to drag on interminably. I was half-expecting the groundsman and his dog to go up to collect a medal (and a bone), along with the catering manager and others. I watched for a while before making my way home.

Essendon and Brisbane Lions line-up before the 2001 AFL Grand Final.

The following season I went to a handful of games again, whilst maintaining my relatively high TV intake of the AFL. Mind you, anyone who's lived in Australia will know of the relative non-merits of Australian free-to-air TV; sport is one of the only watchable things on the box. Hence, I watched quite a lot of Aussie rules back then. I went to three games in June and early July, including a road trip to Adelaide to take in a bit of sightseeing and get a new ground on the list.

Nearly two seasons in, a Grand Final under my belt, an interstate game done and yet I still couldn't answer the "who do you barrack for?" question.

On Sunday 28 July 2002 I went to Docklands for the game between the Western Bulldogs and North Melbourne Kangaroos. (I'd also been in the stadium the night before to see a touring Leeds United team play Colo Colo of Chile.) The Kangaroos were headed for a top half finish, the Bulldogs on their way to lower mid-table. That afternoon saw the last game and retirement of Bulldogs veteran Tony Liberatore. At thirty-six he was in fact remarkably old for a top-level Aussie rules player, where career spans take a quite different shape to football. Many Aussie rules players are making a big impact with their clubs by about eighteen, and many finish their top-level careers before thirty.

Liberatore was a 5ft 3in midfielder, a 'tagger'. Despite his diminutive stature he'd made the very best of his abilities, looked after himself and had a lengthy career. Football fans – for 'tagger' think a Nobby Stiles, David Batty-type midfield player.

This was my eleventh AFL game. And for the first time I felt myself really willing one team – the Bulldogs – to win. Why? Caught-up in the emotion because it was Libba's last game? Appealing to me because they wore the colours of the Union Flag and the name 'Bulldogs' suggested a certain British*ness*? There are many factors at play when you choose a club to follow in any sport. Often, it's simply in the family, or you're very young and a winning team of that era grabs your attention. But when you're thirty-seven, living in a different country with a budding interest in a new sport, what *are* the deciding factors? I'd ruled-out Essendon, Hawthorn and Richmond for reasons already stated. I'd seen St Kilda a couple of times but there was something I didn't like. Carlton could've been, maybe... but that dark blue was a bit close to the boys from White Hart Lane for an exiled Gooner. Following a team from outside Victoria didn't really appeal and seemed a bit of a contrary, for-the-sake-of-it type of thing to do. That didn't leave many. When I finally felt like I *really* wanted one of the teams I was watching to win, that was it. Their underdog status, relative unfashionability, western suburbs working-class blue-collar kind of aura made them all the more appealing. I didn't want to jump on a bandwagon. My choosing of the Western Bulldogs as *my* team was echoed a decade later when, at Oakland Coliseum outside San Francisco, I felt myself willing the A's to victory.

The following day I told a workmate that I'd finally picked a team. "It'll be a rollercoaster following them!" He laughed.

There was only a month or so left in the season. The Bulldogs probably needed to win four of their last five to put them in contention for a top eight finish and thus finals action in September. Two wins and three defeats saw them finish twelfth.

The following season I went to seven Bulldogs games, which included their only three wins. They finished bottom. In 2004 I went to five games. From there the club's form improved and I started going more regularly. I was fully aware that my growing interest in the Western Bulldogs was another kind of *Arsenal replacement* thing. I was enjoying it though.

Over the next few seasons I went quite regularly for someone who lived two hours from Melbourne, had a demanding job and young family. I also wanted to get in a few 'away grounds' or at least different grounds to add to the list. Some of the smaller AFL clubs played a couple of home games a season in different cities or towns around the country in order to help *build their brand*. It's good for tourism, with thousands of fans visiting places they might not normally go to. I assumed there were big $ incentives involved as well. I saw the Bulldogs play St Kilda in Launceston, Tasmania in 2003. I also went to Perth for an away game against Fremantle, the Gabba in Brisbane and the Gold Coast for away games in Queensland, Sydney at the SCG and a couple of trips to Canberra. There were also a couple of family holidays which included Bulldogs 'home' games in Darwin (about two thousand miles from the Bulldogs' base in Melbourne's west) in 2007 and 2009.

Western Bulldogs vs Geelong, Docklands Stadium, Melbourne, 2006.

I started taking my kids to sport in 2010 and 2011. Henry, the oldest, was still a few months off five when I dragged him along to a Melbourne Victory vs Boca Juniors friendly in mid-2010. For a few years an Aussie rules game was just too long for my young children to watch. At a few games they were packing up their drawing books and ready to leave at the long break.

"It's only half-time." I told them.

For a few seasons I eased-off on the Aussie rules games a bit. Trips to Melbourne with my sons took in more 'soccer' games than previously, and we chucked-in the odd Melbourne Storm rugby league game as well.

In 2015 I went to just three Western Bulldogs games, one of which was a pre-season game at Ballarat (one of those outlier grounds only used occasionally for top-level games) so I could get a new ground on the list.

In 2016 I didn't go to *any* Western Bulldogs games in the regular twenty-two game season. They had a good season though, finishing seventh – meaning they'd get to play in the Finals. Seventh position that season was a bit of an oddity though. The three teams directly above only won one more game each than Bulldogs, and teams who finished in the top three spots had only two more wins. Points-wise, seventh wasn't as lowly a spot as it had been in previous seasons. Even so, at the start of the finals the Western Bulldogs were quoted at 67-1 to win the Premiership in that handicapped eight-horse race. They'd need to win four games in a row to do it. But this was also the year that Leicester City won the English Premier League and Chicago Cubs went on to win the World Series after over a century. The year of the under(Bull)dogs?

Finishing seventh meant a tough run of games. One defeat and you're gone. First game away from home and then if you manage to stay the distance, two more games away from home, culminating in a Grand Final against a team who have *probably* had two home games and week off during the finals.

On Thursday 8 September the Western Bulldogs travelled to Perth to play sixth-place West Coast Eagles in an Elimination Final. Melbourne to Perth is a long old haul, and very often a tricky place to go for Melbourne clubs. The Bulldogs' last regular season game had been in Perth against the other WA side, Fremantle. They'd lost by 20 points.

I watched the West Coast vs Western Bulldogs game on TV. I hadn't been to a game all season; my support drifting a bit in the previous few years. The Bulldogs fielded many players I didn't know. Thinking that my evening's TV viewing would end with a Bulldogs defeat, I was prepared with a couple of magazines beside me on the couch to get stuck into once West Coast pulled away, score-wise. It didn't happen. The Bulldogs won comfortably 99-52. They kicked fourteen goals to West Coast's seven. It was the first time the Bulldogs had won a finals game outside Victoria. My magazines stayed where they were. Buoyed, I decided I'd go their next game, against the loser of the following night's Geelong vs Hawthorn game.

On Friday 16 September the Western Bulldogs faced Hawthorn in the Semi-Final at the MCG. I took my sons Henry, a Bulldogs supporter, and Louis, somehow a St Kilda fan. We went with an old work friend of mine, Zack Harvey and his wife and daughter. They were Hawthorn fans. The Bulldogs faced a daunting task against the team that had won the last three Premierships. At quarter-time Hawthorn were ahead 22-11, and at half-time by a single point. In the third quarter the game turned with the Bulldogs kicking six goals to surge into an 18-point three-quarter-time lead. That surge continued early in the last quarter with the Bulldogs getting out to a 32-point lead. All over. A late rally by Hawthorn closed the gap to 23 points at the end. It was an exciting, surprising win for the under(Bull)dogs.

Next up, away to Greater Western Sydney Giants; a not well-liked, but well-drilled franchise team. The finals was down to four teams. On the Friday night Geelong lost to Sydney at the MCG. Sydney had finished top of the ladder at the end of the regular season, albeit on the same points as Geelong and Hawthorn. They would play their fifth Grand Final in twelve seasons the following week. The Giants vs Western Bulldogs game was scheduled for the Saturday evening.

The Giants are the newest addition to the AFL, having their debut season only in 2012. At this point a couple of things should be put in context. Tasmania is a hot-bed of Aussie rules football. Many great players have come off that picturesque island of half a million or so people to play in the VFL, then AFL. Peter Hudson, Royce Hart and Matthew Richardson are just three on a lengthy list of Tasmanians who have played top-level Aussie rules. To the romantic, purist or even just *fair-minded* person an expansion of the AFL from sixteen to eighteen teams should've included a Tasmanian team. Maybe one of the established clubs from either Hobart or Launceston, or an amalgamation of several clubs, or a brand-new start – a club the whole state could get behind. It didn't happen. Instead, new teams were established in the Gold Coast and Western Sydney – both traditionally rugby league territories. Both have growing populations, so there's a double whammy incentive to expand here. From a commercial perspective it made business sense, but was it the *right* thing to do?

The Saturday of the Giants vs Bulldogs game I had a long-planned trip to take my sons to Melbourne to celebrate Henry's birthday – a sushi train, shopping and the stage show of Roald Dahl's *Matilda* on the agenda. We had a fun afternoon. Then we rushed back to the car. I didn't have a working car radio so while the likes of Jack White, Kasabian and the Black Keys played through the speakers, my sons kept checking the Bulldogs app on my phone for the score. At half-time the Bulldogs led by 9 points. I hot-footed it home as fast as possible without drawing too much attention to my driving. We got back in time to see the closing seconds of the third quarter which ended with Sydney Franchise a single point ahead. I poured myself a very large glass of white wine.

The final quarter began. I started-off perched on a barstool. Then, as the last quarter unfolded, I just paced around the room.

***

The scoring went like this (Greater Western Sydney score first):

61-60

62-60

68-60

74-60   Still early, but not looking good.

74-66

74-67

74-68

74-69   About halfway through the quarter.

74-75

74-81

80-81

80-82

81-82

82-82   3:53 to go. GWS attacking in waves.

82-88

83-88   Bulldogs in the GWS 50-metre area. Free shot on goal. Tory Dickson lets the clock wind down. The siren goes. The Bulldogs have won. He kicks for goal, but it hits the post for a point.

83-89   The Western Bulldogs are in the Grand Final for the first time since 1961 – the first team to come from seventh position to get there. My kids tell me I cried. During the last few minutes and at the end of the game the TV camera turned to an ecstatic Tony Liberatore in the crowd. His son Tom was playing.

"My first Bulldogs game was the last game he played." I told them. I took a big gulp of wine. And another. And then I started to calm down.

***

I hadn't been a Western Bulldogs member for a few years at this point. There was no easy way of getting a ticket at face value. I wasn't going to queue-sleep outside a ticket agency for three days. It had been a tough year financially with limited income in my fledgling business, but I had some dough in reserve – 'emergency money'. I went to bed undecided.

I woke up early on the Sunday morning. On one level I was surprised at how I felt about it. I hadn't been to many games in recent years. Yet I felt a wave of euphoria. Even if you *weren't* a Bulldogs fan this was the stuff of sporting fairy tales: the working-class underdog club, only one previous Premiership (in 1954), making the Grand Final from seventh. They were a club that no one really disliked, one that fans of other clubs admitted to having a soft spot for.

I went online. Corporate packages; there wasn't going to be any change out of four figures. I scrolled through the various options. All were offering similar deals. I justified it to myself in part because I hadn't been to many games in recent years and hadn't done a flight and accommodation combo for an interstate game since 2011. I also justified it on another level – one that told me this might never happen again in my lifetime, and even if it did, even if the Bulldogs went on a roll and played in three or four in a ten-year period, the first one would always be the most memorable. $1400; I hit 'pay'.

My match ticket had a face value of $285. The remaining grand and more was for the most expensive breakfast I will ever eat. It was a nice breakfast though. With entertainment. And I snaffled down about six beers to accompany it.

I was one of maybe a thousand people in a hospitality area at Etihad Stadium, the other top-level Melbourne Aussie rules ground. It was just two miles across the city from the MCG where the Grand Final was due to start at 2.30 p.m. We had a compere, TV comedian

Dave Hughes and a panel of speakers which included an ex-Aussie rules coach, and the then Collingwood player, the extrovert Dane Swan.

I was on a table of ten which comprised a father and son, two couples and four blokes on their own. The father and son, it transpired, did this every year. Neither were fans of either club. The two couples were excited and chatted amongst themselves. Us four blokes shared our Western Bulldogs *journeys*. One of them had flown down from Queensland.

"Do we have any Sydney supporters in the room?" Dave Hughes, MCing, asked. A little bit of cheering and handclapping from maybe ten per cent of the room. "And do we have any Doggies fans in the room?" The inevitable much bigger roar went up.

"It's a long time, fifty-five years, since the Bulldogs played in the Grand Final. Is there anyone in the room who was at the game?" I looked around. Five or six hands were raised. Hughes then asked one of them for a brief anecdote about the day.

"And is there anyone in the room who was at the 1954 Final, when the Bulldogs won their only Premiership?" A hand went up on a table near the front.

"Wow!" said Hughes, "and where in the G did you watch the game from?"

"I played in it," came the reply.

Included in our $1400 corporate package was a match programme. Well, at least I didn't need have to shell-out $15 now. After the breakfast we filed-out of Etihad Stadium and onto buses to take us across town to the MCG.

I've been to many a sporting event on my own and never given it a thought. But the really big games – FA Cup Finals, European finals,

The Ashes and stuff – I've done with friends. I did feel something was missing as I walked across Yarra Park to the MCG. This was a day I wanted to talk through with someone.

Sydney were favourites. They'd finished top during the regular twenty-two match season, but had had an early stutter in the finals, and like the Bulldogs, were playing for the fourth week in a row. I didn't feel particularly confident about the outcome, but the Bulldogs had had a remarkable run of form to get here. Like fans of the smaller clubs in many sports, reaching the ultimate stage can almost feel like it's enough to just get that far. Sydney were playing their third Grand Final in five years. No Bulldogs player had ever played in a Grand Final.

I worked my way up to the fourth tier of the Great Southern Stand and found my seat. It was perfect. I was on the end of a row with the entrance just behind me and I was sitting in line with the goals looking towards the city. First bounce was still some time off, so I went down to the bar bought a couple of beers and found myself somewhere to perch. I didn't want to sit in my seat until all the official preamble started. I read a bit of the programme and flicked through Facebook for a bit. I felt a bit of a fraud in some ways. My *journey* as a Bulldogs fan was only fourteen years – the last few of which had been pretty much from my armchair. There were people in the MCG who'd waited fifty years for this.

The AFL does the pre-match pomp stuff pretty well, even if it is a bit drawn-out. The pre-match entertainment included music from the Living End – who are always good live; seen them at many festivals over the years, a bloke called Vance Joy, and Sting. Sting of The Police. The last time I saw Sting on stage was with The Police at Hammersmith Palais in 1979.

Welcome to Country, national anthem and other formalities done

– it was nearly 2.30 p.m. The Bulldogs won the toss and chose to kick to the city end. (In Aussie rules *your* end is the one you're attacking, not like football where *your* end is the one you defend.) In the few seconds either side of the first bounce a big roar engulfed the MCG.

The official attendance was 99,981 – just short of that magical number. Like all major sporting events a big chunk of tickets had gone to neutrals through sports associations, corporates, affiliated bodies, hospitality, government and others. It wasn't apparent though, with the crowd looking to favour the Bulldogs by maybe 70-30. The Bulldogs, not surprisingly, had captured the neutral support. They were the underdog, they were from Victoria, they hadn't won a flag since 1954, and they were a popular 'second team' for fans of some of the bigger Melbourne clubs.

I sat back and watched the game unfold. But I didn't sit back for long – it was edge-of-the seat stuff. The Bulldogs edged a low-scoring first quarter 12-8. At half-time Sydney led by 45 to 43. The third quarter was a tighter, low-scoring affair with Sydney adding only eight points to their score. The Bulldogs rattled-up two goals and six behinds to take a three-quarter-time lead of 61-53. I started to believe it was possible. The couple to my right – who I'd exchanged few words with for the first three quarters of the game – suddenly became my new best friends. I looked at the older couple in front of me – they were late sixties, early seventies maybe. Early in the last quarter she came back from the bar with a beer and a red wine. She handed him the beer, then held up her hand. She was shaking like a leaf. Red wine was spilling all over her hand and the sleeve of her jacket. After a minute she got up and went to the area behind the stand. She was shaking her head, tears in her eyes.

"I can't watch this," she said, overcome with emotion. "I can't watch."

Seven minutes to go. The Bulldogs led by just a point; 67-66.

They powered forward.

With five minutes to go the Bulldogs' lead had gone out to 15 points. While I couldn't comfortably say that we all *knew* they'd done it then, the atmosphere had changed. The tension was gone. The crowd noise was one of building celebration, not anxiety or raucous encouragement.

With two minutes and eighteen seconds to go Liam Picken kicked a goal to make it 88-67. Sydney weren't coming back from that. The Bulldogs were going to win the Premiership after sixty-two long years.

A minor score on the final siren made it 89-67.

I have never seen so many people cry. The outpouring was initially more one of relief than celebration. The couple next to me jumped up and down, hugging. Then I hugged them, together, briefly (I am a reserved Englishman, after all). The older woman in front of me had returned to her seat just before the end. She stood almost motionless for a while, her arms raised in the air, fists clenched. All around me people were on their feet, jumping up and down, arms aloft.

As was the custom for all AFL games the winning team's club song was blasted through the stadium's PA system. A sixty-thousand people singalong ensued.

As with just about everything AFL match-related the post-game ceremony and acknowledgments were a lengthy affair – probably half an hour all-up. Speeches from winning and losing captains, with predictable but genuine messages for their respective fans, match officials (there are several of them) getting their medals, and more.

The players are well-trained. They acknowledge the club and tournament sponsors and the opposition team's endeavours. After

Sydney captain Kieran Jack spoke, it was the presentation of the Norm Smith Medal for best-on-ground (man-of-the-match), deservedly won by the Bulldogs' Jason Johanissen. Then it was all twenty-two Bulldogs players up to receive their medals. The captain, Easton Wood, came to the podium last for his medal and remained there. The Bulldogs' coach, Luke Beveridge, received his medal. He then asked Bob Murphy, Bulldogs club captain, up to the podium. Murphy had been at the club since 1999, making his debut in 2000. In the 2016 season he was injured in the third week and never returned to the team. Murphy walked across the podium and Beveridge handed him *his* medal. The coach and club captain embraced. A few moments later the Premiership trophy was handed jointly handed to Murphy and Easton Wood with Luke Beveridge looking on with a kind of parental or older sibling-like approval.

Then it was the obligatory team celebration photo with the trophy. Some players were lying down, others jumping up and down. And then with most Sydney fans departed or departing, the Bulldogs did a lengthy lap-of-honour. In a reminder of both how well-behaved Aussie rules fans generally are, and that there is still a genuine connect between players and fans of a club, the players got right up to the fence shaking hands, sharing hugs and pausing for selfies with the supporters.

The club song was played again, and again.

Finally, a few Bulldogs supporters started to make for the exits. The game had finished probably forty-five minutes earlier. I said my farewells to the people around me; we're all smiles.

I walked back across Yarra Park, up Spring Street and then waited at the tram stop at the 'Paris end' of Collins Street. The tram took me back to Southern Cross station. It was only a short wait before my two-hour journey back to the country. A solo Bulldogs fan walked past, bedecked in red, white and blue. We smiled at each other. Tired yet elated, I know this is a day that will live long in the memory.

Footnote: A day or two after the game Bob Murphy returned his medal to Luke Beveridge. Luke Beveridge reportedly then donated the medal to the club museum. Bob Murphy played seventeen of the Bulldogs twenty-two games the following season before retiring. The Bulldogs finished tenth in 2017, missing out on the finals – a rare occurrence for a reigning Premier.

I LIKE TO WATCH

Rocky

"We've got a player here, he could be a Brazilian. And he comes from Lewisham." – David Dein, Arsenal Vice-Chairman, 1983-2007, on the young David Rocastle.

It seems strange, as a middle-aged man, to talk about sporting heroes or 'legends'. I tend to think that should be the preserve of younger people. It's also perhaps a little odd that this particular sporting hero was younger than me.

I followed Arsenal for many years. I saw my first game at Highbury in 1973 and started going regularly in 1978. They weren't a great team, but they had a great player – the mercurial Irish midfielder, Liam Brady. He was my first football idol. Brady was one of the younger players in that team and pretty much a regular from the age of eighteen. He left Arsenal in 1980 after a run of four cup final appearances in three years. They won only one of them.

Upon leaving school in 1983, I really ramped up my football-going. I no longer needed a Saturday job to have any kind of social life. I'd unenthusiastically joined the Monday-to-Friday rat-race a few weeks after leaving school and had some disposable income and Saturdays free. Games outside London were on the agenda for the first time in that 1983-84 season.

It was an era of under-achievement – a not unfamiliar post-war position in London N5. But I loved it. I felt attached to something. Around this time Arsenal Football Club was far more important to me than it should've been. Between about 1980 and 1986 Arsenal had the odd cracking win, but never looked in danger of either getting relegated or winning the title. Cup runs fizzled out just as we got excited about them. A 1-1 draw at Aston Villa in the last eight of the League Cup in early 1986 was a highlight, with Arsenal fans making up an estimated third of the 26,093 crowd on a damp, cold Wednesday night in Birmingham.

For many fans during this period of on-field mediocrity there were more exciting attractions off-field. Looking back, it's not that difficult to see the attraction in light of many things. From 1983 until 1989 I rarely missed a home game and regularly travelled away. The majority of games then were played on Saturdays. Remarkable as it may seem now, many games in the early 1980s weren't even filmed by the club and very few appeared in any capacity on TV.

On Saturday 28 September 1985 I set off at lunchtime to travel the twenty-odd stops on the Piccadilly Line to Arsenal. Newcastle United were the visitors. Arsenal were already doing their typical *middling thing* in the First Division. Reading one of the red top papers on the train, I saw that Arsenal were expected to give a debut to an eighteen-year-old midfielder from South London by the name of David Rocastle. I knew his name from the club programmes, which regularly detailed youth and reserves games.

Genuine fans always liked to see players make it through their club's youth system into the first team. It doesn't happen so often at the top-level now; too risky. Many of these young players had been connected with the club for five or more years before getting a chance. These *grown-your-own* players meant more to fans than a big money signing coming in and bossing it. It also afforded the youngster more time, more chances to win the crowd over. Fans were more forgiving of a home-grown young player making his way in the game than a transferred-in wizened old pro making a mistake.

Rocastle's debut against Newcastle was a dour 0-0 draw – a not particularly unusual outcome at the time. He had a good debut though. I particularly remember him making one mazy run through central midfield –the game's undoubted highlight. David Rocastle went on to feature regularly in the side for the rest of that season. I was at Luton Town for an FA Cup tie when he scored his first Arsenal goal. Curiously, considering where his later goals came from, it was a header in a 2-2 draw. He was a bright youngster in a talented but underachieving team that gently jogged to an upper mid-table finish that season and exited the cups in the last eight and last sixteen.

In the summer of 1986 Arsenal brought in a new manager, George Graham. Graham shook things up and within weeks it was clear his focus was on youth. Over the course of a year he reshaped the side almost completely. Prima donnas and big-time-Charlies were soon on their way. Graham found players who had started their careers under the previous manager but were often just in and out of the side and built the core of the team around them. That core was young and many of them were from London and surrounding areas: Rocastle himself, Tony Adams, Michael Thomas, Martin Hayes, Paul Merson and Paul Davis. Graham brought in an early bargain signing from Colchester, Perry Groves. A few years later Kevin Campbell broke into the team. Graham supplemented youth with the signings of hard-working and effective journeymen types like Kevin Richardson, Alan Smith and Nigel Winterburn. Within another few months he'd added Lee Dixon, Brian Marwood and Steve Bould to the squad. It was a team built very much in a particular mould, and curiously that mould was just about as far away from George Graham the player as it was as possible to be.

The 1986-87 season started in a similar vein to previous years. Some good wins, lots of draws and more defeats than was going to help Arsenal break into the top four. They went four games without scoring a goal in September but followed up with a narrow 1-0 win at eventual champions Everton. The Everton win was the start of a run of nine wins and a draw in ten games. Something had clicked. In mid-November I was at Southampton's tiny, packed Dell to see Arsenal win 4-0 to go top of the First Division. They didn't seem to be afraid of anyone. The young Arsenal team ultimately faded in the league that season, but they won the Littlewoods Cup – a first trophy in eight years.

The semi-final of the Littlewoods Cup was a two-legged affair. Arsenal drew rivals Tottenham. The first game was on a Sunday at Highbury. Arsenal's slump had started by then and Tottenham came away with a relatively comfortable 1-0 win. A couple of weeks later we headed over to White Hart Lane for the second leg, more in hope than any real expectation. Arsenal's bright-looking season was now in danger of imploding. It was a dank, rainy, late winter afternoon and the White Hart Lane pitch was just about half mud.

Supporter and media expectations were different then than in the post-millennium Premier League era. Arsenal had a new manager, a young team and had been treading water for a long time. Regardless of what was going to unfold that afternoon at Tottenham, or over the rest of the season, there was a clear feeling amongst Arsenal fans that things had changed. The club was on the up.

Arsenal went 1-0 down in the first half, making it 2-0 on aggregate. It was a real downer. There was many a shaking head at the Park Lane end of the ground at half-time wondering where Arsenal's season had gone. Then, in an almost unthinkable act of hubris Tottenham Hotspur Football Club announced over the tannoy how their fans could apply for tickets to the Littlewoods Cup Final. With forty-five minutes still to play Arsenal had been very publicly dismissed by their biggest rivals. The announcement caused consternation on the terraces. More importantly, the Arsenal players in the changing room heard it.

The second half got underway. Arsenal promptly came out, got stuck-in and scored twice to take the game to extra time. Spurs had a hatful of second-half chances to kill the game but couldn't apply the finishing touch. Two tired teams battled out extra time. There were no penalty shoot-outs then. A simple toss of the coin determined where the replay would be played. Tottenham again. Not as daunting as it should be really, Arsenal having won there that afternoon and a few weeks earlier in the league.

On Wednesday 4 March 1987 we headed again to White Hart Lane. The Park Lane end of the ground housing the Arsenal fans was packed; uncomfortably so. The Hillsborough disaster was still two years away, but the portents were there that evening, and at other games in the 1980s. Fans of many clubs had near-disaster experiences to tell. Looking back at the way supporters, ie paying customers, were treated by clubs, the police and the football authorities it was just awful. Treat people like animals…?

The reason the Arsenal end was so packed compared to the Spurs areas of the ground was that Arsenal sold-out their allocation quickly. Many Arsenal fans then bought tickets for Spurs' sections of the ground. Once inside the ground those fans approached the stewards and police with the "I'm an Arsenal fan and have accidentally ended up here" line and got themselves reallocated to the Arsenal section. Hence a heaving Arsenal end contrasting with comfort, even gaps in the Spurs standing areas.

The teams battled it out to 0-0 at half-time. Tottenham then took the lead through the prolific Clive Allen (forty-nine goals all competitions that season) in the second half. That remained the score until about five minutes to go when Arsenal substitute Ian Allinson, a free transfer a few years earlier from Colchester, popped-up with a miss-hit equaliser. In the last minute, Arsenal scored another scrambled goal, taking the aggregate score to 4-3 to Arsenal. For the first time in the tie, after three games and 300 minutes of football, Arsenal were ahead. The scorer was David Rocastle.

For Arsenal fans of a certain generation (ie, too young for the 1971 Double) this was a pivotal moment in the modern history of the club. Along with Michael Thomas's Anfield winner in 1989, Rocastle's White Hart Lane goal that Wednesday night defined a new Arsenal — an exciting, aggressive young Arsenal. David Rocastle was still two months short of his twentieth birthday when he scored that goal. It was possibly the scrappiest of a distinguished career.

Although Arsenal went on to win the Littlewoods Cup that season, beating a strong Liverpool team in the final, it's the semi-final that more Arsenal fans remember. It was a key moment in the early George Graham era. And it was the type of game and performance that defined the era: the against-the-odds comeback win. One-nil-down-two-one-up *and all that*. David Rocastle, the young midfielder who scored that winner characterised the growing Arsenal spirit in the early George Graham years. Rocastle was a Londoner, modest yet passionate. It felt like he was *one of us*. It wasn't difficult to imagine

David Rocastle standing on Arsenal's North Bank.

The commonly-viewed footage on YouTube of this game is from Thames Television's highlights programme. After his goal and after the final whistle the camera naturally focuses on David Rocastle. Look at Rocastle's face. It's not the face of a hardened pro. It's not the face of a budding prima donna. He's in front of the Arsenal end, applauding the Arsenal fans and celebrating with them. There's a look of humility about him, and a look of genuine excitement. He hugs a couple of invading, celebrating Arsenal supporters, then walks away to the tunnel. He'd just scored what would become one of the most talked about goals in Arsenal history.

Between 2014 and early 2018 Chilean international Alexis Sanchez played for Arsenal. For most of that time he was arguably their best player. His commitment was never in doubt. He's a professional footballer, and a very professional one. As committed as he was on the pitch and as ultra-professional as he was off it, fans knew that Arsenal didn't run through his veins. By twenty-five Sanchez had played top-level club football in Chile, Argentina, Italy, Spain and England. Arguably no team *ran through his veins*. This isn't to denigrate Alexis Sanchez. This is the modern game. There's no point complaining about it if you still follow a Premier League club or one of the dozen or so Championship sides who have burning Premier League ambitions. That's the way it is. But it doesn't stop my generation of football fans looking back misty-eyed on a different time, a time when we more easily identified with many of our club's players. In the case of Arsenal between late-1985, when he made his Arsenal debut, and mid-1992 when he left for Leeds, no player epitomised the new Arsenal more than David Rocastle. No player was more popular at Highbury. We related to many of the players then in a way fans can't now. Adams, Thomas,

Hayes, Davis, Merson, and then later Kevin Campbell and Ian Wright – were all from London or close by. And we had those *hardworking northerners* who'd been around the traps awhile who found their feet under George Graham: Alan Smith, Lee Dixon, Nigel Winterburn, Steve Bould, Kevin Richardson and Brian Marwood. Richardson and Marwood's stays were relatively brief but high on impact. The others carved-out long, successful careers at Arsenal. We loved them all – because we knew they *cared*. Above all, we loved David Rocastle because he felt like one of us. Rocastle's seemingly fearless approach to the game, his middleweight-like physique, his boyishness and enthusiasm endeared him to the rank and file at Highbury.

I remember a goal at Anfield. Wednesday 2 November 1988. It was an early round in the Littlewoods Cup, away to Liverpool. The crowd was 31,951 and I was among six or seven thousand Arsenal fans stretched across the Anfield Road end – a good turn-out for a midweek four-hundred-mile round-trip. It ended 1-1, but Arsenal dominated and should've won. Although Arsenal went on to lose in the second replay, this game was another marker in the changing nature of the Arsenal-Liverpool rivalry. Arsenal were no longer scared of Liverpool. Rocastle's goal that night, in front of the Arsenal end, was struck from the corner of the penalty area. It looked almost as if he'd toe-punted it. There was very little back-lift, but he hit it with exceptional power and it rocketed it into the left-hand corner.

Seven months later Arsenal won the league at Anfield.

Then there was that goal at Man United from distance. The goal at Villa from way out. Those jinky runs at Highbury from the right wing or inside right channel which often ended with a shot, and sometimes a goal.

And there was that Littlewoods Cup semi-final second leg against Everton at Highbury in 1988. Arsenal won the first leg at Goodison 1-0 with a deft turn, shot and goal from Perry Groves. (You never really knew whether Groves planned these things or not, but this one came off.) Everton came to Highbury one down, but the then champions were a strong team and far from out of it. They had a defender at the time, a self-professed hard man, Pat van den Hauwe (he called his autobiography *Psycho Pat*). van den Hauwe played at left-back for Everton, Rocastle on the right for Arsenal. They were up against each other – the hard-nosed seasoned pro versus the gladiatorial young Londoner (who could've been a Brazilian). They battled it out all game. At one point it looked like van den Hauwe had done Rocastle. He'd gone in late, studs showing, looking to take the Arsenal midfielder out of the game. As the lunge came in Rocastle timed his *advance retaliation* perfectly, leaving van den Hauwe in a heap. He then fed the ball to Groves who passed it to Thomas who scored. While this was happening van den Hauwe remained prone on the ground, David Rocastle just a few feet away with his hands, briefly, on his hips.

Arsenal fans identified with David Rocastle in a way I hadn't seen before. Charlie George was a bit before my time and Charlie Nicholas was deified more for his *icon* status as opposed to on-field achievements. There have been great players signed from other clubs – many of whom attracted the fans' affections and who went on to view Arsenal as *their* club. But players who come through the ranks grab and retain a different kind of affection that genuine fans don't often feel for other players. It *does* happen. Ian Wright for example, and some of those famous George Graham back four signings. But in general, the great signings are *respected*, and often affectionately. But they are not *loved* the way David Rocastle was loved on the terraces of Highbury.

There are a few moments in Ian Wright's documentary (*Rocky & Wrighty: From Brockley To The Big Time*) about their different paths to Arsenal's first team, that capture Rocastle perfectly. Early in the film David Rocastle is standing on a South London railway platform, on his way into training at Arsenal. There is a glint in his eye while being interviewed. Simultaneously he looks both shy – about himself, yet confident – in his ability.

In 1988-89, Arsenal won the league; the old English First Division. They won it on goals scored, beating the ultimately second-placed team in the last minute of the last game of a tumultuous season. Much has been said and written about that season – with Hillsborough a major turning point in post-war British football.

Arsenal hadn't won the league since 1971 and in beating Liverpool at Anfield they deposed the dominant club of the previous fifteen years. David Rocastle played in all thirty-eight Arsenal league games that season, scoring six times. He was a star of that league-winning team, but in some regards, he didn't stand out as much that year the way he had done in the previous two seasons. Had he peaked? Or were some of the other players just catching-up with him? Certainly, an Arsenal defence that now included Dixon, Winterburn and Bould seemed – to us mere mortals standing on the North Bank – more committed than the one a few years previously.

The years 1983-2000 were my peak Arsenal-supporting years, with about 1986-1990 being the *peakiest*. This was when my interest was at its highest, I went to the most games and spent, proportionately, the most money on football. My own appearances record was season 1987-88 when I went to fifty-two Arsenal games. In 1988-89 Arsenal played fewer games due to early cup exits, but I went to thirty of the thirty-eight First Division games that year. I didn't go to Anfield on 26 May though. Even worse, I didn't even watch it on TV. Shell-shocked after the home games against Derby and Wimbledon I'd given up on the season.

Arsenal struggled a bit in 1989-90 – well, comparative to the previous title-winning season. Having followed their fortunes since the mid-1970s though, it really wasn't that bad. The following season George Graham made some big signings in Andy Linighan, Anders Limpar, and probably Arsenal's greatest-ever goalkeeper, David Seaman. Seaman was a fixture for the next decade and more. Linighan, another centre-half (Graham was telegraphing his priorities by this stage) became a useful, if sometimes nervous-looking addition to the squad. In 1993 he broke the deadlock of the most boring FA Cup Final in living memory to land Arsenal the trophy for the first time in fourteen years. Anders Limpar, was a high impact, albeit short term-ish signing. He didn't play that many games – and ultimately there were more that he drifted out of than into, but occasionally... Bang! matchwinner. Three timely, complementary signings.

David Rocastle, now suffering from on-off injury problems (thirty-eight league games in 1988-89, thirty-three in 1989-90 and eighteen in 1990-91), began to drift away from the team. As they became more of a rounded team he became less of a focal point. The 1990-91 league-winning team only lost one game.

In mid-1992 the almost unthinkable happened. George Graham sold David Rocastle to Leeds United for £2.5M. That was a lot of dough for a footballer back then. In that first Premier League season there were only a handful of higher value transfers, which included notables like Alan Shearer and Teddy Sheringham. Rocastle reportedly cried when the club sold him. As did many Arsenal fans. Yet underneath, as mercenary as it sounds and as Graham acted, I think we knew we'd already seen the best of the swashbuckling, smiling warrior from previous seasons.

Injuries ravaged the rest of Rocastle's career. Curiously, even while supposedly fit, he didn't feature that often for Leeds in his spell there. The club's biggest signing seemed to be kept on the outer by Leeds' authoritarian manager, Howard Wilkinson. A message to other players?

Leeds played twice at Arsenal in that 1992-93 season – a league game in February, and an FA Cup tie in January in which Rocastle came on as a second-half substitute. A year or so later I was at Maine Road, Manchester – David Rocastle had moved on to Manchester City by then. Seeing him playing in their pale blue just didn't look right; a bit like seeing a scorned woman trying to make the most of a new partner who doesn't quite do it for her. A year or two later I saw him play for his next club, Chelsea, at Arsenal. He was given a hero's reception despite being ensconced in Chelsea's all blue.

When it ended at Chelsea he had trials with other clubs, short spells with Norwich and Hull, some time playing in Malaysia before his career wound down in his early thirties. What wasn't publicly known was that David Rocastle was gravely ill. He died from cancer in March 2001.

Throughout most of 2000 I was working in Central London, near Harley Street and Devonshire Place where all those specialist medical practices are. One lunchtime I was walking back to work when I saw David Rocastle standing in the street, outside one of those practices. My sharp, double-take glance at him registered. He knew that I knew who he was. I thought he looked a bit anxious. I didn't say anything; I didn't want to. He knew that I'd recognised him. I might be an annoying pain-in-the-arse, maybe a piss-taking or even aggressive Spurs fan. I looked away and walked on. There's some expression along the lines of "you should never talk to your heroes because they will disappoint you". But I didn't have that in mind when I walked past David Rocastle, Respectful of his privacy, I just didn't want to bother him.

A year or so later I was living in Australia and David Rocastle was dead. Looking back, I obviously wish I'd detoured just twenty yards or so that day and offered a few words about how much I'd enjoyed watching him play half a generation earlier. I'd seen his debut. I was there when he scored his first goal at Luton. I saw probably three quarters of his games for Arsenal. He had been my favourite player.

David Rocastle died the weekend of a North London derby at Highbury. A minute's silence was planned as a mark of respect. There were concerns that Spurs' fans might disrupt or disrespect the tribute, and what might happen if they did. The minute's silence was observed impeccably. Some things are more important than rivalries.

In May 2001, six weeks after his father died, nine-year-old Ryan Rocastle led the Arsenal team out for the FA Cup Final against Liverpool in Cardiff. Arsenal fans chanted Rocastle's name long and loud.

Playing for Arsenal between 1985 and 1992, David Rocastle bridged two eras – the sporadic, fleeting and occasionally exciting fourteen years between the Double and his debut, and the modern Arsenal of trophies, increased expectation and high-placed finishes. He started his Arsenal career in a desperately under-achieving team. He ended it in a team that has been in the top three or four clubs in England ever since, winning fifteen trophies in the thirty years to 2017.

David Rocastle was a key player in the late 1980s resurgence of Arsenal Football Club. I don't recall hearing a single word of criticism of him from any Arsenal fan. He was also one of those rare players whose appeal also spread to fans of other clubs. He clearly loved the game. He was a key player in the Arsenal team when Arsenal meant a lot to me; an important player in a developing team; the player with the biggest heart of all. For my generation of Arsenal fans, David Rocastle felt like one of us.

Fortunately, David Rocastle's career has been fairly well-documented in print, and particularly on film – unlike say Duncan Edwards or Robin Friday. He played at the start of the era when televising games and annual club videos became more common. There is no shortage of great Rocastle moments on YouTube. And there is plenty to read online. Obituaries and articles after his death outline his career and have a poignance not found in simple match reports. For those wanting to know (and see) more of David Rocastle I recommend:
Ian Wright's documentary *Rocky & Wrighty: From Brockley To The Big Time,* James Leighton's book *Rocky: The Tears and Triumphs of David Rocastle,* David Stewart's documentary *89* about Arsenal's 1988-89 title-winning season.

If you can find footage of goals Rocastle scored in the following games, you will start to see why this modest young Londoner was so revered at Arsenal:

Tottenham Hotspur away, Littlewoods Cup, 4 March 1987.
Liverpool away, Littlewoods Cup, 2 November 1988.
Middlesbrough home, Division One, 19 November 1988.
Aston Villa away, Division One, 31 December 1988.
Southampton away, Division One, 25 March 1989.
Manchester United away, Division One, 19 Oct 1991.

***

That David Rocastle died at just thirty-three undoubtedly increases the affection in which he is held. That's not to be cynical, because he was still loved by Arsenal fans once he'd left and was wearing the colours of other teams.

A young life cut short is very sad. In the case of David Rocastle, I think it was difficult for so many people to comprehend someone they remember as a supreme athlete being so gravely ill and dying at such a young age.

David Rocastle was Arsenal's most exciting player at the time the club meant most to me. Of all the sportsmen I've ever seen ply their trade, he was the player I most liked to watch.

I LIKE TO WATCH

The author's list of stadia, grounds and racetracks visited, and different sports seen

Football: Arsenal (Highbury and Emirates), QPR, Tottenham Hotspur (old White Hart Lane), West Ham United (Upton Park), Chelsea, Brentford, Crystal Palace (also saw Charlton Athletic and Wimbledon play home games at Selhurst Park), Wimbledon, Charlton Athletic, Millwall (both Dens), Fulham, Leyton Orient, Barnet (Underhill), Wembley Stadium (old and new), Watford, Luton Town, Wycombe Wanderers (Adams Park), Reading (Elm Park and Madejski Stadium), Oxford United (Manor Ground), Swindon Town, Bristol City, Bristol Rovers, Newport County (Rodney Parade), Millennium Stadium Cardiff, Brighton and Hove Albion (Goldstone Ground), Gillingham, Aldershot Town, Southampton (The Dell), Portsmouth, AFC Bournemouth, Ipswich Town, Norwich City, Colchester United (Layer Road), Peterborough United, Coventry City (Highfield Road), Aston Villa, West Bromwich Albion, Wolverhampton Wanderers, Leicester City (Filbert Street), Nottingham Forest, Derby County (Baseball Ground and Pride Park), Mansfield Town, Burton Albion (Pirelli Stadium), Stoke City (Victoria Ground), Grimsby Town,

Hull City (Boothferry Park), Sheffield Wednesday, Sheffield United, Barnsley, Bradford City, Huddersfield Town (John Smith's Stadium), Rotherham United (New York Stadium), Leeds United, Scarborough, Middlesbrough (Ayresome Park and Riverside Stadium), Sunderland (Stadium of Light), Newcastle United, Liverpool, Everton, Manchester United, Manchester City (Maine Road and Eastlands), Stockport County, Bolton Wanderers (Burnden Park and Reebok Stadium), Oldham Athletic, Burnley, Accrington Stanley, Blackburn Rovers, Bedford Town, Wealdstone, Harrow Borough, Southall, Celtic, Rangers, Hampden Park, Airdrieonians (Excelsior Stadium), St Mirren (St Mirren Park), Hibernian, Heart of Midlothian, Dundee United, RC Lens, Parc Des Princes Paris, Bayern Munich (Allianz Arena), Parken Stadium Copenhagen, Skonto Riga, Dynamo Kyiv, Legia Warsaw, Stadion Śląski (Chorzów, Poland), Sporting Gijón, Deportivo La Coruña, Celta Vigo, Barcelona, Chicago Fire (Toyota Park), Racing Club de Avellenada (Argentina), River Plate, Boca Juniors, Vexembong Da (in Cholon district of Ho Chi Minh City, Vietnam), 700th Anniversary Stadium (Chiang Mai, Thailand), Heidelberg United (Melbourne), South Melbourne, Melbourne Knights, Olympic Park (Melbourne), MCG, Etihad Stadium (Melbourne), Sydney Olympic (Kogarah Oval), Adelaide United, AAMI Park (Melbourne), Hunter Stadium (Newcastle, NSW), Epsom and Huntly Reserve (Central Victoria), North Sydney Oval, Geelong.

Test cricket grounds: Lord's, The Oval, Trent Bridge, Headingley, The Riverside (Durham), The Gabba, MCG, Adelaide Oval, SCG, Bellerive Oval (Hobart), WACA (Perth), Seddon Park (Hamilton, NZ), Basin Reserve (Wellington, NZ), University Oval (Dunedin, NZ), Eden Park (Auckland, NZ), Kensington Oval (Barbados), Wankhede Stadium (Bombay), Asgiriya Stadium (Kandy, Sri Lanka),

Galle International Cricket Stadium (Sri Lanka).

Other cricket grounds (includes ODIs and representative games played at Test, county, state and club grounds): Swansea (Glamorgan), Southampton (Hampshire, was near The Dell), Uxbridge (Middlesex), Scarborough (Yorkshire), *Edgbaston, Fenner's (Cambridge University), *Rose Bowl Southampton, Victoria (state games at Richmond, Junction Oval and Geelong Football Ground), Manuka Oval (Canberra), Etihad Stadium Melbourne, Queen Elizabeth Oval (Bendigo), *Feroz E Shah Kotla Grounds (New Delhi), PT Jawaramarlal Nehru Stadium (Goa), *SSC (Colombo, Sri Lanka). (*denotes a Test ground, but I didn't see a Test match there.)

Australian rules football: Princes Park (Carlton, Melbourne), MCG, Etihad Stadium (Melbourne), Geelong, Football Park (Adelaide), York Park (Launceston, Tasmania), Manuka Oval (Canberra), Queen Elizabeth Oval (Bendigo), SCG, Olympic Stadium Sydney, Tio Stadium (Marrara, Darwin), Subiaco Oval (Perth), The Gabba (Brisbane), Metricon Stadium (Gold Coast), North Ballarat Oval.

Rugby union: Cardiff Arms Park, Twickenham, Wembley Stadium (new one), Etihad Stadium (Melbourne), Suncorp Stadium (Brisbane), Eden Park (Auckland, NZ), Waikato Stadium (Hamilton, NZ), Baypark Stadium (Mt Maunganui, NZ).

Rugby league: Brookvale Oval (Sydney), Sydney Football Stadium, Etihad Stadium (Melbourne), AAMI Park (Melbourne), Mt Smart Stadium (Auckland, NZ).

Baseball: Boston Red Sox, New York Yankees (old and new), New York Mets (Citi Field), Toronto Blue Jays, Philadelphia Phillies,

Pittsburgh Pirates, Baltimore Orioles, Washington Nationals, Atlanta Braves, Cleveland Indians, Chicago Cubs, Chicago White Sox, Colorado Rockies, Oakland A's, San Francisco Giants, Los Angeles Dodgers, LA Angels of Anaheim, San Diego Padres.

Horse racing: Windsor, Lingfield Park, Ascot, Market Rasen, Caulfield, Flemington, Moonee Valley, Bendigo, Kyneton, Geelong, Hanging Rock (Victoria), Yea (Victoria), Dowling Forest (Ballarat, Victoria), Randwick, Tocumwal (NSW), Cairns, Hollywood Park (Los Angeles), Hipódromo Argentino de Palermo (Buenos Aires), Tor Służewiec (Warsaw).

Harness racing: Bendigo, Shepparton, Moonee Valley, Maryborough (Victoria), Gold Coast, Harold Park (Sydney), Gloucester Park (Perth), Forbury Park (Dunedin, NZ).

Greyhound racing: Newcastle-Upon-Tyne, Belle Vue (Manchester), Romford, Crayford, Wimbledon, Swindon, Doncaster, Owlerton (Sheffield), Nottingham, Shawfield (Scotland), Bendigo, Hobart, Wentworth Park (Sydney).

Where ground, stadium or track names have changed I have tried to use the most recent name or a previous name which easily identifies it. For example, the stadium in Docklands, Melbourne is occasionally known as 'Docklands' but has had a number of sponsors with naming rights over twenty-odd years and has been known as Colonial Stadium, Telstra Dome, Etihad Stadium and Marvel Stadium. AAMI Park in Melbourne is sometimes referred to as 'Melbourne Rectangular Stadium'. There may be some errors – which I take full responsibility for. The *important thing* is the reader knows which ground, stadium or track is referred to.

Different sports attended by the author: football, rugby union, rugby league, Australian rules football, international rules (Australian rules-Gaelic football hybrid, played occasionally between Australia and Ireland), American football, cricket (Test, domestic three and four day, ODI, T20, domestic 40, 45, 50, 55 and 60 overs), baseball, horse racing, harness racing, greyhound racing, bullfighting, roller derby, rowing, tennis, snooker, stock car racing, Formula One, monster trucks, cycling, boxing, Thai boxing, hockey, ice hockey.

I LIKE TO WATCH

Acknowledgments

I've attended thousands of different sporting events with hundreds of different people over many years. However, the person I have to acknowledge (blame?) the most in turning this whole thing into a bit of an obsession for me is Owen Francis, whose company, knowledge and good humour I have enjoyed most often. It's been a lot of fun.

In compiling these stories and anecdotes I have relied largely on memory and the input of a few friends. However, YouTube has been invaluable refreshing me on many of the goals I've seen, just *where* Steve Waugh struck that 4 at the SCG and other things. Delving through different Wikipedia pages offered up info and links to other sites that were invaluable in helping me include detail and specifics. Google Maps helped me work out distances, journey times and the juxtaposition of grounds, stadia and race tracks in different towns and cities.

Thanks to Em Burgess-Gilchrist and Dave Gibbs for their comments and suggestions on early versions of I Like To Watch. Thanks also to Louise Harnby for her invaluable input.

Selected further reading

Among The Fans (2011), Patrick Collins

Angels With Dirty Faces: The Footballing History of Argentina (2016), Jonathan Wilson

Ashes 2011: England's Record-Breaking Series Victory (2011), Gideon Haigh

Backpass magazine

Diary of the Real Soul Crew: The Complete Chronicles (2010), Annis Abraham Jnr

History of Football in Australia, A (2014), Roy Hay & Bill Murray

Inside the Divide: One City, Two Teams… The Old Firm (2012), Richard Wilson

Life In Football, A (2016), Ian Wright

Maximum City: Bombay Lost and Found (2005), Suketu Mehta

Rocky: The Tears and Triumphs of David Rocastle (2016), James Leighton

Running With The Firm (2014), James Bannon

Steaming In (1989), Colin Ward

Football Tourist, The (2013), Stuart Fuller

Idler Book of Crap Towns, The (2003), Sam Jordison and Dan Kieran

Rivals Game, The: Inside The British Football Derby (2008), Douglas Beattie

Turf Wars: A History of London Football (2016), Steve Tongue

When Saturday Comes magazine

Wink From The Universe, A (2018), Martin Flanagan

Suggested viewing

89: Arsenal's Triumph Against The Odds (2017), David Stewart, Amy Lawrence

The Real Football Factories International (2008), Danny Dyer

Rocky & Wrighty: From Brockley To The Big Time (2017), Tom Boswell, Ian Wright

Start them young. The author with his son, Henry at Victoria vs Queensland, Junction Oval, Melbourne, 2005.